T0330244

Banking on Multinationals

Banking on Multinationals

Public Credit and the Export of Japanese Sunset Industries

MIREYA SOLÍS

Stanford University Press
Stanford, California
2004

Stanford University Press
Stanford, California

Printed in the United States of America
On acid-free, archival-quality paper.

Library of Congress Cataloging-in-Publication Data

Solís, Mireya.
Banking on multinationals : public credit and the export of Japanese sunset industries / Mireya Solís.
p. cm.
Includes bibliographical references and index.
ISBN 0-8047-4887-X (cloth : alk. paper)
1. Investments, Foreign—Japan. I. Title.
HG5772 .S65 2004
332.67'352—dc22 2003025170

Original Printing 2004
Last figure below indicates year of this printing:
13 12 11 10 09 08 07 06 05 04

Typeset in 10.5/12 Bembo

To my mother, Mireya, whose generosity and passion for life have brought me immeasurable joy and inspiration

And in loving memory of my father, Carlos, whose courageous pursuit of the truth knew no bounds

Contents

Tables and Figures

TABLES

FIGURES

Acknowledgments

In writing this book I acquired many intellectual and personal debts that I can never fully repay. Susan Pharr, my mentor of so many years, challenged me to unravel the intricacies of Japanese politics, provided wise guidance, and has become a valued friend. Lawrence Broz and David Weinstein tirelessly and cheerfully read many dissertation chapter drafts and offered many insights that greatly enhanced the final product. Shujiro Urata of Waseda University opened the doors of the former Japan Eximbank to me, making my fieldwork possible and allowing the project to succeed. Despite his many commitments, during my two years in Tokyo I could always count on his good advice and help in overcoming the challenges of tracking down obscure documents; interviewing government officials, businesspeople, and academics; and even touring Japanese subsidiaries in Southeast Asia.

Although I spent many hours of solitary work poring over Japanese documents and typing draft after draft on the computer, this book taught me that academic research is in fact a collective effort. Numerous colleagues and friends volunteered perceptive comments that profoundly affected my thinking. I am of course responsible for any of the book's shortcomings, but would like to extend my deepest gratitude to Robert Art for reading the entire manuscript and offering invaluable advice; to Saadia Pekkanen for pressing me to refine my methodology and maintain theoretical rigor; and to Peter Evans, Bill Grimes, Tim Kessler, Ulrike Schaede, and Steve Teles for reading the work-in-progress and volunteering insightful suggestions. Two anonymous reviewers provided thorough and helpful feedback. Their suggested revisions were on the mark and greatly improved the quality of my arguments.

Many institutions provided generous financial and logistical support. Thanks to the Fulbright Program, the Ford Foundation, and the Mexican government's CONACYT fellowship program, I was able to pursue my graduate studies at Harvard and to undertake my fieldwork in Japan. Jorge Domínguez encouraged me to pursue higher education in the United States.

This book could not have been written without the generous support I received as a fellow at the Research Institute for International Investment and Development of the former Japan Eximbank. Mr. Kinoshita, Mr. Kijima, Mr. Tanaka, Mr. Tejima, and Mr. Someya provided me with an excellent work environment, went out of their way to answer my questions, and gave me access to very rich data on Japan's public loans for overseas investment. Mr. Kuroyanagi in particular became a friend and a mentor. At the institute I also struck a cherished friendship with Ms. Mutsuko Yamaguchi.

The Institute of Advanced Studies of the United Nations in Tokyo was my host for a nine-month fellowship and generously facilitated my research. Writing the dissertation was made possible by the financial support of Harvard's Reischauer Institute and the Center for US-Mexican Studies at the University of California, San Diego. At UCSD, I profited from many conversations with Van Whiting on regionalism and Japanese business strategy, and I learned a great deal from teaching a seminar with Steph Haggard. I have only the fondest memories of San Diego because it was at a conference there over free appetizers—which no graduate student will ever pass up—that I met my husband, Todd A. Eisenstadt.

My alma mater, El Colegio de México, was also a very supportive place to make the final revisions to my dissertation. My former teachers generously greeted me as a colleague. I especially want to thank María Celia Toro, director of the Center for International Studies, and Ana Covarrubias, the center's academic coordinator and my former classmate. I also want to acknowledge a very special friendship with another former classmate, Luz María de la Mora, which has only grown stronger over the years. At Brandeis University, I very much enjoyed teaching inquisitive students and interacting with collegial faculty.

Financial support from the US-Japan Relations Program at Harvard University provided me with essential time away from teaching to turn the dissertation into a book manuscript. Susan Pharr, Frank Schwartz, and the program fellows provided an environment conducive to refining my manuscript. I am also very grateful to acquisitions editor Muriel Bell and assistant editor Carmen Borbon-Wu at Stanford University Press for their support. As I ship off this manuscript to the press, I am about to begin a new position at the School of International Service at American University, where Robert Pastor, Louis Goodman, Nanette Levinson, Quansheng Zhao, and the SIS faculty have welcomed me warmly.

This book is dedicated to several generations of my family. From two generations past, I was able to meet only my maternal grandmother, Carmen. Even so, I was blessed with an intimate bond to this remarkably witty and cheerful woman. My parents, Carlos and Mireya, raised me a happy child and exemplified the high ethical standards that I am forever striving to meet.

My brothers, Carlos and Fernando, have always been a source of companionship and joy. My sister, Luz Elena, is quite simply my best friend. My mother and sister contributed indirectly to this book by selflessly giving of their time whenever I called on them. And through Todd, I acquired a most loving second family, the Eisenstadts.

A few years ago, Todd and I embarked on a lifelong adventure, seeking to achieve our professional goals and to raise a family. It has been quite a ride: moving our residence across countries, landing jobs and book contracts, and facing the challenges of parenthood (with many sleepless nights writing lectures and changing diapers). I couldn't have hoped for a more loving and supportive companion.

This book is also for my two daughters, Natalia and Paola. They bring happiness into our lives every day and remind us what is really important. May they too chase their dreams.

Abbreviations

AFL-CIO	American Federation of Labor-Council of Industrial Organizations
ARDECO	Aluminum Resources Development Corporation
ASEAN	Association of Southeast Asian Nations
BOP	balance of payments
CDC	Commonwealth Development Corporation
CTVs	color televisions
DI	develop-for-import policy
EIAJ	Electronics Industry Association of Japan
EPA	Economic Planning Agency
FDI	foreign direct investment
FECL	Foreign Exchange Control Law
FIL	Foreign Investment Law
FILP	Fiscal Investment and Loan Program
FOREX	foreign exchange
GAO	General Accounting Office
GATT	General Agreement on Tariffs and Trade
GSP	Generalized System of Preferences
IJPC	Iran-Japan Petrochemical Complex
IMF	International Monetary Fund
IPE	international political economy
JAF	Japan Aluminum Federation
JAIDO	Japan International Development Organization
JBIC	Japan Bank for International Cooperation
JCFA	Japan Chemical Fiber Association

JDB	Japan Development Bank
JFS	Japan Finance Corporation for Small Business
JODC	Japan Overseas Development Corporation
JSA	Japan Spinners Association
KfW	Kreditanstalt für Wiederaufbau
LDP	Liberal Democratic Party
METI	Ministry of Economy, Trade, and Industry
MFA	Multi-Fiber Agreement
MHW	Ministry of Health and Welfare
MITI	Ministry of International Trade and Industry
MMAJ	Metal Mining Agency of Japan
MNCs	multinational corporations
MNE	multinational enterprise
MOF	Ministry of Finance
MOFA	Ministry of Foreign Affairs
MOPT	Ministry of Posts and Telecommunications
NAA	Nippon Asahan Aluminum
NAAC	Nippon Amazon Aluminum Company
NHK	Japan Broadcasting Corporation
NLM	Nippon Light Metals
NTBs	nontariff barriers
ODA	official development assistance
OECD	Organization for Economic Cooperation and Development
OECF	Overseas Economic Cooperation Fund
OLI	ownership, location, and internalization approach
OMA	Orderly Market Agreement
OPIC	Overseas Private Investment Corporation
SMEs	small and medium-sized enterprises
TFB	Trust Fund Bureau
VERs	voluntary export restraints
VTRs	videotape recorders

Japanese and Korean Terms

Amakudari. Postretirement positions in the private sector for top bureaucrats.

Chaebol. Korean business conglomerates.

Endaka. Yen appreciation.

Gaiatsu. Foreign pressure.

Jūsen. Housing loan corporations.

Kadenka. Electrification boom.

Kankoku sotan. Recommended production cuts.

Keidanren. Japan Federation of Economic Organizations.

Keiretsu. Business groups.

Kokusanka. National production.

Kūdōka. Hollowing-out.

Shingikai. Deliberation councils.

Shōken. Commercial rights.

Sōdankai. Consultative body.

Sōgō shōsha. General trading companies.

Zaidan hōjin. Private foundation.

Zoku. Policy tribes.

Banking on Multinationals

Introduction

THE JAPANESE GOVERNMENT has led the world in publicly financing the expansion of its multinational corporations. This relatively unknown fact presents us with a fundamental puzzle related to Japanese industrial policy. Indeed, the Japanese state's self-assumed role as banker to multinationals seems counterintuitive given existing perceptions about the nature of its intervention in the economy. Why would a state known for its penchant for market control not object to losing jurisdiction over mobile transnational corporations and even offer low-cost financing to promote their overseas expansion? Why would a state widely credited with protecting infant industries and promoting exports subsidize the offshore relocation of production through foreign direct investment (FDI)?[1]

This book explains Japan's emergence as the world's largest provider of FDI financing as part of a national economic strategy to secure its access to key natural resources and to facilitate industrial restructuring, as well as a political strategy to subsidize inefficient but politically powerful producers.

This first systematic study of Japan's public FDI loan program offers insights into the unusual ability of stagnant sectors and small firms to invest and prosper overseas, a topic that has long occupied students of Japanese multinationalism. I offer a political-economy model of FDI that highlights the powerful influence of preferential financing on the sectoral composition of Japanese investment flows. The argument developed here is that the Japanese government, armed with substantial public credit, helped declining sectors and weak firms to regain international competitiveness through offshore manufacturing. In other words, preferential FDI loans lowered the cost of an international adjustment strategy.

Far from touting Japan's preeminent role as banker to multinationals as evidence of mercantilism in Japanese foreign economic policy, this book seeks to analyze the domestic politics of FDI subsidization, in which public financial institutions and their responsible ministers compete for resources and control, where Treasury bureaucrats and politicians battle over the strings attached to soft FDI credit, and where the private sector and the Japanese government, although regular partners in overseas endeavors, are often at odds over long-term commitments to large-scale FDI projects.

This book also traces the impact of recent changes in the Japanese political economy on the institutional framework of FDI financing. The post-1990s economic recession, the onset of coalition governments, and an unprecedented challenge to bureaucratic authority all influenced the nature of the public FDI program. Advocates of overt FDI subsidies to comparatively disadvantaged industries gained clout, and they may produce long-lasting changes in what had been a relatively disciplined program of public credit.

At the analytical core of this book lies a political-economy model of state FDI financing. It tests the argument that government FDI loan programs significantly influenced the industrial composition of Japanese foreign direct investment. In order to explain the allocation patterns of public FDI credit, the model first identifies the main rationales for government support of overseas investment: solving market failure in natural resource procurement and industrial adjustment, or politically compensating core support industries that need to relocate production abroad in a last-ditch effort to stay in business. It then develops hypotheses about which sectors should pursue overseas ventures backed by public credit, and tests whether the model's predictions for the industrial composition of Japanese FDI are more accurate than the expectations of traditional economic theories of overseas investment.

Second, the model takes on the single most divisive issue related to public FDI financing: uneven rates of subsidization for different producer groups. It underscores the systematic battle between bureaucrats and politicians to expand soft lines of credit by amending the mandate and budgetary design of public financial institutions.

Last, the model addresses the factors responsible for neutralizing political opposition to state subsidies for offshore production. It explains why the Japanese labor movement did not mobilize—unlike its US counterpart—against public FDI subsidies, and why rifts in the business community between domestic and international firms did not derail state FDI financing either.

This book also aims to dispel the notion of Japanese exceptionalism. While primarily concerned with explaining how Japan's public program of financing overseas investment unfolded, it also aims to place the Japanese experience in comparative perspective. Japan leads the way, but it is by no means the only government extending loans to foster the expansion of its multinational corporations. I challenge conventional views on the convergence of home-government policy by showing that there are persistent differences in the degree to which several governments "bank on" multinationals. The book addresses the question of why some states attempt to solve market failure with FDI loans, while others abstain. Empirically, it provides the first quantitative international comparison of large public FDI loan programs. And in order to test the broader applicability of the theoretical model it presents a mini case study of South Korea and concludes with a discussion of the factors conducive to the emergence of public financing of overseas investment in different nations.

Findings and Implications

The Japanese state shouldered the burden of financing multinationalism to a degree unparalleled elsewhere in the industrialized world. But one should not jump to the conclusion that the country's absolute lead in providing public FDI credit makes Japan the ultimate mercantilist nation, which, unconstrained by international regulations, awarded heavily subsidized credit to strategic sectors that promised to act as engines of growth for the economy. This characterization of Japan would be very misleading.

Japanese public financial institutions affected the sectoral composition of Japanese overseas investment by influencing the FDI strategies of some, but not all, manufacturing sectors. The Japanese state assisted mostly comparatively disadvantaged industries to embark on foreign production, while innovative and profitable Japanese industries self-financed their overseas expansion strategies. Its focus on declining sectors and weak firms responded to a genuine concern about raw materials supply and industrial restructuring, and also to the political demands of well-organized sectors in distress. Paraphrasing Albert Hirschman, it is possible to say that Japanese industries used their "voice" (lobbying) to pay for their "exit" (overseas expansion).

In addition, the Japanese state did not act cohesively as a banker to industry. Rather, bureaucratic rivalries prevented the streamlining of the institutional setup for FDI financing. Moreover, bureaucrats and politicians were at odds over the wisdom of opening soft FDI financing windows for Japanese industry (that is, extending public loans with very low interest rates, and sometimes without securing adequate collateral). Politically negotiated budgetary rules were a key determinant of the behavior of Japanese public financial institutions as either economic maximizers or political appeasers. In other words, budgetary design influenced the quality of government lending: public institutions that enjoyed generous transfers from the general account (approved by the politicians) could provide easier credit terms, whereas agencies that borrowed from the Treasury and through bond issues or generated their own resources were less likely to provide subsidized loans.

How successful was Japan in its public financing of overseas investment? Measured by three indicators (initial goals, sustainability, and burden on public finances), the public FDI loan program had a mixed record. Some industries were more successful than others in achieving their FDI aims. Public FDI loans to the textile and aluminum industries, for example, had different objectives: to protect market share in foreign countries in the former, and to guarantee the supply of a key industrial input in the latter. Japanese textile makers captured a substantial portion of East Asian markets through local production, but the aluminum smelters were not as successful. Japanese-owned refiners abroad produce very expensive ingot in a market where spot purchases are on the rise. Consequently, their share of Japanese imports decreased.

Judged by long-term sustainability, public FDI credit does not fare very well either. Mirroring domestic adjustment assistance, it was very hard to withdraw state support and make targeted industries eventually pay for their overseas ventures. Worse, some "national projects" were a recurrent drain on public financial resources. The Japanese government had to offer additional injections of capital and interest relief to keep many of these ventures afloat. But the financial record of the Japanese state as banker to transnational corporations has been largely positive. Despite the burden of national projects and the growing share of soft FDI loans to political constituencies, most of the FDI credit program is still subject to budgetary rules that discipline allocation decisions.

This study of the domestic politics of Japanese FDI has broader implications for the fields of Japanese and international political economy. The myth of the strong Japanese state has gone unchallenged in political-economy studies of FDI that subscribe to the idea of a strategic Japanese government directing the multinational moves of private firms (Bergsten, Horst, and Moran 1978; Ozawa 1978; Dunning 1992). More recent insights from studies of government-business relations in Japan, however, suggest that accepting without further scrutiny the image of the strong, autonomous Japanese state may be quite misleading.

Ever since Chalmers Johnson (1982) introduced his pathbreaking model of the Japanese developmental state, in which the Ministry of International Trade and Industry (MITI) plays a crucial role in the process of economic growth and industrial restructuring, most work in the field has aimed to show the limits of Japanese state power and the important role of politicians and the private sector in shaping industrial, energy, and structural adjustment policies (see Ramseyer and Rosenbluth 1993; Friedman 1988; Samuels 1987; Sheard 1991). A different challenge to the notion of the developmental state points to the limits of MITI's power over other bureaucracies that affect industrial policy. As Calder (1993) shows, MITI bureaucrats were constrained in bringing about their vision of economic transformation by a lack of control over public industrial credit.

Finally, time must figure in any assessment of the developmental state argument. Pempel (1998: 146; 1999) describes the unraveling of embedded mercantilism in Japan during the 1990s. The new forces of capital mobility, political realignment, and economic contraction have weakened core elements of the past system, such as protection of domestic markets, restrictions on foreign direct investment, regulated financial markets, and stable compensation for farmers and large and small enterprises.

The developmental state model and its critics have produced a sophisticated understanding of the Japanese political economy. Yet the puzzle of Japanese state financing of FDI continues to confound conventional wisdom about Japanese government-business relations with its strict demarcation of two policy areas: one modern and efficient (trade and industrial policy), and the other stagnant and subsidized (agriculture and construction, for example). This book shows that compensation and efficiency coexisted much more closely than has been understood, even within FDI financing. In providing public FDI credit, some government financial institutions engaged openly in subsidization; others were more insulated from interest-group pressure by built-in institutional mechanisms.

This book revisits a key debate over the Japanese developmental state: whether industrial policy was guided by bureaucratic growth objectives, or whether it was held captive by special interests that wanted state subsidies. Japan first embarked on FDI financing in a strategic attempt to solve market failure and instituted strict rules to prevent rampant subsidization. Over time, though, politicians became more and more interested in providing discounted FDI loans to groups that supported them politically. And the book details the mechanism by which these soft financing windows were opened: in a contest between the bureaucracy and politicians to shape the budgetary design of public financial institutions.

The argument that declining industries, if politically assisted, can be internationally mobile has profound implications for our understanding of national adjustment strategies, the political behavior of sunset industries, and the interaction between home states and multinational corporations. The incentive structure for firms facing adjustment is not only guided by the protection and free-trade options but also affected by the costs of setting up factories abroad. This book broadens our understanding of industry response to decreasing competitiveness to include not just domestic insulation, but also international adjustment; and it demonstrates the possibility of private sector lobbying for FDI subsidies, not only protectionism.

This study of the political economy of Japanese FDI redefines the scope of home government action to include financially targeting specific industries for resource security or industrial upgrading purposes. In fact, several other countries also bank on multinationals, even if their FDI credit programs have yet to match the Japanese.

Plan of the Book

Part One analyzes Japanese state financing of overseas investment from a theoretical and comparative perspective. In Chapter 1 I point to the shortcomings of available theory in analyzing the use of preferential credit in home government policy, and in explaining the participation of depressed industries in Japanese FDI. Then I develop a political-economy model of FDI that stresses the key role of preferential public financing in explaining the sectoral composition of Japanese overseas investment. In Chapter 2 I compare the historical evolution of Japanese FDI with that of other countries and identify the areas of convergence and divergence in the makeup of Japanese overseas investment flows.

Part Two raises the dilemma between promotion and control that the Japanese government faced in implementing its FDI policy. FDI sponsorship allowed Japanese multinationals to escape Japanese bureaucratic regulation and gain access to foreign sources of capital. Chapter 3 describes how, for most of the postwar period, the Japanese government addressed this issue by perpetuating a very restrictive system of capital controls to interdict FDI projects it deemed ran counter to its industrial policy goals. The chapter also discusses the implications of the liberalization of capital controls for Japanese FDI policy and highlights how bureaucratic politics affected the timing and manner in which these capital restrictions were lifted.

Chapter 4 discusses the politics of Japanese preferential financing for overseas investment. It constructs the first comprehensive database of Japanese public FDI loans, traces the impact of budgetary rules governing public financial institutions on rates of FDI subsidization, and discusses the critical junctures where Treasury bureaucrats and politicians clashed over the expansion of soft FDI credit.

Part Three offers three case studies of the role of public credit programs in facilitating the international industrial adjustment of troubled Japanese industries. Chapter 5, on textiles, details the emergence of Japan's first manufacturing multinationals. Public credit and co-investment with general trading companies led to full-fledged multinationalization of the textile industry (in sharp contrast with the experience of textile sectors in the rest of the industrialized world, which remained domestic and highly protected industries).

Chapter 6, on aluminum smelting, presents one of the most dramatic cases of state support for the overseas relocation of a dying industry. Far from accepting the dictates of comparative-advantage law, the Japanese state relied on the "national project" formula to pay for the creation of mammoth aluminum smelters abroad. But the nationally endorsed smelters were saddled by huge yen debt, which compromised their competitiveness and self-sustainability.

Chapter 7, on consumer electronics, offers a reminder that not all Japanese industries needed public FDI credit. The book's political economy model explains why government support for electronics FDI was moderate. Consumer electronics firms had substantial experience with foreign production before the value of the yen increased dramatically and possessed sufficient resources to invest overseas on their own. The state never targeted consumer electronics as an industry for growth, and the industry did not fall into a structural recession that required state-orchestrated curtailment of its capacity. Consequently, no close connections between this industry and bureaucrats or politicians ever developed, and electronics firms largely self-financed their overseas expansion.

The book concludes with an evaluation of Japan's attempt to craft comparative advantage through FDI credit. It highlights the implications of FDI policymaking for broader Japanese government-business relations, and for the field of international political economy more generally. The Conclusion expands the comparative purchase of the book's model of state FDI financing with a case study of South Korea. A comparison of the United States, Japan, and South Korea reveals three important preconditions for the emergence of active FDI loan programs: market failure in resource supply or industrial restructuring; the existence of robust indicative credit programs; and national labor adjustment institutions that temper union opposition to FDI subsidies. The result is a new research agenda that explores the role that governments can play as bankers to multinationals and the internal politics that inhibit or promote public FDI financing.

PART ONE

Japan's Foreign Direct Investment in Theoretical and Comparative Perspective

CHAPTER 1

Preferential FDI Financing and International Industrial Adjustment

EARLIER ANALYSES of the swift expansion of Japanese multinational corporations (MNCs) have neglected a key issue: the fundamental role played by the Japanese state through its preferential financing program.[1] The Japanese government's decision to support multinationals is both little known and counterintuitive given our current understanding of Japanese industrial policy.

Why does the Japanese state, better known for its attempts to control markets, protect infant industries, and maximize national exports, administer the world's largest public loan program to assist in the relocation of manufacturing overseas? Why does the Japanese state seem unconcerned about the loss of control over mobile multinational corporations and the erosion of the domestic export base through FDI? For a government widely credited with picking "winners," the public FDI loan program is even more remarkable for its emphasis not on leading industries, but on structurally depressed industries that traditionally have not been mobile across borders. The task at hand, therefore, is to explain why a developmental state like Japan subsidized the overseas transfer of part of its industrial base, and why it targeted mostly sunset industries rather than the rising stars of the economy.

I argue that it is possible to understand the Japanese government's actions once we take into account the industrial policy goals that the government is pursuing with FDI financing: raw materials procurement and industrial restructuring through the relocation abroad of declining industries. However, Japan's public loan program for FDI has not been guided exclusively by national strategy. Lobbying and rent-seeking have also been powerful motives. Indeed, subsidized FDI credit is a useful political tool to appease economically weak but politically powerful constituencies that need to relocate to low-cost locations abroad to stay afloat. By bringing the state back in, I am able to explain one of the most enduring puzzles in the patterns of Japanese

FDI: the remarkable ability of stagnant sectors and small firms to participate actively in overseas investment projects.

This chapter lays out several key research questions: Why has Japan committed such an inordinate amount of public resources to foster MNCs? Why have FDI subsidies to different producer groups varied so widely? Why has little domestic opposition emerged to a public credit program with such an explicit bias in favor of Japanese transnational capital? I question long-standing views in the field of international political economy (IPE) that declining industries can resort to only domestic adjustment measures and that home governments do not deploy active FDI industrial policies. In this chapter I develop a political-economy model of state FDI financing to explain why some governments but not others generously finance the expansion of multinational corporations; and the degree to which sunset industries rely on this discounted public credit to cross borders.

State FDI Credit and the Offshore Relocation of Sunset Industries

The interaction between states and multinational corporations has received wide attention in the IPE literature, although most studies have centered on the bargaining relationship between host governments and MNCs. The relative lack of interest in the actions of home states derives from two core propositions in the literature: that home government FDI policies do not differ significantly, and that overseas investment measures have a very limited impact on industrial policies. The conventional view is that policy convergence among home governments—in both the regulation and the promotion of FDI—has been a powerful force.

Past differences between countries with strict controls on capital outflow or FDI review mechanisms (France, Japan, South Korea) and nations with free movement of capital and little interest in monitoring FDI projects (Germany, the United Kingdom, the United States) have largely disappeared.[2] The uniformity in FDI policies resulted from the willingness of interventionist governments to relax their supervision of overseas investment projects by dismantling capital controls; and the requirement that firms get advance government approval for their foreign investment projects has been replaced with a requirement that they merely notify the government before or after they begin (Safarian 1993; Bailey, Harte, and Sugden 1994; Van Hoesel 1999).

To promote overseas investment, home governments always adopted nearly identical measures: providing some form of investment insurance, and allowing foreign tax payments to be credited against domestic tax liabilities so that companies would not be taxed twice.[3] The lack of variation in different nations' public policies to promote FDI made them uncontroversial:

"Since the policies are so similar, no home country has gained much competitive advantage for its multinational enterprises, nor is there much conflict among home countries regarding those firms" (Bergsten, Horst, and Moran 1978: 40).

Equally important to the dominant view on home government FDI policy is the argument that there is no industrial policy on FDI in advanced market economies (Bergsten, Horst, and Moran 1978: 16; Dunning 1993: 74–75). In other words, home governments have not devised systematic policies to promote overseas investment; instead, most measures influencing outward FDI flows have been put in place with other industrial policy goals in mind: balance-of-payments adjustment, taxation, or exchange rate management. The policy portfolio on outward FDI in major source nations, therefore, affects only the total volume of capital outflow, leaving no margin for the preferential targeting of individual sectors.

Only two major exceptions to this pattern of indifferent or ineffective home governments are recognized in the IPE literature: European attempts to breed "national champions," and the comprehensive FDI policy framework in Japan. The success of the European policy on national champions has been questioned given the difficulties of identifying winners, maintaining the international competitiveness of firms that receive generous subsidies or market protection from the government, and forcing business compliance with the government's preferred production and marketing strategies (Safarian 1993a; Moran 1993: 10–11).

Far more enduring in the literature has been the perception of a centralized Japanese state strategically coordinating trade, industrial, and FDI policies (Bergsten, Horst, and Moran 1978; Ozawa 1978; Dunning 1992). Ozawa, for example, believes that "the most important supportive feature in Japan's overseas industrial expansion is the role of the Japanese government in encouraging, assisting, and occasionally even participating, albeit indirectly, in private overseas investment ventures" (1978: 33). And Dunning portrays a highly strategic and cohesive state orchestrating economic policy across issue areas: "Japan set up a single agency to ensure that outbound MNE [multinational enterprise] activity was consistent with national economic objectives. Unlike other developed countries, Japan has evolved in a holistic and integrated strategy towards outward direct investment. Even today such a strategy is inseparable from its more general industrial, trade, and technology policies, as well as from its policies towards inward direct investment" (1992: 59–69).

CHALLENGING THE CONVENTIONAL VIEW OF HOME GOVERNMENT FDI POLICY

My analysis of Japan's public financing of overseas investment challenges the notions of both FDI policy homogeneity and Japanese exceptionalism.

The conventional view of home government FDI policy disregards the role that states can play as bankers for transnational corporations. This is a major omission because several governments have attempted to facilitate the overseas expansion of their multinational corporations with preferential financing. Not only has this one important policy tool been left out of the discussion of home government policy, but more important, there are marked differences in the degree to which states loaned money for overseas investment, so the "convergence thesis" does not apply.[4] Furthermore, public credit is a useful instrument of industrial policy because it permits the targeting of individual sectors and projects. By providing public credit, some states, but not all (and to varying degrees), directly financed MNC expansion to meet their industrial policy goals.

The problems of construing Japanese FDI policy as the tool of a monolithic developmental state are dealt with in more detail throughout the book. In contrast to the prevailing view of a cohesive and strategic Japanese FDI policy, I find in Japan a fragmented system, with economic bureaucracies contesting their jurisdiction over FDI financing and public financial agencies competing vigorously to expand their scope of operations. And FDI loans have largely gone not to vibrant new industries, but to sectors struggling to survive in the international marketplace.

STATES AS BANKERS FOR MULTINATIONAL CORPORATIONS: JAPAN IN COMPARATIVE PERSPECTIVE

The record of major source countries in the control and promotion of overseas investment underscores the degree to which national FDI policies have or not converged (see Table 1.1). In some areas home government policy has been remarkably homogeneous: balance-of-payments safeguards, tax benefits, and investment insurance programs. In one fundamental area, the monitoring of capital outflows, past differences in the regulatory approach of home states diminished. The four countries in Table 1.1 that more actively screened international capital transactions (France, Japan, South Korea, and Taiwan), substantially liberalized rules on the outflow of capital and review procedures for overseas investment projects. In the past, the governments of these countries examined and approved every single FDI project. In the early 2000s, most of these nations operate similar review systems, granting automatic approval to small projects, requesting prior or ex post facto notification for larger investments, and requiring government approval for FDI only in restricted sectors or for unusually large projects. In the area of control of overseas investment, therefore, policy homogenization seems to be at work.

But there is no trend toward convergence in the area of public credit for overseas investment. A cross-national comparison of public FDI credit programs reveals that state FDI financing has not been uncommon (most source countries have at least one public financial institution with a mandate to extend loans to the private sector for overseas production), but that there is great variation among states in their commitment to financing multinationals (see Table 1.2).[5] The Japanese state is the leading lender for private multinational investment in three crucial dimensions: the absolute size of the lending program, the relative importance of FDI credit in the overall operations of public financial agencies, and the share of FDI actually financed with public credit.

At the end of the twentieth century, the Japan Bank for International Cooperation (JBIC) had disbursed FDI loans equivalent to $72 billion.[6] Germany's Kreditanstalt für Wiederaufbau (KfW) and the Export-Import Bank of Korea (Korea Eximbank) trailed far behind with only $2.6 billion (although South Korea's figures are more impressive if one considers that the FDI loan program was not started until 1976). In the first half of the 1990s, the Taiwan Eximbank undertook FDI financing more aggressively (loaning $509 million), whereas the US Overseas Private Investment Corporation (OPIC) disbursed a meager $281 million in direct loans for overseas investment in its first twenty years of operations.[7]

The gap in total FDI financing reflects the different priorities that promotion of MNC expansion had in these public credit agencies. The core mission of OPIC is to insure against FDI political risk such as expropriation, currency inconvertibility, or war (Shelp 1980: 187). FDI loans always played a subordinate role, representing a mere 1.5 percent of total OPIC operations. FDI financing was also of minimal consequence to the KfW's mission, accounting for a mere 0.6 percent of financing (see Table 1.2). For the Eximbanks of South Korea and Taiwan, FDI lending was a more prominent activity, representing 4.8 percent and 7.1 percent of their total loans, respectively. Once more JBIC stands out for the much greater importance it attached to MNC promotion: FDI loans represented 20 percent of all credit.

With these differences in mind, it is no surprise that the US and German public FDI programs had a minor impact on the overseas expansion of their MNCs. Public loans for overseas investment represented a mere 0.08 percent of US and 0.53 percent of German FDI flows. The importance of public FDI loans as a share of total overseas investment was much greater in the three other countries listed in Table 1.2: 4.4 percent for Taiwan, 9 percent for South Korea, and 10.3 percent for Japan. The state is clearly an important factor in the analysis of multinational corporate expansion in these Asian countries where the government acts as FDI banker.[8]

The variation in the policy strings attached to FDI credit once more underscores differences in the public commitment to promoting MNCs among key source nations. Interestingly, the United States and Japan operate at opposite ends of the policy spectrum. The United States has one of the

TABLE 1.1

Home Government Policy on Outward Investment

	Control			Promotion		
Country	Government approval required	Capital controls	Sectoral restrictions	Tax benefits	Insurance/ Protection	Financing
United Kingdom	No	Standby balance-of-payments (BOP) controls	None	Foreign tax credit	Bilateral treaties; MIGA; ECGD insurance system	Modest; CDC (1.5 percent of all flows in 1990–96)
United States	No	Standby BOP controls; interest equalization tax (1965–74)	None[a]	Foreign tax credit	Bilateral treaties; MIGA; OPIC insurance system	Modest; OPIC
Germany	No	Standby BOP controls	None	Foreign tax credit	Bilateral treaties; MIGA; Hermes insurance system	Modest; Kf W
France	Yes	Standby BOP controls	None	Foreign tax credit	Bilateral treaties; MIGA; COFACE insurance system	Modest; Proparco (0.1 percent of all FDI flows in (1990–96)
Japan	Yes; but since 1998 only ex post facto notification required for most projects	Pervasive BOP controls until the reform of FECL, 1980, 1998	Closer monitoring of several restricted sectors	Foreign tax credit; tax deferral on loss reserves	Bilateral treaties; MIGA; MITI insurance system	Substantial; JBIC

South Korea	Yes; but since 1990s prior notification required for projects of less than $50 million	Pervasive BOP controls until deregulation in 1990s	Real estate until 1996	Foreign tax credit; tax deferral on loss reserves	Bilateral treaties; MIGA; KEIC insurance system	Substantial; Korea Eximbank
Taiwan	Yes; but since 1996 automatic approval for projects of less than $20 million	Pervasive BOP controls until deregulation in 1987	Investments in PRC require special approval	Foreign tax credit; tax deferral on loss reserves	EIBC insurance system	Increasingly substantial; Taiwan Eximbank

[a] Although there are no sectoral restrictions for FDI specifically, American multinationals are limited by the Trading with the Enemy Act and legislation covering defense technologies.

ABBREVIATIONS: CDC: Commonwealth Development Corporation; COFACE: Compagnie Française d'Assurance Commerce Extérieur; ECGD: Export Credit Guarantee Department; EIBC: Export-Import Bank of China; KEIC: Korea Export Insurance Corporation; KfW: Kreditanstalt für Wiederaufbau; MIGA: Multilateral Investment Guarantee Agency; MITI: Ministry of International Trade and Industry; OPIC: Overseas Private Investment Corporation; PRC: People's Republic of China; Proparco: Société de promotion et de participation pour la coopération économique; JBIC: Japan Bank for International Cooperation.

SOURCES: Safarian 1993; Bailey, Harte, and Sugden 1994; Van Hoesel 1999; Japan Eximbank *Gyōmu Binran* (several issues); and the *Annual Reports* of OPIC, KfW, and the Korea Eximbank.

TABLE 1.2

States as Bankers to Multinational Corporations

Country	Institution	Mandate	Policy conditions for FDI financing	Amount of FDI loans (million US$)	FDI loans as a share of all financing (percent)	FDI loans as a share of all FDI flows (percent)
United States	Overseas Private Investment Corporation (OPIC)	Investment insurance; direct loans; loan guarantees	Direct loans only for small enterprises; projects must not have a negative effect on US jobs, exports, environment, or local workers' rights	281.4 (1971–92)	1.50	0.08
Germany	Kreditanstalt für Wiederaufbau (KfW)	Domestic investment; foreign aid; export, FDI, and project finance	Loans exclusively for small enterprises	2,636.1 (1963–99)	0.66	0.53
Japan	Japan Bank for International Cooperation (JBIC)	Export, import, FDI, and project finance; untied loans; foreign aid	None	72,022.8 (1953–99)	20.10	10.30
South Korea	Korea Eximbank	Export, import, and FDI financing; loan guarantees; foreign aid	No lending for real estate, banking, or insurance	2,661.9 (1976–99)	4.80	9.00
Taiwan	Taiwan Eximbank	Export, import, and FDI financing; loan guarantees; insurance	Ministry of Economic Affairs approval required	509 (1989–96)	7.10	4.40

NOTES: The years for which public FDI financing is reported do not coincide mostly because of the different dates in which these public financial agencies launched their FDI loan programs. For OPIC, figures after 1993 are not reported because the annual reports no longer distinguish between the FDI financing and insurance programs.

SOURCES: Japan Eximbank, *Gyōmu Binran*, several issues; *Annual Reports* of OPIC, KfW, and the Korea Eximbank.

most restrictive approaches to the public financing of overseas investment. Since its creation in 1971, OPIC has confronted objections that government FDI lending and insurance results in corporate welfare and threatens labor interests. To assuage fears of rampant subsidization, OPIC was designed as a self-sustaining agency in order to discipline its financing activities and to minimize the burden on the US Treasury.[9]

But sound management principles were not sufficient to silence critics of state subsidization of economic activity. Because of the continuing controversy surrounding OPIC's operations, in the mid-1970s the US government announced a plan to privatize the agency. Although the privatization did not happen, the debate over the need for a public agency like OPIC did not subside, and the agency continued to face reauthorization every five years (GAO 1997).[10]

The concerns of organized labor had a much more significant impact on the mandate of OPIC. The 1971 Burke-Hartke bill symbolized the clout of a labor lobby that resented the loss of employment opportunities due to the overseas relocation of production by US multinationals. This legislative proposal contemplated far-reaching limitations on the freedom of American firms to invest abroad: it proposed the establishment of a system of presidential licensing for all FDI projects—with the employment effect as a major criterion for approval; it mandated corporate disclosure of international activities; and it pushed for a reduction in offshore manufacturing (Bergsten, Horst, and Moran 1978: 111–12; Brennglass 1983: 59).

The Burke-Hartke bill was considered too extreme and was defeated. However, the government took the unions' concerns about the export of jobs through FDI seriously enough to reform the OPIC charter in 1974. Since then, OPIC has insisted it attaches a high priority to protecting domestic employment: it "will not support a 'runaway plant,' i.e., the substitution of existing US facilities with a foreign plant to produce for the same US or export markets" (OPIC 1997). Every time OPIC evaluates a project for FDI financing it must carry out preliminary studies to verify that the project will not harm US jobs or exports, will not have a negative effect on the environment, and will not result in the deterioration of workers' rights in the host country.

The list of requirements for FDI loan approval is not as exhaustive in other countries. In Germany, the KfW only finances the overseas investment projects of small enterprises—just as OPIC does. The Korea Eximbank does not supply FDI loans for projects in real estate, banking, and insurance. And the Taiwan Eximbank's credit allocation decisions are under the close surveillance of the bureaucracy; each FDI project must be approved by the Ministry of Economic Affairs (Van Hoesel 1999: 82).

The Japanese government gives its main FDI credit agency great freedom to act. The JBIC is not limited to financing small enterprises (in fact most of JBIC's FDI loans have been awarded to large firms); it is not banned from loaning money to the financial sector; it does not have to receive bureaucratic approval for each FDI project (the Ministry of Finance supervises JBIC's FDI lending program but is not involved in the routine approval of loans); and it does not have to prove that no harm will come to domestic labor, exports, or the environment.

The lack of national policy restrictions on public FDI lending in Japan is all the more significant because no international rules limit public FDI subsidization. In the area of government export credit, members of the Organization for Economic Cooperation and Development (OECD) have established a sophisticated regime that covers minimum interest rates, maturity periods, and use of tied aid.[11] In sharp contrast, there has been no attempt at international rule-making to curb soft FDI financing. Unconstrained by domestic labor opposition or international restrictions, the Japanese government was free to develop the largest public program in the world to support the internationalization of Japanese firms.

PUBLIC CREDIT AND THE MIGRATION OF JAPANESE SUNSET INDUSTRIES

In order to explain why the Japanese state has emerged as the most active public financier of foreign direct investment, we must understand its goals. The literature on government export financing is a good starting point for analyzing the motivations behind public lending for corporate international activity.[12] Usually, governments award export credit to accomplish two objectives: avoid financial market failure; and neutralize predatory financing by rival export credit agencies (Eaton 1986; Ray 1995; Rodriguez 2001; Evans and Oye 2001). Since Japan was the first country to launch an FDI public loan program and no other country has come close in its FDI credit disbursements, it is possible to rule out the second objective.

The market-imperfection rationale (that commercial banks bypass projects they deem too risky but that would yield positive economic externalities) accounts better for the emergence of Japanese government FDI financing. In particular, Japan has used FDI credit to solve cases of market failure in raw material procurement and to achieve industrial adjustment. Owing to uncertainty, high costs, or factor price rigidities, private firms have frequently shied away from actively participating in these projects. With the aim of guaranteeing the supply of key raw materials and of restructuring declining industries, the Japanese government has used public FDI credit to encourage private sector investment in these areas.

States may intervene to guarantee raw material supply if imperfect capital markets, insufficient communication and transport infrastructures, and economies-of-scale barriers dissuade entrepreneurs from investing in natural resource extraction and processing (World Bank 1993). In addition, arm's-length transactions have been scarce in many international raw materials markets owing to the vertical integration strategy of a handful of multinational corporations or host states' nationalization policies (Vernon 1983; McKern 1976). In these cases, state leverage may be essential to negotiate preferential supply contracts (Kojima 1978) or to protect ownership rights over natural resources in foreign countries (Lipson 1985; Krasner 1978; Rodman 1993).

In other words, states have intervened to guarantee the procurement of natural resources in different ways: through the acquisition of overseas colonies, the protection of ownership rights of multinationals, and preferential FDI financing of raw materials extraction projects.[13] That colonies may benefit the metropolis by locking in the supply of raw materials is an old observation in the imperialism literature. As Frieden (1994) points out, the nature of foreign investments in raw materials extraction (their distant physical location and large sunk costs) enticed home governments to solve the problem of contract enforcement and property rights protection through formal integration.[14] However, in the second half of the twentieth century, the US government shied away from formal territorial control, relying instead on its disproportionate political influence to protect American raw materials investments in the developing world from the threat of forced nationalization (Gilpin 1975; Lipson 1985).

Japan's solution to the problem of raw material supply was very different, though. At the end of World War II, Japan lost the overseas colonies that had supplied key raw materials to Japanese industry before 1945. And the country was not able or inclined (after the absolute failure of its prewar aggressive militarism) to acquire formal colonies or to project its military power abroad to obtain the raw materials it needed for economic recovery. Instead, the Japanese government emphasized reparations and economic cooperation to reestablish economic links with neighboring Asian countries.[15] Preferential financing for overseas investment projects in raw materials exploitation soon became a core component of the economic assistance strategy of the Japanese state.

Market failure in industrial restructuring may also prompt a state response through FDI financing. Unfavorable shifts in comparative advantage can trigger government support to smooth the industrial adjustment process. Decreased international competitiveness can be the product of economic forces (mature technologies, rising wages, inflation and revaluation spirals) or of political outcomes (international government negotiations over export restraints, for example). In these instances, government support is channeled to ailing industries in an effort to smooth the industrial adjustment process and reallocate resources to growth sectors of the economy.

Government intervention of this kind is predicated on the existence of market failure as well. In this case, rigidities in wages, prices, and specific factors of production hinder the movement of resources across industrial sectors (Itoh et al. 1991; Patrick 1991; Trebilcock 1986). Structural adjustment assistance can be used to mitigate the effects of an abrupt loss of competitiveness (widespread bankruptcy and massive unemployment), thereby preempting more economically disruptive political demands for isolation from the international market (Ruggie 1983; Katzenstein 1985).[16]

It is well known that the United States and Japan have managed the process of industrial change very differently. Trade policy has been the fundamental tool with which the US government has sought to address the difficulties of declining industries. In Hufbauer's opinion, three major factors account for the exclusive use of trade measures to deal with decline: a nonintervention ideology; a long tradition of resorting to tariff policy to respond to changes in international trade; and constraints of the federal budget, which imply that off-budget measures (such as trade restrictions) are the only realistic option (1991: 99).

Protection had important implications for the apathy that many declining US industries exhibited toward offshore relocation. For example, Ramstetter argues that the central reason for only minimal US investment in Asia's primary metals, motor vehicles, and textiles is the protection these industries enjoyed from foreign competition in their domestic markets (1991: 232). Ramstetter's findings suggest that import protection may deter FDI and therefore may have prevented corporations from lobbying for more government credit to finance it.

For a trade-surplus country such as Japan, though, which is always bickering with its main trading partners over structural access barriers, the imposition of overt protectionist measures to shield declining industries was not an easy option.[17] Studies of Japanese industrial adjustment policies have often noted an interesting phenomenon: structurally depressed industries exhibit moderate import penetration ratios, despite the fact that international pressure has forced the Japanese government to abstain from overt protectionism (see Patrick 1991; Sekiguchi 1991). The standard explanation is that Japanese adjustment policy centered on rationalization subsidies and cartel policy, while a host of nontariff barriers (such as regulation of the distribution sector and land policy) and collusive business practices helped keep the market closed (Schoppa 1997; Schaede 2000; Elder 2003; Tilton 1996). I argue instead that another key dimension of Japanese adjustment assistance was FDI subsidization, which allowed firms to survive in lower-cost locations.

Several factors made the selection of FDI credit to solve market failure in industrial restructuring particularly attractive to the Japanese state. First, it offered a way to shelter Japanese firms from unrestrained market competition. Supported by subsidized public loans, Japanese firms could hope to regain international competitiveness by relocating to low-cost locations overseas. Second, the Japanese government used FDI credit as a side payment to Japanese manufacturers in compensation for their acceptance of discriminatory trade measures imposed by Japan's trading partners (voluntary export restraints, VERs, for example). Japanese firms accepted export caps but obtained cheap government loans to manufacture directly in local markets (see Chapter 5). Third, the rapidly growing pool of financial resources at the disposal of the government (the product of an improving balance of payments and the expanded base of postal savings) also facilitated the selection of public credit to promote foreign direct investment. Finally, the absence of labor union opposition to public funding of FDI helped eliminate one of the most important disincentives to state FDI financing for industrial adjustment.

The twin goals of FDI financing are reflected in the allocation of public loans for overseas investment: the largest shares of public FDI credit were allocated to depressed industries (textiles, iron and pulp, iron and steel, chemicals, and nonferrous metals received 35 percent of all FDI loans). The Japanese government first introduced FDI loans to make possible Japan's participation in natural resource projects overseas. To this strategic attempt at solving the problem of market failure in resource procurement was soon added the goal of facilitating industrial adjustment. Government FDI loans in manufacturing backed sectors with eroding export competitiveness (due to wage increases or currency realignments), and downstream processing industries undergoing structural decline due to rising energy costs (see Chapter 4).

Japan's support for troubled sectors began with the textile industry, when in the 1960s it entered a structural process of decline due to wage hikes. Next, the Japanese government lent its financial muscle to heavy industries dependent on cheap resources and energy (lumber and pulp, iron foundries, copper smelting, aluminum refining, and others) when they abruptly lost competitiveness in the post–oil shock years. In more recent times, the Japanese state financed more assembly-oriented industries (automobiles and electronics) threatened with loss of market share due to yen appreciation. Troubled industries received access to long-term, low-cost, fixed-interest-rate loans to pay for their overseas relocation.

Thus did government FDI financing powerfully shape the industrial composition of Japanese FDI by encouraging the exit of disadvantaged industry. The observation that Japanese declining sectors and small investors actively invest abroad is not new,[18] but this distinctive Japanese practice has not yet been convincingly accounted for. This book breaks new ground by focusing on the politics behind Japan's use of preferential FDI financing to facilitate the international adjustment of economically weak but politically influential constituencies. I underscore the bureaucratic rivalries, the overlap problems among FDI credit disbursing agencies, and the varying levels of subsidization made available to Japanese business interest groups.

Alternative Explanations for the Overseas Relocation of Declining Industry

Three different strands of theory are confounded by declining industry FDI: political models of industrial adjustment, microeconomic theories of FDI, and macro models linking loss of comparative advantage with overseas investment.

DECLINING INDUSTRIES AND THE POLITICAL MARKET FOR ADJUSTMENT ASSISTANCE

The political behavior of declining industries has been thoroughly analyzed by those who study international political economy. A common approach is to explain an industry's demand for protection according to its position in the international division of labor (Gourevitch 1986; Bhagwati 1988; Nelson 1988). In other words, industrial sectors without comparative advantage and besieged by imports are the most vocal advocates for closing the national market (Baldwin 1985). In turn, their success in translating their own preferences into economic policy hinges on two factors: the ability of member firms to overcome collective action problems by forming a tariff lobby group (small numbers and excludable benefits are key to successful organization; see Olson 1971); and their command of key resources (votes and contributions) to elicit the support of elected officials (Baldwin 1985: 11, 14; Hillman 1989: 10, 26).[19]

Central to this discussion is the widely shared view in the literature that demand for protection is the dominant response of declining industries because they "do not have the opportunities for adjustment available to mobile factors" (Hillman 1982: 1180). Since FDI is not an alternative for stagnant industries, the political efforts of these sectors focus exclusively on protectionism.

The literature on industrial adjustment shares some of the basic assumptions of political market models of tariff determination: declining industries will have strong incentives to organize politically to ensure their survival, and their political clout (measured by financial resources or vote mobilization) will largely determine their lobbying success (Patrick 1991: 13; Trebilcock 1986). However, this literature has provided further explanations of declining industry's policy choices. Uriu, for example, notes the impact of industry structure (degree of concentration and size of workforce) on the preferences of stagnant industries (1996: 15–17). Fragmented industrial sectors in which small firms have few financial resources to undertake economic adjustment on their own or industrial sectors with large adjustment costs due to extensive labor forces will have a stronger preference for political solutions: compensation, stabilization, and preservation (ibid.: 13). The literature on political demands for adjustment thus considers a broader range of policy options than is addressed by endogenous tariff theories. Government adjustment assistance can take many forms: subsidies and cartels to facilitate rationalization or diversification, worker retraining and unemployment compensation, and trade protection (Patrick 1991; Peck, Levin, and Goto 1987; Hufbauer 1991; Sekiguchi 1991; Ramseyer 1981; Tan and Shimada 1994).

Although the literature addresses the politics of national adjustment, it does not systematically entertain the possibility of government support for the overseas migration of industries that have lost comparative advantage. Hillman (1982) rules out the possibility that sunset industries could restructure and thrive by moving overseas; Uriu (1996: 13) deems FDI an economic adjustment option available only to firms with self-generated financial and technological resources; and Patrick (1991: 25) notes that some states (Taiwan, Korea, and Japan) provide FDI incentives, though he does not detail the nature and impact of such programs or their political dynamics. Missing in the literature on the political market for adjustment assistance, therefore, is an acknowledgment that sunset industries may also lobby for subsidized FDI credit, and that the state may use preferential financing to facilitate the international industrial adjustment of declining sectors. Moreover, following Milner's (1988) insight that multinationals will resist protectionism, the politics of public FDI financing suggests that states may preempt the demand for overt protection by opening the path to multinationality.

The possibility of achieving international industrial adjustment through subsidized FDI credit changes the political economy of Japanese adjustment. Regarding labor, Uriu (1996) elegantly demonstrates that large workforces often complicate the tasks of adjustment and encourage industries to search for political solutions—that is, some form of compensation from the state (such as subsidies or cartels).[20] However, if soft FDI credit is available, the opposite is true. Firms with extensive workforces could refrain from demanding that the government supply this form of assistance, for the simple reason that it implies international mobility for only one factor of production (capital).[21] Moreover, purely domestic enterprises could resent government subsidies to internationally mobile enterprises. This book adds a new dimension to the discussion of Japanese industrial adjustment by taking into account how the interests of labor and domestic capital clash with those of transnational corporations.

FIRM-SPECIFIC ADVANTAGES AND FOREIGN DIRECT INVESTMENT

Dunning's (1992) eclectic paradigm is one of the most influential theories of FDI because it successfully integrates the various strands of microeconomic FDI theory into a comprehensive approach to explain international production. In Dunning's formulation, each case of foreign direct investment is the result of a combination of ownership, location, and internalization advantages (the OLI approach).

The central tenet of conventional FDI theory is that firms must possess ownership advantages to offset the costs of manufacturing in a foreign environment. Some of these advantages are firm size, technological and capital intensity, and product differentiation, to name a few. The theory is founded on the existence of some form of structural market imperfection through which oligopolists exploit their firm-specific advantages in foreign locations.[22] A second major tenet of conventional FDI theory is that firms will exploit their proprietary advantages through direct investment (not exports or licensing) when market exchange is more costly than internalization of transactions.[23] Therefore, international production occurs when firms internalize transactions across borders. Finally, the eclectic paradigm poses that firms will select an investment destination by evaluating the quality and availability of location-bound assets (such as natural resources, labor costs, and technology).

Microeconomic theory rules out FDI in sectors with mature technologies: "Direct investment does not occur in standardized goods produced by competitive industries such as textiles, clothing, flour milling and distribution" (Kindleberger 1969: 13–14). And it finds a strong correlation between firm strength and multinationality: "We can say that multinational firms are R&D intensive, large, profitable, and fast growing relative to other firms in their industries. Furthermore, their industries exhibit the same characteristics relative to industry as a whole" (Lipsey 1991: 277).

It is therefore difficult to reconcile microeconomic theories of FDI with the overseas relocation of Japan's stagnant industries. The eclectic paradigm considers FDI as the terrain of the large, profitable, and innovative corporation. This model well explains the international adjustment of strong firms (for example, large corporations self-financing the transfer of labor-intensive operations to lower-cost economies in order to remain competitive). But this approach is hard pressed to explain why small investors with seemingly insufficient resources, large firms on the brink of bankruptcy, or companies in industrial sectors characterized by competitive structures, mature technologies, or lack of export competitiveness also have turned to foreign production.[24]

At the root of the problem are the constraints imposed by the microeconomic orientation of this theory—that is, its almost exclusive focus on the ownership advantages generated by the firm itself. The deliberate effort of home governments to strengthen the outward investment capabilities of firms, especially weak ones, has remained largely outside this framework. This is a large omission in the case of Japan, where the government intentionally lowers the cost of capital to finance overseas investment projects.

LOSS OF COMPARATIVE ADVANTAGE AND OVERSEAS RELOCATION

Other FDI models look more explicitly at the relationship between shifts in comparative advantage and the decision to transfer manufacturing abroad. In his well-known product cycle theory, Vernon (1966; 1970) posits that innovative companies (who were serving the international market through exports) may decide to invest in low-cost overseas locations once technology is standardized and production costs become a larger factor in competitiveness.

There are, however, important limitations in applying Vernon's theory to declining industry FDI. The product cycle model is applicable only to certain kinds of industries and firms: the technological innovators. There is no room in this approach for FDI in standardized, technologically mature industries: "Multinational enterprises are not identified with the manufacture of such standardized products as steel bars and rods, gray cloth, or plywood; but they are identified with products whose specifications are in flux" (Vernon 1970). Most important, Vernon does not address the issue of differing responses to the loss of comparative advantage once the technological innovator is forced to cut production costs. Eroding export competitiveness does not always result in FDI in low-cost economies, but may instead trigger lobbying campaigns for trade protection. Governments can affect the investment decision by lowering the costs of overseas relocation (through preferential FDI financing) or by erecting import barriers.

Kojima's (1978) macroeconomic theory of FDI has also been widely discussed in the field of international production.[25] Kojima argues that "American-style FDI" replaces trade with foreign production: firms from the home country invest in industries in which they are comparatively advantaged and the host country is comparatively disadvantaged. In contrast, "Japanese-style FDI" is trade-enhancing: Japan invests in maturing industries that can be competitively developed by host nations, favoring industrial restructuring in both countries and expanding the basis for trade.

Kojima's model has been strongly criticized, but suffice it here to point out that Kojima does not address the crucial question of why there has been so little US investment in mature industries, and why—when he wrote in 1978—there had been so little Japanese investment in oligopolistic industries.[26] This mystery could be solved by paying more attention to the incentive structure that firms in declining sectors face, either to pursue protection or to adjust through FDI. This model also does not provide an in-depth consideration of the role of home states in the multinationalization of industry. By providing protection, subsidies for capacity curtailment, and soft FDI financing, governments can decisively affect the adjustment strategy of firms in troubled industries.

Bhagwati (1982; 1987) offers one of the few models to directly link interest group lobbying with government policy on international factor mobility. He argues that the only adjustment options lobbies for senescent industries can press for are trade protection and an inflow of foreign labor. Bhagwati claims that foreign direct investment is not an option for declining, labor-intensive industries because "these are unprogressive industries where, with no Hymer-like firm-specific know-how to take advantage of, the migration of domestic entrepreneurship is likely to mean merely that the migrant entrepreneurs will have to operate in unfamiliar, relatively riskier foreign situations, without any offsetting technological advantage, and hence at a competitive disadvantage with local producers" (1982: 155).

Significantly, Bhagwati acknowledges only one major exception to his hypothesis concerning the lack of capital mobility (FDI) in senescent industries: the Japanese textile industry (ibid.: 180). The puzzle of a labor-intensive, technologically mature industry investing actively overseas remains a puzzle in Bhagwati's framework. This suggests that a political-economy model of outward investment should also incorporate the lobbying responses of capital and labor in favor of or against an FDI prescription for declining industries.

Sunset industry relocation thus presents a formidable challenge to available theories. Political models of industrial adjustment focus on protection or domestic restructuring strategies, while assuming that structurally depressed industries are not internationally mobile. The predominant microeconomic model neither predicts FDI by mature industries or weak firms nor anticipates that domestic political institutions can influence industry to choose overseas relocation. Moreover, work to date linking shifts in comparative advantage to overseas investment does not solve the puzzle of declining industry FDI either. Missing in these macro models is a systematic discussion of the incentive structure that prompts mature industries to select FDI as an adjustment strategy, and the recognition that public support is necessary for troubled sectors to afford the costs of investing overseas.

A Political-Economy Model of FDI: The Politics of Public FDI Credit

The political-economy model set forth here stresses the influence of government FDI financing (the independent variable) on the sectoral composition of overseas investment (the dependent variable measured by the industry shares of total foreign investment flows).[27] In this book I explore whether we can attribute the prominent role of weak industries and small enterprises in Japanese FDI flows to the availability of a substantial public loan program for overseas investment. And I assess the interplay of economic and political motives behind the government's decision to promote the multinationalization of sunset industries.

The political-economy model proposed here unfolds in three stages: identifying different multinationalization patterns (self-financing versus public financing); analyzing the politics behind the allocation and subsidization of public FDI credit; and establishing the conditions that neutralized domestic opposition to publicly financed multinationalization.

PREFERENTIAL CREDIT AND THE INCENTIVES TO INVEST ABROAD

The availability of preferential credit affects the firm's incentive structure to go multinational. In the United States and Europe, companies that pursue industrial adjustment through FDI (for example, by relocating labor-intensive manufacturing overseas) must rely on their own financial means. Weak and financially strapped companies in these countries, therefore, cannot afford to set up production abroad. In contrast, Japanese declining industries are financially assisted by the government to set up foreign production facilities.

The distinction between self- and public financing is also helpful in establishing different multinationalization patterns *within* Japanese manufacturing. Preferential financing was not of equal importance to all Japanese industries investing abroad. Some Japanese sectors (food, electronics, general machinery, precision instruments) self-financed their FDI strategies, whereas others (textiles, lumber and pulp, nonferrous metals, iron and steel, chemicals, and transportation machinery) relied heavily on FDI loans from the Japan Eximbank. Dependence on state financing from sectors in the second category was by no means minor: all of these industries financed between 25 and 70 percent of their FDI expenses with public money (see Chapter 4). Many of the more multinationalized Japanese sectors leaned significantly on public financial institutions offering FDI credit, and not coincidentally, many of these sectors had difficulty gaining or maintaining international competitiveness given their labor or natural resource intensity.

In order to show the variation in multinationalization patterns within Japanese manufacturing, this book analyzes the international industrial adjustment experiences of three industrial sectors: textiles, aluminum smelting, and consumer electronics. The case studies analyze the outward investment activities in these sectors throughout their life cycle: from infancy through growth, maturity, and eventually decline. I selected these three industries for the following reasons. One, they capture the process of industrial change in Japan: the shift from light manufacturing to heavy industry and assembly-line production. All faced substantial erosion in their international competitiveness and confronted the challenge of adjusting through downsizing or foreign relocation. Two, these three industries played a leading role in Japanese FDI flows, so a study of their individual experiences provides us with a representative sample of the multinationalization process in Japanese industry. And three, this selection allows us to compare industries with high value (textiles and aluminum) and low value (electronics) in the independent variable.

These case studies thus shed light on the powerful role of public credit in the internationalization of depressed Japanese industries, and also point to the limited influence of the Japanese government over industries capable of self-financing their foreign investments. The argument advanced here is that public credit affects the composition of Japanese FDI flows precisely because it helps some industries but not others. Obviously, the next task is to explain why certain industries were targeted and why they received different levels of FDI subsidization.

THE POLITICS OF FDI CREDIT ALLOCATION AND SUBSIDIZATION

This political-economy model of FDI financing identifies three primary rationales for government support of overseas investment: two economic criteria to solve market failures in either natural resource procurement or industrial adjustment, and a political motivation to reward lobbying groups that supply votes or financial contributions to the ruling party.

These motivations suggest testable hypotheses about patterns of public credit allocation and allow the conceptualization of government FDI financing as a policy tool subject to bureaucratic or political manipulation. In other words, bureaucrats and politicians compete to control the allocation (and especially the subsidization) of the vast amount of public overseas investment loans. The focal point of this competition is the institutional budgetary design that allows interest groups and their political brokers to influence public FDI disbursing agencies, or prevents them from doing so.

The Japanese government found FDI credit an attractive solution to the problems of raw materials procurement and industrial restructuring for reasons already mentioned. Briefly, deprived of other alternatives (such as domestic self-sufficiency or colonial control over resource rich areas), and compelled by its trading partners to avoid overt protectionism, the Japanese government turned to indicative credit. It is important to note, however, that the purpose of the Japanese government's generous support of overseas investment was not only to solve market failures. The state used preferential financing with a more explicit political goal in mind: to please important electoral constituencies.

Two arguments related to interest groups and politicians underscore the

TABLE 1.3
Explaining Self-Financed and State-Financed Multinationalization

Industrial characteristics	Industries
Favoring self-financed international production[a]	Electronics
High technological intensity	Chemicals
Large product differentiation	Machinery
Good export performance	Transportation equipment
Large firm size	Food products
Industrial concentration (oligopoly)	Metal products
High capital intensity	
Managerial capabilities	
Favoring state-financed international production[b]	Lumber and pulp
Intensive consumption of energy and raw materials (bureaucrats aim to counter market failure in natural resource procurement)[b]	Nonferrous metals Iron and steel Petrochemcials
Structural or cyclical decline (bureaucrats aim to counter market failure in industrial adjustment)	Textiles Machinery part makers
Suppliers of funds or votes to the ruling party (politicians aim to reward key support groups)	

[a]Firm-specific advantages that conventional economic FDI theory identifies as necessary for foreign production.

[b]Characteristics of firms and industries that should entice the government to provide assistance via low-cost FDI loans.

political angle in Japanese public FDI financing. The first views the relationship of big business and politicians as an exchange of financial contributions for policies agreeable to capital (Magee, Brock, and Young 1989; Okimoto 1988). The second focuses on the exchange of votes for trade protection, subsidies, and other benefits. In this case, small and medium-sized enterprises (SMEs) that make up a large portion of the Japanese electorate emerge as the main constituency to be appeased by politicians (Calder 1988; Okimoto 1988).[28]

These rationales for public funding of FDI suggest several hypotheses about the patterns of FDI credit allocation. Table 1.3 lists the characteristics of firms and industries that should trigger government support for international production. Included are sectors that consume vast amounts of energy and raw materials; industries in deep recession; and sectors that provide key financial contributions or votes. Whether politics affected the multinationalization of Japanese industry becomes a testable proposition because most of the sectors in the "political" box are different from those identified by economic theory.[29] In other words, my political-economy model retains the insights of economic theories to explain FDI by expanding industries, but adds an institutional and political dynamic to explain FDI by stagnant sectors and small firms.[30]

In addition to explaining public FDI credit allocation patterns, my political-economy model also seeks to unravel the politics behind the varying degrees of subsidization awarded to different interest groups through public FDI loans. It analyzes how the lending behavior of public financial institutions differs toward various producer groups. Some institutions are highly disciplined in their credit decisions, carefully screening borrowers, demanding collateral, and charging interest rates close to market levels (I call them efficient credit allocators); other agencies use more soft financing and monitor their clients only casually (I call them pork dispensers).

Budgetary rules seem to be crucial in explaining the contrasting behavior of public FDI loan agencies in Japan. Those that provide soft financing have few budgetary constraints because they are funded generously from the general account (by both capital injections and annual appropriations). More disciplined lending agencies must borrow (from the Treasury and through bond issues) or use their own resources (earnings) to carry out their activities. Control over these budgetary rules has been a high priority for politicians and bureaucrats with clashing preferences over the degree and distribution of FDI subsidies (see Chapter 4).

OVERCOMING DOMESTIC OPPOSITION TO STATE-SUPPORTED MULTINATIONALIZATION

The expansion of multinational corporations has traditionally generated opposition at home on the grounds that it fosters deindustrialization or harms the domestic workforce. Proponents of the deindustrialization (or hollowing-out) thesis highlight the negative effects of outward FDI on the competitiveness of the domestic economy: curtailment of the technological base, employment loss, and the creation of a low-productivity service economy (Bluestone and Harrison 1982).

However, the claim that FDI is responsible for economic hollowing-out has not been demonstrated empirically.[31] In fact, the mainstream view is that foreign direct investment is not detrimental to the home economy. FDI does not replace exports, but instead enhances the international competitiveness of firms and promotes higher-value-added exports (Moran 1993: 11; Caves 1982). In other words, FDI and exports are complements, not substitutes.

But if FDI does not promote deindustrialization, others argue that it does disadvantage labor unions in a variety of ways: it produces labor redundancy in low-skilled jobs, compresses domestic wages, and reduces union membership; most important, it shifts the bargaining balance in favor of capital.

Unions find it difficult to resist management demands for lower wages or layoffs when they must negotiate with multinational corporations ready to exercise their exit option.[32]

Concerned about the deleterious effect of "footloose enterprises" on the clout of organized labor, American union leaders have systematically opposed foreign direct investment by US enterprises. For instance, in 1994, Thomas Donahue, vice president of the American Federation of Labor–Council of Industrial Organizations (AFL-CIO), complained: "The world has become a huge bazaar with nations peddling their workforces in competition against one another, offering the lowest price for doing business. The customers, of course, are multinational corporations" (quoted in Piazza 2002: 4).

Union contestation of offshore relocation and outsourcing plans has regularly pitted labor leaders against managers of US multinationals. In 1998, for example, when General Motors announced its intention to relocate much of its manufacturing to Mexico, workers struck, idling most of GM's North American workforce for fifty-four days. To settle the strike, GM promised further investments in two US plants and the scaling down of the outsourcing plan; the union had to accept some layoffs (500) and a campaign to increase worker productivity.

The US textile union also waged a high-profile campaign against offshore manufacturing. Charging textile MNCs with condoning sweatshop conditions in their overseas outsourcing networks, the union asked US consumers to boycott American MNCs that rely on cheap and exploited foreign labor (Piazza 2002: 1–2, 188).

Considering these union battles against FDI in the United States, the minor resistance in Japan from disadvantaged groups—labor and domestic firms—is all the more remarkable. With the swift expansion of Japanese FDI after the yen appreciation of the mid-1980s, the familiar charges of hollowing-out *(kūdōka)* were increasingly heard in the media.

But as in the United States, no direct link between outward investment and deindustrialization in Japan has been established. Academic studies note that FDI is not correlated with the unemployment rate and has not harmed the export performance of Japanese industry (Nakamura and Shibuya 1995; Minotani 1996; Ishiyama 1999).[33] Where Japan and the United States do differ is in the fact that Japanese organized labor did not launch a campaign based on the "export of jobs" issue to oppose foreign investment by Japanese companies. Despite the far more substantial public funding of Japan's MNCs, Japanese unions did not seek the support of local politicians to block soft FDI loans.

The weak resistance of Japanese unions to industry relocation could be explained by the traditional weakness of Japan's organized labor movement. Because it lacks strong industrial-level unions, Japan has been identified by some as a case of "corporatism without labor" (Pempel and Tsunekawa 1979). Nevertheless, enterprise unionism was very effective in some areas.[34] Japanese enterprise unionism assigned the highest priority to employment security and scored high marks in ensuring management and government commitment to this principle. During the 1970s, labor extracted special legislation to protect laid-off workers in the state-denominated structurally depressed industries (Kume 1998: 170–71). Far from being powerless, Japanese unions were able to defend their core interest (employment security) even in contracting sectors. Why Japanese unions did not challenge the huge public FDI credit program to assist overseas industrial relocation is, therefore, in need of explanation.

I posit that the muted opposition of unions to state financing of overseas investment is the result of three factors. First, the public FDI credit program concentrated on stagnant industries receiving large subsidies for labor adjustment. Consequently, FDI was not considered the root cause of decline for these industries, and workers in these sectors benefited from state relief programs. Second, organized labor did not suffer the brunt of employment cuts and, consequently, viewed overseas expansion more benignly. As this book's case studies on textiles and electronics reveal, most of those who lost their jobs were female employees and part-timers. Since its core interests (union member employment) were not affected, Japanese labor did not attempt to politicize FDI policies. And third, the Japanese government was careful to avoid possible criticism for fostering *kūdōka*. Adjustment assistance packages for industries in structural recession frequently contained clauses on the promotion of FDI *and* the maintenance in the homeland of higher-value-added activities. The thrust of FDI credit policy is not to transfer whole manufacturing sectors abroad, but to relocate overseas the uncompetitive segments of the industry while maintaining research and development (R&D) and high-value-added activities in Japan.

Another potential source of opposition to FDI is domestic firms hurt by MNC activity. Multinationals that target the domestic market with reverse imports put increased pressure on domestic Japanese firms. Although for most of the postwar period, Japanese multinationals used their foreign factories primarily to serve local and third markets, in more recent years shipping part of the offshore production back to Japan became more common. All three of the industries in this book's case studies report increased import penetration ratios, though the level of conflict differed markedly from one industry to another. Industrial fragmentation may explain this divergence in outcome. Firms unconstrained by *keiretsu* loyalties were more vocal in their opposition to multinational operation (see Chapters 5 and 6). The political-economy model of FDI developed here, therefore, pays special attention to the protection of unionized workers and to the development of *keiretsu* links to explain the minimal contestation of the world's largest preferential credit program for overseas investment.

This chapter laid out the motivations behind Japanese government's financing of foreign direct investment, as well as the political factors that influence differential rates of FDI subsidization. The following chapter describes in much more detail the evolution and industrial composition of Japanese foreign direct investment.

CHAPTER 2

The Rise of Japan as an FDI Power

FOREIGN DIRECT INVESTMENT has profoundly affected the distribution of worldwide production, the organization of international trade, and the speed of technology transfer among countries. Despite the broad geographic reach of multinational corporations, these firms continue to be headquartered in a small number of developed nations. Indeed, close to 98 percent of the world's outward investment stock is concentrated in developed market economies. Moreover, one or two home countries (the United Kingdom and the United States) have generated the bulk of direct investment capital over time, and more recently Japan has joined them as a major investing power.

This chapter traces the evolution of the multinational corporation and places the unfolding of Japanese multinationalism in comparative perspective. It discusses the forces of convergence that have influenced Japanese FDI patterns, as well as the enduring peculiarities of Japan's overseas investment. The leading role of structurally depressed industries and small firms in Japanese offshore manufacturing sets Japanese multinationalism apart and underscores the powerful role of government preferential financing in the international adjustment of struggling Japanese producers.

Japanese FDI Flows in Comparative Perspective

The multinational corporation developed in earnest during the late nineteenth century. The colonial trading companies (such as the East India and Hudson Bay Companies) were predecessors of the modern transnational firm; foreign direct investment took off only in the 1860s and 1870s. Several factors spurred the growth of multinational corporations: progress in communications and transport technology, the Industrial Revolution (which generated greater demand for raw materials, manufacturing know-how, and investment capital), and Great Britain's commitment to free international exchange. Moreover, the political risk of operating in foreign countries was mitigated by the absence of large-scale conflict, the expansion of colonial empires (and the granting of special privileges to enterprises headquartered in the metropolis), and the development of international property rights to protect MNCs against the risk of expropriation (Jones 1996; Lipson 1985).

Just as it led the way in the Industrial Revolution, Britain pioneered in the development of the transnational firm.[1] Although most British investment overseas was directed to the acquisition of portfolio assets, significant amounts were channeled as well to managerial enterprises. In 1914, Britain was the undisputed FDI power, with cumulative outward investment worth $6.5 billion, roughly 45.5 percent of the world's total. The United States trailed behind with a mere $2.65 billion (or 18.5 percent of the total) (Dunning and Archer 1987: 63).

The reach of British corporations was indeed global, with a marked preference for European high-income markets and lands of recent settlement (such as Australia and South Africa) and resource-rich countries in Asia and Latin America. Initial British investments abroad were highly skewed toward infrastructure projects (railroads), overseas plantations, mines and oil fields, and financial services (insurance on overseas trade and investment). These ventures abroad were backed by the early formation in England of an efficient capital market and fueled by the desire to capture higher returns on capital abroad and the supply of foreign raw materials. British manufacturing investment abroad centered on consumer industries, such as soap, beer, thread, and patent medicines. Some investment also took place in producer industries, mainly textiles. British investors concentrated on consumer industries that were trademarked so that they could enjoy the benefits of product differentiation and name recognition. In producer industries, Britain reaped the benefits of its lead in the Industrial Revolution, particularly in textiles (Stopford and Turner 1985; Dunning and Archer 1987; Wilkins 1988).

England's lead in the expansion of the multinational corporation began to erode in the interwar period as it failed to develop at home and invest abroad in new industries such as chemicals and electrical machinery; and the loss of the Empire and slower domestic rates of growth rendered the balance-of-payments situation more precarious. The UK's direct investment abroad in the postwar period continued to be heavily focused on consumer industries, and was increasingly concentrated in the Commonwealth area where British companies could still profit from preferential treatment (Dunning and Archer 1987).

After World War II, the United States emerged as the leading source of offshore investment capital. The position of US multinational corporations was so dominant that according to some observers the term *multinational corporation* was taken as synonymous with the *US oligopolistic corporation* (Wilkins 1974; Gilpin 1975). Indeed, cumulative US outward investment grew at a staggering pace, increasing from $7.2 billion in 1946 to $31.9 billion in 1960, and to $124.2 billion in 1975 (see Table 2.1). In other words, during the first half of the postwar period US cumulative FDI amounted to almost half of the world's total. Although US multinationals have established operating bases on all continents, foreign direct investment is concentrated in developed economies (Europe and Canada) and neighboring countries (Latin America and of course Canada). One of the most noteworthy characteristics of FDI flows in the postwar period is that they have largely become a North-North phenomenon. Since 1975 more than three-quarters of all FDI has taken place in industrialized nations (Brewer and Young 1998: 59).

Another major difference in the nature of FDI in the late twentieth century is that natural resource investments have receded in importance. In its early stages, US FDI was also heavily oriented toward primary activities (agriculture, mining, and especially oil), and manufacturing. In 1970 these sectors accounted for 70 percent of cumulative US outward investment. In the second half of the postwar period, investment in raw materials, ores, and fuels contracted, while financial services and manufacturing became the mainstays of US direct investment abroad. In 1990 these sectors represented more than 90 percent of cumulative US outward investment. In manufacturing, sectors with advanced technologies, differentiated goods, and scale economies have led the way throughout in the offshore investment drive (Wilkins 1974; Ramstetter 1991). For example, in 1950 electrical and general machinery, automobiles, chemicals, and food products accounted for 60 percent of cumulative US FDI in manufacturing. Forty years later, these same sectors amounted to 70 percent of cumulative FDI in manufacturing by US corporations.

Although the United States continues to be the largest foreign investor in the world, its days of undisputed supremacy are gone. With the recovery of the European and Japanese economies, and their increased capital exports, the US share of worldwide investment began eroding in the late 1970s. In 1975 the United States still contributed 45 percent of the cumulative outward investment by developed market economies, but this share fell to 28 percent in 1990 and grew again slightly to 30 percent in 1997 (see Table 2.1). The UK ranked second to the United States during the postwar period, although its share of world cumulative FDI has also decreased. Other European countries with large FDI flows are the Netherlands, Switzerland, and Germany. Both Japan and Germany rose from the bottom of the FDI rankings (ninth and eighth place, respectively, in 1960) to become top overseas investors. Japan, however, surpassed Germany to rank third among FDI powers in 1990, with a 13 percent share of cumulative FDI from OECD countries. The Japanese

TABLE 2.1

Japan Joins the Ranks of FDI Powers: The Evolution of Outward Investment Stock, 1960–1997

	1960			1975			1990			1997		
Country	Amount (billion US$)	Share of total outward investment stock (%)	Rank	Amount (billion US$)	Share of total outward investment stock (%)	Rank	Amount (billion US$)	Share of total outward investment stock(%)	Rank	Amount (billion US$)	Share of total outward investment stock (%)	Rank
United States	31.9	47.6	1	124.2	45.1	1	430.5	27.5	1	865.5	30.1	1
United Kingdom	12.4	18.5	2	37.0	13.4	2	230.8	14.7	2	371.1	12.9	2
Japan	0.5	0.8	9	15.9	5.8	6	201.4	12.9	3	282.3	9.8	3
Germany	0.8	1.2	8	18.4	6.7	5	148.5	9.5	4	280.8	9.8	4
Netherlands	7.0	10.5	3	19.9	7.2	4	109.1	7.0	6	209.6	7.3	5
Switzerland	2.3	3.4	6	22.4	8.1	3	66.1	4.2	8	161.9	5.6	7
France	4.1	6.1	4	10.6	3.9	7	110.1	7.0	5	189.7	6.6	6
Italy	1.1	1.6	7	3.3	1.2	10	59.0	3.8	9	125.0	4.3	9
Sweden	0.4	0.6	10	4.7	1.7	9	49.5	3.2	10	75.3	2.6	10
Canada	2.5	3.7	5	10.4	3.8	8	84.8	5.4	7	143.9	5.0	8
Other	4.0	6.0		8.5	3.1		75.2	4.8		169.4	5.9	
Total	67.0	100.0		275.4	100.0		1,565.1	100.0		2,874.5	100.0	

SOURCES: United Nations Centre for Transnational Corporations data compiled by Grazia Ietto-Gillies (1992); and OECD, *International Direct Investment Statistics Yearbook* (several years).

recession during the 1990s has exerted its toll on FDI, however. At the end of the 1990s, Japan and Germany were tied in third place with close to 10 percent of the world's cumulative outward direct investment.[2]

Japan has come a long way from the $0.5 billion in cumulative FDI it reported in 1960 to the $282 billion registered in 1997. Japan resumed postwar foreign direct investment in 1951, but in the early years there were very few investment projects abroad because the priority for business and the state was reconstruction at home. Indeed, the Japanese government, worried about the balance of payments, implemented strict controls on the outflow of capital (see Chapter 3).[3]

Most Japanese investment during this period (1951–70) went to the development of natural resources. Of particular importance were five large-scale projects: Goa Iron Ore (1951), Alaska Pulp (1953), Minas Steel in Brazil (1957), Arabian Oil (1958), and North Sumatra Oil (1960). Japanese trading companies also invested early on in commercial outposts in the territory of their main business partners. During the 1960s, the textile industry led a rise in offshore manufacturing investment. Cotton spinners that had invested early in South America to obtain access to cheap supplies of cotton were joined later by synthetic fiber firms investing in Asia to reach protected domestic markets. Overall, however, Japanese FDI flows from 1951 to 1970 remained modest: $3.6 billion, of which $0.9 billion was in manufacturing (see Table 2.2).

A new era in the Japanese outward investment drive dawned in 1972. This year, known as *gannen,* or "first year," saw an unprecedented explosion in outward investment flows. In 1972 and 1973 alone FDI flows amounted to $5.8 billion, almost twice the accumulated Japanese FDI of the previous twenty years. Several factors were responsible for the surge in Japanese outward investment. The demise of the Bretton Woods system of fixed exchange rates brought a serious revaluation of the yen, from 360 to 308 per dollar. Japanese exporters were immediately hurt by the strong yen and sought to produce locally to offset currency realignments. Moreover, the value of foreign assets in yen terms decreased, facilitating an FDI strategy. Domestic wage increases also strained the competitiveness of Japanese labor-intensive industries (particularly textiles), encouraging them to seek cheap labor overseas (Komiya 1988: 262). Finally, Japan's balance-of-payments situation improved notably, and the government gradually liberalized the regime governing capital outflows during 1969–72. In the aftermath of the "Nixon shocks,"[4] strong revaluatory pressure on the yen prompted government action to facilitate even more capital exports. The government passed three consecutive yen stabilizing policies that sought to promote imports and FDI by reducing interest rates on the public credit available for these operations, and by offering foreign currency loans to tame currency risks (Japan Eximbank 1983).

But the FDI boom was short-lived. The first oil shock in 1973 drove the

TABLE 2.2

Manufacturing Abroad: The Evolution of Japanese FDI, 1951–1999

	First period (1951–1970)		Second period (1971–1984)		Third period (1985–1999)	
	Amount (million US$)	Share of manufacturing (%)	Amount (million US$)	Share of manufacturing (%)	Amount (million US$)	Share of manufacturing (%)
Food products	60.8	6.3	949.0	4.4	24,813.0	11.2
Textiles	189.8	19.7	1,946.0	9.1	7,381.0	3.3
Lumber and pulp	212.4	22.1	973.0	4.6	5,231.0	2.4
Chemicals	59.6	6.2	3,822.0	17.9	26,330.0	11.9
Iron and steel, nonferrous metals	137.9	14.3	4,678.0	21.9	17,170.0	7.8
General machinery	67.2	7.0	1,568.0	7.3	17,970.0	8.1
Electrical machinery	70.9	7.4	3,182.0	14.9	65,168.0	29.5
Transportation equipment	102.5	10.7	2,663.0	12.5	29,581.0	13.4
Other manufacturing	61.5	6.4	1,594.0	7.5	27,130.0	12.3
Manufacturing total	962.7	100.0	21,375.0	100.0	220,776.0	100.0
Agriculture	57.7		722.0		1,682.0	
Forestry, fisheries	27.2		383.0		1,077.0	
Mining	1,126.7		10,558.0		16,233.0	
Construction	37.8		670.0		4,670.0	
Commerce	403.1		10,793.0		61,005.0	
Finance, insurance	321.9		6,825.0		132,553.0	
Other nonmanufacturing	659.1		17,490.0		214,786.0	
Nonmanufacturing total	2,633.6		47,441.0		432,006.0	
Total	3,596.3		68,816.0		654,939.0	

SOURCE: Compiled from Ministry of Finance statistics.

Japanese economy into one of its worst postwar recessions. Economic deterioration was evident in the worsening balance of payments, rising inflation, and low or even negative growth rates. The transformation of the international energy market and its impact on the Japanese economy had the effect of reducing outward investment. In 1974 outward investment was only $2.4 billion, down from $3.4 billion the year before. Lower firm profitability due to the contraction of internal and external demand limited corporate liquidity, and the hostility of many Asian nations toward what was perceived as Japanese "overpresence" acted as powerful disincentives for Japanese companies to undertake foreign production (Yoshihara 1978). In addition, balance-of-payments concerns again constrained outward capital flows. For example, directives were passed to the Japan Eximbank to limit its overseas investment loans (Japan Eximbank 1983).

The energy price hikes in 1973 and 1979 unleashed even larger forces that further promoted the transnationalization of the Japanese economy. Immediately after the first oil shock the Japanese government embarked on an "economic diplomacy" initiative, with Japanese officials touring the capitals of oil-producing nations to obtain guarantees of petroleum supply in exchange for Japanese commitments to expand economic cooperation. The ties developed between Japan and these countries went far beyond oil sale contracts and petroleum exploitation projects; they included oil-refining ventures, petrochemical complexes, projects for iron and steel production, and shipbuilding.

Moreover, Japanese industries that relied on oil saw their international competitiveness plummet almost overnight. Many responded by moving their production facilities to countries with ample energy sources, notably the aluminum smelting and textile synthetic fiber industries. Unstable international raw material markets and higher production costs in Japan led to an exodus of many Japanese heavy industries. Petrochemical firms, iron foundries, steel makers, copper smelters, and others invested actively abroad during these years, often in integrated ventures that comprised natural resource extraction and processing on foreign soil.

Manufacturing FDI in assembly industries increased as well during the 1970s and early 1980s. Concern over protectionism acted as a powerful lever on the decision to invest abroad. For example, after the United States capped Japanese exports of televisions to the US market in 1977, Japanese television companies hurried to open shop in the United States: Mitsubishi in 1977, Toshiba in 1978, Sharp in 1979, Hitachi in 1979, and Japan Victor in 1982.

The automobile industry followed suit. Transportation equipment's outward investment jumped from $1.7 billion in 1980 to $4.1 billion in 1981. The Japanese carmakers' investment rush was due mostly to the export quota imposed by the United States in 1981 and their need to embrace local production to avoid further protectionist threats. Between 1981 and 1984 Honda, Nissan, and Toyota opened US factories, and a few years later all major Japanese automobile firms were manufacturing in North America. Table 2.2 summarizes the trends in Japanese outward investment during its second period (1971–84).

Mining—which includes oil exploration—was at the top of Japanese productive investments abroad with outflows of $10.6 billion. Heavy industries also played a leading role in the outward investment drive (iron and steel and nonferrous metals with $4.7 billion, and chemicals with $3.8 billion). Machinery industries exhibited increased dynamism in their outbound ventures, and textiles continued to represent an important portion of total investment flows.

In the mid-1980s, the value of Japanese outward investment almost doubled in one year, from $12.2 billion in 1985 to $22.3 billion in 1986. Japan's FDI peaked in 1989 at $67.5 billion. Although the burst of the Japanese economic bubble in the early 1990s slowed outward investment (it reached a low of $34 billion in 1992), it recovered to $67 billion by 1999. In the third period (1985–99) Japanese FDI was greatest in real estate, finance, insurance, and commerce. Manufacturing FDI also multiplied in absolute terms, with a cumulative value of $221 billion between 1985 and 1999. The electronics industry alone accounted for 30 percent of manufacturing FDI, and transportation equipment, chemicals, and general machinery also held significant shares in manufacturing overseas investment (see Table 2.2).

This tremendous increase in the value of Japanese offshore investments can be attributed to the combination of several factors. Import restrictions and local content requirements proliferated in industrialized countries, pushing further manufacturing in these markets (Urata 1991). Moreover, the steep appreciation of the yen reduced the international competitiveness of Japanese goods.

After the signing of the Plaza Agreement on exchange rates in 1985, the value of the yen increased rapidly, from 236.95 per dollar in September 1985 to 127.56 in January 1986. During the late 1980s, the annual average exchange rate ranged between 126 and 144 yen to the dollar, and the Japanese currency again appreciated dramatically in the early 1990s. Between 1991 and July 1994 the value of the yen increased an additional 38 percent, with the exchange rate reaching 98.5 yen to the dollar. In the late 1990s, the yen remained very strong (in 1999 the exchange rate of the yen to the dollar was 102). Assembly industries were particularly disadvantaged by the currency realignment. These sectors lost profits and cut back on equipment investment (an average reduction of 46 percent between 1992 and 1993) and R&D (a 10 percent decrease in the same two years) (Nagaoka 1995: 3–4).

To offset their decreased competitiveness, assembly industries intensified their FDI. Electronics in particular redoubled its overseas investment efforts. Whereas $3.2 billion in electronics FDI was registered between 1971 and 1984, the following decade saw an increase of more than twenty times in outward investment flows (to $65 billion).

Throughout the 1980s and 1990s, Japan not only maintained its interest in manufacturing in North America and Europe but also recovered an Asian focus. Between 1986 and 1993 close to 30 percent of Japanese investment took place in Asia and increasingly targeted members of the Association of Southeast Asian Nations (ASEAN). In many of these countries, Japan has emerged as the top foreign investor (Doner 1993: 162). Indeed, the dynamic relocation of Japanese electronics firms in Asia has generated a growing body of research on the implications of the emerging Japanese-led regional production networks (Urata 1991; Doner 1993; Bernard and Ravenhill 1995). The export of Japanese FDI capital has tightened the trade and production interdependence among countries of the region with growing intraindustry and intrafirm transactions. Even as Asian nations embark on the production of electronic and automotive goods, firms in these countries still remain heavily dependent on their Japanese business partners for the supply of key technologies and parts (Bernard and Ravenhill 1995).

Distinctive Features of Japanese Foreign Direct Investment

Multinational corporations have become giants in the international marketplace through their extensive and sophisticated networks of production and trade. Leading technologies, financial prowess, and capital mobility have brought them great political and market power. However, there is little consensus among IPE scholars on whether these are truly "global" multinational corporations—companies that, unconstrained by national regulation, adopt similar corporate strategies to meet intense world competition.

Some believe that through their investments across the globe MNCs have shed their nationality. In this view, multinational enterprises have acquired global interests and assets, and home governments are progressively incapable of forcing MNC compliance with domestic policies (Grieder 1997; Ohmae 1996). Others disagree, pointing to the enduring influence of home domestic structures in all key areas of corporate operation (governance, R&D patterns, trade and FDI strategies) (Doremus et al. 1998; Pauly and Reich 1997). The debate over convergence in MNC behavior has profoundly shaped the study of Japanese multinationalism and must be revisited here.

With five decades of postwar history, the profile of Japanese offshore investments is increasingly close to that of other industrialized nations, notably the United States and Great Britain. Table 2.3 highlights the convergence process that has taken place as Japan has matured into a full-fledged FDI power. In 1970, Japan was clearly different from the United States and the UK, both in the geographic areas of operation of its multinationals and in the main economic activities those companies selected.

Japanese companies invested heavily in developing countries, especially in Asia (56 percent and 21 percent, respectively). Twenty years later, the geographic distribution of Japan's offshore investments was closer to that of the UK and the United States. In the early twenty-first century developed countries are the main recipients of Japanese managerial capital, just as they have been for the United Kingdom and the United States since the 1970s. Japan stood out in 1970 for its extensive FDI in trade and mining (the latter represented 30 percent of the cumulative total). Foreign direct investment in the tertiary sector is still proportionately larger in Japan than in the UK and the United States, mostly because of the huge investments in foreign real estate. But by 1990, Japanese direct investment in the primary sector (agriculture, mining, and oil) had decreased markedly, just as it had for the other two FDI powers.

The evolution of Japanese FDI seems to have resolved the controversy over the unique nature of Japanese outward investment. Several characteristics of early Japanese FDI had fueled a debate over the intrinsic differences of Japanese multinationalism: its greater emphasis on manufacturing activities (Kojima 1978; Ozawa 1978); a preference for joint ventures in developing nations; a significant role for Japanese trading companies (Yoshihara 1978); and active participation by small and medium-sized companies (Komiya 1988) and by firms operating in mature industries (Yoshino 1976). Given the subsequent substantial transformation of Japanese FDI, the prevailing consensus is that, over time, most of the unique attributes of Japanese FDI have disappeared.

First, the nonmanufacturing sector (finance, real estate) has invested more actively overseas in recent years. Second, nowadays, large Japanese multinationals operating in technology-intensive sectors go overseas to exploit firm-specific advantages in industrialized markets without the assistance of local or Japanese partners. And third, the role of trading companies has receded, producing, according to some observers, a "weakening of the influence of the inter-corporate network on the behavior of Japanese FDI" (Yoon 1990: 13).

Some uncommon characteristics of early Japanese multinationalism and FDI persist, however: the large role of industries that have lost or never enjoyed comparative advantage; and the active participation of smaller companies.[5] Indeed, Japanese FDI defies the convergence thesis and current theories of outward investment because of the active role that "loser" industries and weak firms have played in the multinationalization of manufacturing.

The industrial composition of Japanese FDI differs markedly from that of other industrialized nations. Declining industries have frequently left Japan, whereas they have often remained domestic (and protected) sectors else-

TABLE 2.3

The FDI Triad: Comparing the United Kingdom, the United States, and Japan

	Share of total FDI stock (percent)					
	UK		US		Japan	
	1970	1997	1970	1997	1970	1998
Developed countries	73.7	80.5	63.4	74.8	43.9	68.3
Europe	51.9	49.8	32.9	48.1	18.1	24.8
North America	22.0	30.7	30.5	17.1	25.8	43.9
Developing countries	26.3	19.5	36.6	25.2	56.1	31.7
Asia	10.1	7.5	7.5	5.8	21.3	16.4
Economic activity						
Primary	35.4	15.5	46.7	11.1	33.7	4.6
Agriculture	5.0	0.7	11.0	0.1	1.6	0.4
Mining	6.4	n.a	7.9	11.0	31.3	4.0
Oil	24.0	18.4	27.8	9.5	n.a.	n.a.
Secondary	44.9	38.2	41.3	32.4	26.8	30.3
Chemicals	7.8	11.8	7.8	11.0	1.7	4.3
Electronics	n.a.	0.0	10.4	3.7	2.0	7.9
Automobiles	5.7	1.9	6.7	4.0	2.9	4.2
Tertiary	19.8	46.3	12.0	56.5	39.6	63.4
Trade	10.0	7.7	8.4	8.9	11.2	10.3
Banking and finance	n.a.	20.0	n.a.	43.3	9.0	19.7

SOURCES: Compiled from US Department of Commerce data, *Survey of Current Business*, several years; OECD, *International Direct Investment Statistics Yearbook* (1999); Dunning and Cantwell 1987; UNCTC, *World Investment Report* (1992); MOF, FDI statistics.

where. Figure 2.1 shows that the industrial makeup of US and European outward investment changed little during the postwar period through the 1990s.[6] The same sectors were the top investors overseas: machinery, chemicals, and transportation equipment in the United States; and chemicals, electrical and transportation machinery, and food in Europe. Moreover, structurally depressed industries have invested only small amounts overseas. Textiles represented only 1 percent, and metals roughly 5–6 percent of cumulative US and European FDI. Stability characterized the industrial composition of these nations' FDI, as sectors with advanced technology, differentiated goods, and healthy growth rates led the way into multinationalization.

In contrast, the industrial profile of Japanese FDI has changed dramatically. Until 1970, textiles and lumber and pulp dominated Japanese outward investment. By 1980, heavy industries (chemicals, steel, and nonferrous metals) figured prominently in Japan's FDI. By 1990, electric machinery and transportation equipment firms were the most dynamic investors overseas. The sectoral evolution of Japanese FDI closely reflected changes in industrial structure from labor (textiles) to capital (chemicals, steel) and knowledge-intensive industries (electronics). Moreover, Japanese FDI stands out for the large investment flows by industries that were losing comparative advantage (textiles, iron and steel, chemicals) and sectors that never enjoyed international competitiveness (lumber and pulp, nonferrous metals, petrochemicals, food products).

Finally, the Japanese offshore investment drive is also distinguished by the large role of small and medium-sized enterprises (SMEs).[7] In 1977, SMEs made 40 percent of all new equity investments, and their share peaked in 1988 at 60 percent. During the 1990s, SMEs were highly visible in FDI flows, when their new equity investments overseas accounted for 45–57 percent of the total number of investments.[8] The international dynamism of Japan's small firms has not been easily duplicated by other countries. For example, SMEs accounted for 25 percent of all foreign affiliates of UK companies, 23 percent of Swedish firms, and only 6 percent of US corporations (Fujita 1993: 50, 67–68).

Table 2.4 shows the main areas of operation for Japanese SMEs. Japanese SMEs have traditionally been oriented toward commerce and services in their investments abroad, but since the 1990s manufacturing has dominated. Within manufacturing, most small-firm FDI took place in the machinery sector (particularly between 1974 and 1990). In the early stages of SME expansion overseas, light industry investments were very important. For example, the combined share of the textiles and miscellaneous sectors represented more than half of total FDI until 1971. From the mid-1970s to mid-1980s, the processed-food sector registered a large share of SME outward investment. More recently textiles boomed, making between 36 percent and 45

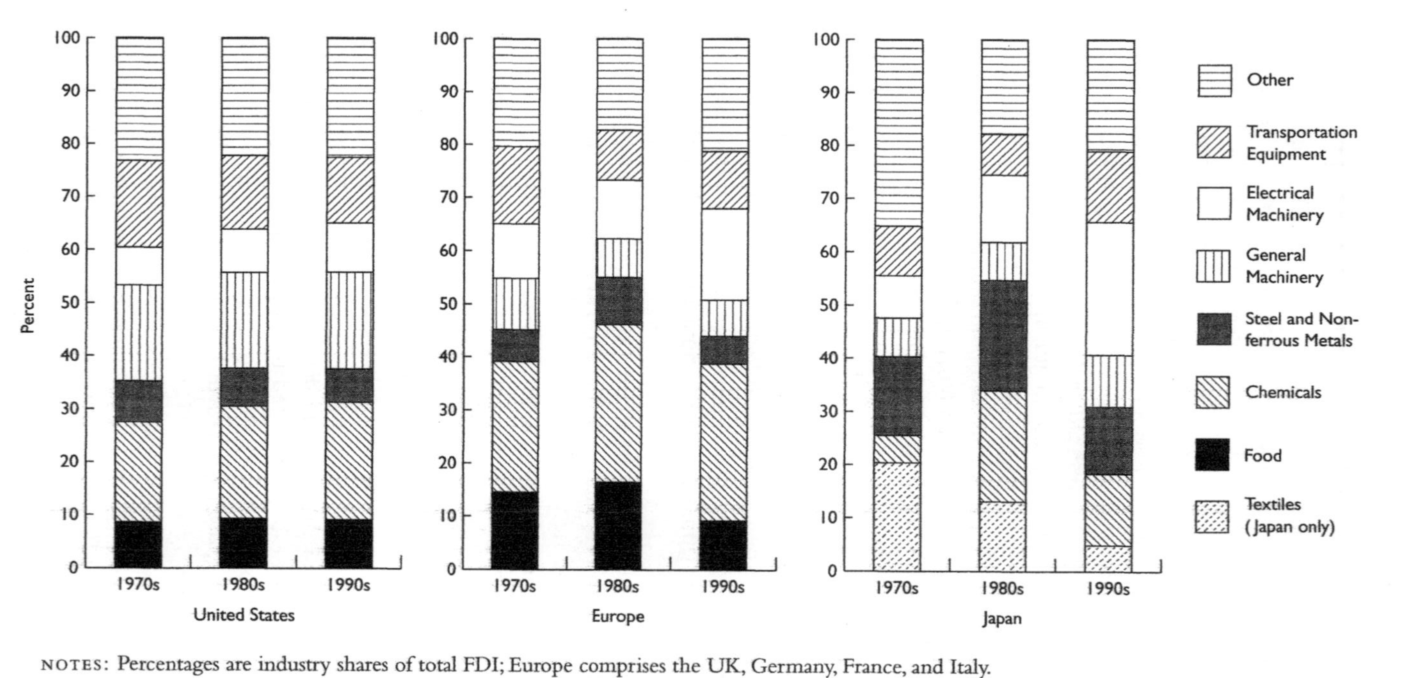

NOTES: Percentages are industry shares of total FDI; Europe comprises the UK, Germany, France, and Italy.

SOURCES: US Department of Commerce, *Survey of Current Business*, several years; MOF's FDI statistics; Dunning and Cantwell 1987; OECD *International Direct Investment Statistics Yearbook*, several years.

Figure 2.1 The Industrial Composition of Outward FDI in Developed Nations, 1970–2000

percent of all SME outward investment during the 1990s. Machinery, textiles, and miscellaneous manufacturing were thus the core activities of SMEs in their operations abroad.

Small-firm FDI has been heavily concentrated by industrial sector and by location of production. Asia has been by far the largest recipient of manufacturing SMEs, followed at a distance by North America. In the recent era of yen appreciation, renewed concentration of Japanese small-firm investment in Asia is evident (with as much as 86 percent of all new equity investments taking place in this region). A few countries dominate as manufacturing bases. Until 1985 almost all investment in Asia took place in Korea and Taiwan. In the middle of the 1980s, the ASEAN countries began to more effectively attract Japanese SMEs that sought to establish or expand their production network abroad. In the 1990s, China, the location of approximately half of all SME investments abroad, emerged as the most important destination for small-firm FDI (particularly from the textile industry). The predominance of developing-country destinations in Japanese SME outward investment sets it apart from other countries' small-firm FDI, which flows mainly to economically developed nations (Fujita 1993: 50).

The high degree of multinationalization of Japanese SMEs is the more remarkable given the compounded difficulties that smaller firms face in undertaking FDI. It has been widely recognized in the literature that SMEs have fewer of the intangible assets that make production in a foreign environment possible: technological innovation, brand names, financial liquidity, or marketing networks. Moreover, the FDI risks are higher for a smaller firm, for which the failure of any single project can doom the company; and the decision to transfer production abroad may be complicated by a lack of sufficient personnel with international expertise or difficulty gathering information about prospective host-country investment conditions.

To sum up, Japanese FDI is remarkable because loser industries and weak firms have found the strength to invest abroad. Their feat may be responsible for the arrival of the multinational age to Japan decades earlier than what mainstream economic theories of FDI would have anticipated given the scarcity of large firms with proprietary technology during the initial stages of Japanese postwar development.

I believe that some of the special and enduring traits of Japanese multinationalism (including the ability of the "weak" to undertake international adjustment) are better understood by factoring in the role of state FDI financing. Although I attempt to explain the active participation of mature industries in Japanese FDI flows, I do not subscribe to the popular flying-geese model of Japanese FDI, first developed by Akamatsu (1962) and still influential among Japanese economists.

TABLE 2.4

A Profile of Multinational Japanese Small Enterprises, 1971–1999 (percent)

Years	Industrial Profile										
	Food products	Lumber and pulp	Textiles	Chemicals	Iron and steel, nonferrous metals	Machinery	Mfg.	Trade	Services	Number of nonmfg. firms	Total number of firms
Up to 1971	6.4	4.3	16.4	6.4	5.9	25.1	439	—	—	—	—
1974–80	12.4	4.6	6.0	8.5	8.5	34.8	718	65.5	10.8	1,571	2,289
1981–85	12.4	2.6	7.7	9.4	7.7	33.3	534	63.0	11.7	985	1,519
1986–90	7.5	2.8	11.1	6.8	10.1	37.9	2,388	32.9	16.6	3,294	5,682
1991–94	4.5	2.8	45.3	4.4	6.4	19.2	1,524	36.9	25.4	1,051	2,575
1995–99	4.3	2.9	35.9	7.4	8.8	28.8	1,412	25.1	21.5	657	2,069
	Location of Manufacturing Investment										
	Korea	Taiwan	Thailand	Phillippines	Malaysia	Indonesia	China	Asia total	North America	Europe	Total number of cases
Up to 1971	15.9	38.7	n.a.	n.a.	n.a.	n.a.	n.a.	88.2	3.0	0.5	439
1974–80	14.9	17.8	n.a.	n.a.	n.a.	n.a.	n.a.	66.2	20.6	5.2	718
1981–85	12.7	12.9	n.a.	n.a.	n.a.	n.a.	5.4	53.9	35.4	7.7	534
1986–90	12.4	11.2	5.4	1.9	3.7	1.1	8.8	66.1	24.7	6.8	2,388
1991–94	1.8	1.1	5.9	2.8	4.1	5.3	59.0	86.0	8.8	3.9	1,524
1995–99	1.4	2.3	7.9	3.8	3.9	5.4	48.8	80.6	13.3	3.6	1,412

NOTES: The number of investments by small and medium-sized enterprises includes individual investments and coinvestments with large enterprises. In April 1984, the value of recorded investments increased from 3 million yen to 10 million yen, and in July 1989 to 30 million yen. Therefore the data set is not continuous.

n.a. = not available.

SOURCES: MITI, Small Business Agency; *Chūshō Kigyō Hakushō*, several issues.

According to the flying-geese formulation, Japan invests abroad (exclusively) in those industries in which it has lost comparative advantage. The main recipients are developing countries where production costs are low and Japanese companies from these mature industries can manufacture competitively. This model anticipates a constant improvement in the industrial composition of both the investor and host nations, as Japan moves into more technologically intensive sectors and proceeds to relocate mature industries abroad. The transfer of new and more sophisticated technologies to the second- and third-tier countries in the flying-geese formation allows them to develop mature industries and become successful exporters to Japan and other international markets (Ozawa 1993).

The serious flaws of the flying-geese model have been adeptly discussed by Bernard and Ravenhill (1995) and Hatch and Yamamura (1996): Japan has not recycled whole mature industries to developing countries; host nations to Japanese MNCs have not benefited sufficiently from substantial technological transfer to undertake autonomous production; and the Japanese market has remained closed to exports from Asian enterprises.

My own insight is that rather than shouldering on their own the burden of offshore relocation, Japan's mature industries and small enterprises have successfully lobbied for state subsidization of their international adjustment strategies (FDI). Through capital controls and generous public FDI financing, the Japanese government has promoted international industrial restructuring, but has preserved the higher-value-added activities onshore, limited the disruptive effect of reverse imports, and minimized job losses among organized labor in order to avoid union contestation of state FDI financing.

Foreign direct investment by inefficient Japanese producer groups is fundamentally a political response to adverse shifts in comparative advantage: business interests have enlisted the support of politicians in rewriting the mandate of public financial institutions to facilitate soft finance, and the public-private partnership in large-scale national projects abroad has also created conflict over the responsibilities of each partner in keeping costly ventures afloat. The politics of selective FDI approval and preferential financing of overseas investment lies at the heart of Japan's ability to promote international adjustment among structurally depressed industries.

PART TWO

Industrial Policy Politics and Japanese Multinational Corporations

CHAPTER 3

Japan's Regulatory Regime Governing Capital Outflows

GOVERNMENTS CAN affect the expansion of multinational corporations most directly by means of their rules on cross-border capital mobility. By establishing monitoring requirements and specific criteria that firms must meet in order to receive FDI project approval, home governments enjoy significant leverage over these enterprises' overseas investments.

After World War II, Japan imposed strict controls over FDI outflows. The Japanese state acted as a zealous gatekeeper, closely monitoring overseas investments by Japanese firms for financial and industrial policy reasons. In the early postwar era, the government sought to influence the overseas investment plans of Japanese companies to ensure they complemented public policy on the balance of payments, natural resource procurement, and industrial restructuring. In this way, the Japanese state tried to resolve the dilemma between control and promotion mentioned in the Introduction. On the one hand, the Japanese bureaucracy feared that internationally mobile Japanese firms would be less compliant with governmental directives; and on the other, it sought to foster overseas investment projects it deemed compatible with larger industrial policy goals. Tight monitoring of FDI projects and generous financing of desirable ventures defined the Japanese state's approach to the thorny question of multinationalization of indigenous enterprises.

This happy resolution of the control/promotion dilemma could not be sustained forever, though. The one leg of the FDI policy framework that gave in was the strict regime governing foreign exchange transactions. Over the years, a gradually more liberal policy on capital outflow eroded the powers of the government to review outward FDI projects. In this area proponents of the convergence thesis are on stronger ground. Most FDI source nations have moved to deregulate capital outflows, and Japan has not been the exception.

But FDI liberalization is far from complete: important pockets of bureaucratic discretion remain in place. Moreover, conventional accounts (Bailey, Harte, and Sugden 1994: 39) of the Japanese move toward deregulation of capital outflows are incomplete. Foreign pressure (*gaiatsu*) from the United States and international institutions is not sufficient to explain either the timing or content of Japan's protracted liberalization of FDI flows. This chapter discusses the bureaucratic clashes between the Ministry of International Trade and Industry (MITI) and the Ministry of Finance (MOF) that led to the convoluted path toward capital outflow liberalization. Just as in other instances of regulatory reform, bureaucratic actors played a central role and offered liberalization measures that left their discretionary power largely untouched (Vogel 1996).

Government Control over International Capital Transactions

Keenly aware of the country's fragile economic condition, the Japanese state emerged from US occupation once again a devoted regulator of all international economic exchange.[1] The government was well endowed in this pursuit with two key pieces of legislation: the 1949 Foreign Exchange Control Law (FECL),[2] and the accompanying Foreign Investment Law (FIL) enacted in 1950).[3] The guiding principle of the FECL—prohibition in principle of all international financial transactions unless publicly authorized—made the state the guardian of Japan's economic contact with other countries.

In particular, the balance-of-payments deficit and meager foreign exchange reserves were powerful threats to Japanese efforts at economic revival. The Japanese government therefore assumed extraordinary powers to concentrate and allocate precious foreign exchange. It was mandatory for all citizens to sell within a month of their acquisition all foreign currency notes to the denominated foreign exchange banks. These banks in turn were required to sell the foreign currency to a special foreign exchange account at MOF. In this way, the government concentrated all foreign exchange (Nakahira and Mizoguchi 1992: 27–28). Next the government set up its spending priorities through a foreign exchange budget. Initially, this task was entrusted to the Foreign Exchange Control Board, but in 1952 it was transferred to MITI (Johnson 1982: 194).

Far-reaching public powers over the allocation of foreign exchange for export credit, outward investment, and import purchases "reflected the belief of government that it, and not the market, was the best judge of how to maximize the benefits that could be derived from available foreign exchange" (Horne 1985: 144). MOF and MITI were intimately involved in the monitoring of international economic transactions. The FECL made MITI responsible for transactions directly related to foreign trade and the establishment or transfer of mining and industrial property rights; and it designated

MOF as the overseer of all remaining financial transactions. The law required consultation and agreement between the two ministries (MITI 1993: 297).

In the area of foreign direct investment, government control was equally strict. Case-by-case screening and government approval of each company's investment plan was mandatory. The grounds for rejection of an FDI petition were very broad. The government could refuse an FDI request if it deemed that the project would negatively influence the Japanese economy or a particular industry, or that it would adversely affect monetary policy. Less explicit requirements for FDI projects were that they would not damage the competitive position of other firms in the industry or result in job loss (Safarian 1993: 272; Bailey, Harte, and Sugden 1994: 14). Always aware of foreign exchange constraints, the Japanese government was willing to authorize only investment projects that promoted exports or secured key natural resources. Because they would accomplish neither goal, real estate acquisition and portfolio investment abroad were frowned upon as activities wasteful of scarce foreign exchange.

Public control over FDI, as sanctioned by the FECL, was so extensive that "if differences of opinion existed between the investor and the government, the government prevailed, the assumption being that it was in a better position to judge both the national interest and the interest of the firm" (Bergsten, Horst, and Moran 1978: 37). In fact, the Japanese government even attempted to influence the behavior of Japanese firms *after* investments abroad had taken place. Japanese bureaucrats expected earnings to be repatriated promptly, unless they were reinvested in the same enterprise. Not surprisingly, enforcement in this area was lax and considerable delays occurred (Bergsten, Horst, and Moran 1978: 37).

PIECEMEAL CAPITAL LIBERALIZATION IN THE 1960S AND 1970S

The tight controls over capital outflow remained in place for thirty years. The Foreign Exchange Control Law devised at a time of weak balance of payments and foreign currency shortages stayed in effect even as Japan acquired commitments to liberalize financial relations through its membership in the International Monetary Fund (IMF) and OECD, and as the country's capital surpluses and financial dealings with the world multiplied. Whatever regulatory liberalization took place during this period was piecemeal, and occasionally restrictions were even reinstated. A gradual liberalization of the rules of capital outflow started at the end of the 1960s and extended through five different rounds. The gist of these limited reform steps was to expand the number of projects subject to automatic approval.

As the 1960s drew to a close, the pressures on Japan to open up its system of foreign exchange transactions intensified. Foreign complaints mounted when Japan failed to relinquish control as expected by the IMF and OECD, even though the country's trade account and balance of payments improved markedly after 1967. In the words of an MITI official: "MITI's basic approach has been to gain time as long as the opponents are not too angry. [The] frustration of the United States, however, has of late been rising noticeably. We have reached a point where an early liberalization of capital transactions becomes mandatory" (quoted in Bailey, Harte, and Sugden 1994: 14).

Moreover, the Japanese government had become more sympathetic toward capital outflows as a way of slowing down the accumulation of foreign reserves and facilitating the transfer of mature industries to developing countries (MITI 1993: 299). In October 1969 the government introduced a system for automatic approval by the Bank of Japan of projects under $200,000 (round 1 of *liberalization*), but case-by-case screening continued in some sectors: fishing, pearl culturing, banking, securities brokerage, and industries where international obligations exist or *where there is the concern that they will exert a negative influence on the domestic economy* (MITI 1993, 300; emphasis added).

On September 1970 the ceiling for automatic approval was raised to $1 million, though again the restricted sectors were exempted (round 2). In fact, new regulations were placed on the textile and leather industries, for which any overseas investment of over $200,000 was to be scrutinized by the Bank of Japan. Bureaucrats were already worried about the potential negative effects of FDI in textiles: reverse imports, competition in third markets between Japanese products manufactured domestically and overseas, and excessive rivalry among Japanese investors. The new restrictions showed capital liberalization to be guided not only by monetary policy but also by industrial and trade policy considerations (MITI 1993: 303).

Liberalization made great strides with the elimination of the lower ceiling for automatic approval of FDI projects in July 1971 (round 3). A more modest step toward deregulation was adopted in July 1972 (round 4), when MOF agreed to automatically approve investments in foreign subsidiaries where Japanese companies held less than 25 percent of ownership but maintained long-term business relations. But the deregulatory wave proved to be short-lived.

The liberalization process came to a halt in 1974 when the Japanese economy experienced a serious recession. The oil shock strained the balance of payments, and the government responded by reimposing restrictions on capital outflows. MOF moved swiftly in the first week of January 1974 to halt all overseas investment projects except those in high-priority areas, such as natural resource development.

MITI also responded promptly to the balance-of-payments crisis, but with proposals that would have made the ministry the locus of public decisions on FDI. In its "Urgent measures on overseas direct investment" of January 1, 1974, MITI's Bureau of International Enterprises called for increased surveillance of FDI. Energy-intensive industries (petrochemicals, iron and steel, and others) would be monitored more closely, but also projects that could cause friction with the host nation due to investment rushes or pollution export (MITI 1993: 304).[4]

MITI's vision of its role as undisputed FDI gatekeeper was clearly outlined in its "Scheme on the adjustment/regulation of outward investment" (also released in January 1974). With this plan the ministry broke new ground in three areas. First, it suggested the creation of a public/private Council on Overseas Business Activities to strengthen administrative guidance. Second, it proposed that MITI evaluate proposals for Japan Eximbank funding. MITI would study the investment plans, rank the projects according to policy guidelines, and then pass on its evaluation to MOF and the Japan Eximbank. Third, MITI suggested using its FDI insurance program to influence the overseas investment decisions of private firms (MITI 1993: 305).

MITI's ambitious plan was never implemented. The outcome is hardly surprising given the core interests it touched: MOF would have been relegated to a secondary position as overseer of FDI flows and also would have surrendered its monitoring authority over the Japan Eximbank; and the Japan Eximbank would have lost its autonomy in the selection of which FDI projects to finance. The liberalization process resumed once the balance of payments improved, and in April 1978 (round 5) the approval requirement was replaced by a prior notification system. Once more, the restricted sectors remained unaffected by the deregulatory change.

The piecemeal liberalization of capital outflow is not surprising, given that the source of government control over capital outflows—the Foreign Exchange Control Law—remained untouched. A cautious government was willing to ease the outflow of capital when the balance of payments permitted, but was prepared to reestablish controls quickly if the economic situation worsened. Moreover, it never relinquished close control and monitoring of the restricted sectors (and of textiles and leather later on). Even though after 1964 Japan was under an obligation to free the movement of capital in and out of its frontiers, fifteen years later it still maintained important restrictions on capital flows.

The Politics of Reforming the Foreign Exchange Control Law

The postwar regulatory framework on capital outflows was finally reformed with revision in December 1980 of the Foreign Exchange Control Law. The attempts to revise this piece of legislation, however, spanned more than two decades.

EARLY ATTEMPTS

The first efforts to change the law date back to 1959 when a committee of public and private sector representatives appointed by MOF and MITI proposed a new "Foreign Economic Law" that would lift restrictions on foreign exchange and trade. The committee also recommended the abolition of the Foreign Investment Law (the provisions of which would be incorporated into the new law).

In the area of capital outflows, the proposed Foreign Economic Law was not very liberal. To avoid negative influences on the domestic capital market, the draft legislation anticipated restrictions on portfolio investment abroad, on the acquisition of foreign real estate, on the establishment of overseas businesses, and on loans to nonresidents. Overseas investments that fostered international trade were to be vigorously promoted, but over time the financial self-sustainability of firms investing abroad was to be encouraged. This provision in particular reflected the view, prevalent at that time, that overseas investment projects should not drain the domestic economy from valuable investment resources. Moreover, the proposed Foreign Economic Law prescribed close monitoring of Japanese companies' overseas performance, making postinvestment surveys and periodic reports mandatory for firms investing abroad (Watanabe 1963).

MOF agreed in principle to the shift from capital interdiction to freedom of foreign exchange transactions (especially since it retained the discretion to impose restrictions as it saw fit), and welcomed the abolition of the Foreign Investment Law. The system of authorized foreign exchange banks was to remain intact. MOF approved only a relaxation of the foreign exchange concentration system and recommended replacing the foreign exchange budget with a less stringent foreign payments plan. Nevertheless, MITI was not satisfied with the proposal, and a bureaucratic difference of opinion proved to be the undoing of the Foreign Economic Law. At the core of the dispute was MITI's refusal to give up its regulatory faculties over inward investment flows. The 1950 Foreign Investment Law allowed MITI to impose restrictions on foreign capital to protect domestic industrial sectors. However, the Friendship and Trade Treaty with the United States prohibited foreign exchange restrictions for reasons other than maintaining currency reserves. Since FIL preceded the treaty, the wider regulatory powers of MITI had not been questioned. However, MITI anticipated opposition to the foreign capital restrictions on industrial policy grounds. MITI disapproved other proposed changes such as the adoption of a foreign payments plan, the abolition of the export approval system, and the dismantling of the rules on letters of credit (MOF 1992: 78).[5]

Disagreement over the contours of a new Foreign Exchange Law was widespread. Even within the committee of experts there was dissension.

Some members preferred to keep two separate laws since FECL was mainly concerned with international balance of payments and FIL was guided by industrial and technology policies. The private sector had its own views on capital liberalization. A survey by the business peak association—Keidanren—on the improvement of the FECL showed strong demand for regulatory revision, but mostly through simplification of the numerous and complex statutes and ordinances of the law. The private sector's vision of reform, therefore, stopped short of a full-fledged liberalization of foreign transactions (MOF 1992: 79).

Japan's approaching membership in the IMF and OECD, forced the bureaucracy to revisit once more the thorny question of deregulating foreign capital transactions. MITI took the initiative in 1963, this time with its own version of a Foreign Economic Law. As in the previous formulation, the draft law promulgated the principle of freedom of international transactions and the integration of FIL into the Foreign Exchange Law. But it still called for restricting foreign exchange transactions for industrial protection or if severe harm to the national economy were predicted. MITI went even further by naming sectors to be specially circumscribed: dyed fabrics, passenger autos, synthetic fibers, petrochemicals, special classes of iron and steel, coal, medical products, and agricultural commodities.

MITI was acting quickly to preempt the strong pressure it anticipated from the OECD to pursue capital liberalization once it was admitted as a member. The ministry therefore deemed it important to promptly pass a Foreign Economic Law that comprised exceptional regulations. The spirit of MITI's draft on foreign exchange legislation, singling out key industrial sectors for protection, also affected another law the ministry was drafting to strengthen its domestic industrial policy powers (the Special Measures Law for the Promotion of Designated Industries) ("Kawase Kanrihō ni Kawaru Shinpō Settei e" 1963, 8; and "Shinkawase Kanrihō no Osuji Matomaru" 1963: 9).

In response, MOF issued the document "On the rejection of the establishment of a Foreign Economic Law" in June 1963. MOF argued that the proposed law would exacerbate international criticism of Japan's regulations on foreign exchange transactions. In the ministry's opinion, restrictions on the introduction of technology and direct investments would be detrimental to the negotiations over OECD membership, while restraints on foreign capital for other than balance-of-payments reasons would contradict the Friendship and Trade Treaty with the United States. But MOF also believed the proposed deregulation of foreign exchange transactions had gone too far. In particular, MITI intended to abolish both the foreign exchange concentration system and the foreign exchange budget, but MOF refused to give up the former since it would eliminate the privileged status of the few officially denominated foreign exchange banks under MOF's supervision.

Finally, MOF was skeptical of proclaiming a new law on freedom of international transactions when restrictions were still necessary on inward and outward investments, especially since transition into an IMF "eighth clause" country could be accomplished by modifying only a portion of the legislation in place—namely the foreign exchange budget (MOF 1992: 80–81).[6]

In financial circles the dispute over the second Foreign Economic Law was seen mainly as a jurisdictional battle between MITI and MOF. On the eve of liberalization, MITI was trying to secure its jurisdiction over international transactions: it wanted capital flow freedom, but strict control on trade. MOF, though, was willing to abandon only the one item (the foreign exchange budget) whose retention would certainly cause friction with the IMF (in fact there were widespread rumors that MOF had consulted and reached a confidential agreement with the IMF in this regard) ("Taigai Keizaihō no Kōbōsen" 1963: 14–15).

Once more, bureaucratic deadlock killed the proposal for a new Foreign Exchange Law, and the only change of significance that was agreed to was the dismantling of the foreign exchange budget (MOF 1992: 79–81). The consequences of this reform were particularly important for MITI, which thereby lost the significant leverage it had enjoyed over private firms through the setting of foreign exchange quotas.

Reform of the FECL was not discussed again until 1977, when Prime Minister Takeo Fukuda used the banner of a new FECL to ease US criticism of expanding Japanese trade surpluses.[7] Jurisdictional conflicts and interest representation redrew the battle lines between the two ministries most involved in foreign exchange policy, MOF and MITI, which, following Fukuda's instructions, were to sit down at the table to hammer out a new law. Again MITI pushed the argument that trade operations were closely intertwined with foreign exchange transactions and that therefore the ministry should have a say in the drafting of foreign exchange guidelines. MOF rejected this as an encroachment by MITI on MOF's turf and argued for a strict separation of duties: with MITI in charge of commodity transactions (trade) and MOF in charge of money transactions (finance) (Horne 1985: 159).

Each ministry perceived the drafting of new foreign exchange legislation as an opportunity not only to set new jurisdictional boundaries, but also to defend its private sector clients from the undesirable effects of liberalization. MOF on this occasion pushed for the total revamping of the FECL; its intention was to bring the new law into line with the deregulation steps that had been taken over the years, not to completely dislodge foreign exchange controls. MOF was enthusiastic about trade liberalization (MITI's jurisdiction), but less keen about relaxing controls on capital transactions. In particular, MOF ardently defended the foreign exchange concentration system—that is, the foreign exchange banks. According to the ministry, the preservation of this system was necessary to control capital flight and other speculative activities.

Nevertheless, in defending the system MOF was also protecting the rents of the few banks authorized to carry out foreign exchange transactions. In particular, the general trading companies resented their exclusion from the foreign exchange business (Horne 1985: 157–58).

MITI for its part interpreted very differently its mandate to reform the Foreign Exchange Control Law. The ministry vehemently opposed the establishment of a new law. MITI argued that reform should center on capital controls because trade was already almost completely liberalized. Therefore, it said, no new law was necessary. Moreover, MITI criticized the exclusive use of financial criteria in determining the constraints on foreign transactions. Regulations should be designed to meet the needs of trade and industrial policy, to comply with international commitments, to respond to abrupt changes in the international economy, and to deal with currency instability or balance-of-payments deterioration (MITI 1993: 307). For these reasons, MITI argued that its jurisdiction should extend to outward FDI regulation (until then the preserve of MOF). MITI proposed to maintain restrictions on outward investment in sectors that were exempted from the OECD liberalization code (banks, securities, fishery, pearl production), in national security areas outside the scope of the OECD code (weapons, narcotics, operations in South Africa and Namibia), or in industrial sectors that could cause exceptional damage to the Japanese economy (such as textiles because of the reverse-import problem) (MITI 1993: 310–11).

With bureaucratic controversy still raging, the government established in October 1978 a consultative body (*sōdankai*) to examine reform of the foreign exchange and trade legislation. The role of the *sōdankai* in introducing substantive innovations was rather limited, since bureaucrats refused to shift the locus of the decision-making process. The *sōdankai* was scheduled to meet only six times, and dissenting opinions were not incorporated into the final report: "The agreement by the two supervising ministries on the general issues to be reported in the proceedings of the Committee's activities reduced the scope for effective dissent" (Horne 1985: 161). Nor was the draft of the bill subject to intensive scrutiny by the LDP or Diet Committees. Political influence was mostly felt in Fukuda's decision to revise the FECL, and in the ratification of the amended bill by its successor, Prime Minister Masayoshi Ohira (ibid.: 162).

The bureaucratic impasse was finally overcome in a meeting between the chief of MOF's International Finance Bureau and the chief of MITI's Trade Bureau on March 17, 1979. Deregulation limits acceptable to each ministry were agreed upon: MOF would keep the foreign exchange banks, while MITI would oversee the existing trade provisions, although the Foreign Investment Law would be abolished (MITI 1993: 308). Moreover, jurisdictional lines were to stay as before, meaning that MITI would not enlarge its authority over overseas investment.

After the agreement among ministries was secured, the *sōdankai* released its conclusions in April 1979. The report envisaged complete freedom for all current account transactions, as well as for capital transactions under normal circumstances (except in the restricted areas). It also called for the formulation of an emergency regulation system to manage capital transactions in unusual situations. The *sōdankai* supported the maintenance of the officially authorized foreign exchange banks, but called for the abolition of the Foreign Investment Law by integrating it into the FECL.

Once the consensus was worked out, the drafting of the law proceeded swiftly. In May 1979 the proposed legislation was submitted to the Diet; it was approved in December 1979 and enacted a year later. A new era of freedom in foreign trade and financial transactions seemed to have dawned in Japan. But because trade legislation remained practically untouched, the foreign exchange bank system continued to operate, and the state enjoyed wide discretionary power to interdict foreign capital, real change was only modest.

A NEW "LIBERAL" LAW, UNRELINQUISHED DISCRETIONARY POWER

The revised FECL provided freedom in principle for cross-border capital flows, but the Japanese state did not withdraw completely from the regulation of capital transactions. State power to intervene in international financial operations was broadly defined. MOF approval was still required in capital transactions deemed to harm the balance of payments, to suddenly affect the national currency or international exchange rates, or to result in large capital outflows that could negatively influence the national monetary and capital markets. In the revised law, MOF retained sweeping authority to intervene in capital markets for monetary policy and financial guidance reasons.

In the area of foreign direct investment, the system of prior notification operated for investments of over 10 million yen (originally it was 3 million yen, but the ceiling was raised in 1984). After receiving notification, MOF had twenty days to determine whether it would require alterations or block the overseas investment project. Once more the MOF had great room for maneuver. It could demand changes or the postponement of an FDI project if it might adversely affect (1) the international money market or the international reputation of the country; (2) the domestic money or capital markets; (3) *the business activities of certain industrial sectors or the smooth performance of the national economy*; or (4) the faithful performance of international treaties, international peace and security, or the maintenance of public order (MITI 1993: 310).

The revised FECL provided for more exacting state monitoring in several restricted sectors where prior notification was still mandatory regardless of the investment amount. The areas subject to more stringent control were almost the same as before: fisheries, pearls, leather, textiles, weapons, drugs, banking and securities, and investment in certain countries (at that time, South Africa and Namibia). The rejection of FDI projects for industrial policy considerations was, therefore, well ingrained in the amended regulatory framework. In particular, the special restrictions were occasionally used to protect industries undergoing competitive adjustment. For example, in interviews with officials from two major ministries in 1983, Safarian (1993: 274, 283) was told that approval would not be given to FDI projects that entailed the import of textiles to Japan.

Given the wide discretionary power of the state to veto FDI projects in the name of monetary or industrial policy, it is not surprising that capital outflow liberalization in Japan appeared so unimpressive to scholars in the field (Robinson 1976: 302; Safarian 1993: 278; Bailey, Harte, and Sugden 1994: 42). The source of government power continued to be the diffuse terms in which public authority on FDI screening was defined: "What is perhaps equally remarkable is that this system in practice has been based on a large degree of discretion in decision making, with the legal basis set in very broad terms" (Safarian 1993: 278). Moreover, the FDI monitoring system lacked transparency. Although the government never formally rejected an outward FDI project, firms that expected a problem contacted the authorities first and did not apply if any disagreement could not be solved (Safarian 1993: 274).

Indeed, the process of capital liberalization in Japan proved to be so tortuous because the regulatory framework (FECL) intimately interlocked the responsibilities of MOF and MITI. In other words, the consent of both ministries was indispensable for the passage of a new law. But each ministry used the negotiations over capital liberalization to push for a more advantageous jurisdictional demarcation, to protect client industries, and to press for more deregulation on the rival ministry's turf.

In the end, the revised law protected the fundamental interests of each ministry: MOF retained the foreign exchange banks system, and MITI prevented more thorough deregulation of trade items. Significantly, in the new "liberal" law the Japanese state did not relinquish its hold over FDI. It still enjoyed wide discretionary authority to thwart FDI projects for the sake of monetary or industrial policy. The state's role as gatekeeper of capital outflows escaped the campaign to liberalize foreign exchange legislation largely unscathed.

A New Regime for Japanese Capital Outflows: The Big Bang and Foreign Exchange Liberalization

During the 1990s, Japan underwent dramatic restructuring and liberalization of its financial markets. After the economic bubble burst, the country experienced the worst economic recession in more than forty years. The financial sector was among the most affected industries. A massive bad-loan crisis and the end of the "convoy system"[8] (with the unprecedented bankruptcy of several important financial institutions) signaled that the previously regulated and compartmentalized financial regime was unable to cope with the exacting competition from global finance (Horiuchi 2001). Although the government attempted some reforms early in the crisis (for example, softening the boundaries between the banking and securities sectors in 1993), the deepening banking crisis, public outcry at the government rescue packages for poorly managed housing loan institutions, and the loss of competitiveness in financial services persuaded Prime Minister Ryutaro Hashimoto to launch a structural reform of the entire financial system.[9]

THE POLITICS OF THE BIG BANG

The liberalization package known as Big Bang was first announced in November 1996. Unlike its British namesake (which focused narrowly on reforms in the securities market), the Japanese deregulatory program was to touch every aspect of the financial system (Laurence 2001). The goal of the Big Bang was to create a free, fair, and global capital market by the year 2001 (M.J.B. Hall 1998). Its proponents promised to introduce market competition (eliminating entry barriers and other cumbersome regulations), to increase the transparency of transactions and eliminate the moral hazard of implicit government guarantees, and to facilitate the internationalization of Japanese finance, both by lowering the transaction costs of international dealings and by eliminating barriers to the operation of foreign financial firms and investors in the Tokyo market. The specific reform measures included the elimination of foreign exchange controls; the liberalization of cross-border capital movements; free entry into the banking and securities industries; permission to establish holding companies; the development of new financial products such as derivatives; and the adoption of international accounting standards (Laurence 2001: 181; Radin 1998; M.J.B. Hall 1998: 140–46).

Significantly, this ambitious blueprint for a reformed Japanese financial marketplace identified foreign exchange (FOREX) liberalization as the first crucial step toward effective deregulation. Amending the FECL both signaled the resolve of the government to engage in genuine liberalization and provided further incentives to deregulate since Japanese market participants would face more international competition due to the liberalization of cross-border capital transactions (Higuchi 1998).

A NEW FOREX REGIME: IMPLICATIONS FOR FDI OUTFLOWS

The purpose of the amended Foreign Exchange and Foreign Trade Law (henceforth referred to as the Foreign Exchange Law) is to promote the globalization of Japanese financial markets by eliminating remaining barriers to the free and speedy flow of capital across Japanese borders. The Committee on Foreign Exchange recognized that the previous Foreign Exchange Control law had stopped short of full liberalization. Two core pillars of the previous regime were considered increasingly anachronistic and an obstacle to the international flow of capital at low cost: the prior notification rule and the centralization of FOREX transactions in government-authorized banks. These two traits of the previous system diminished competition in currency transactions (keeping service fees high) and delayed capital movements (through the cumbersome process of prior notification and licensing). The committee concluded that the resulting increase in transaction costs for currency dealings was partly responsible for the lack of international competitiveness of the Japanese financial system (Committee on Foreign Exchange 1997).

The new Foreign Exchange Law, which took effect on April 1, 1998, did away with the two central features of the former regime governing capital outflow. It abolished the system of government authorized FOREX banks and established an ex post facto reporting requirement for international capital transactions. The reformed Foreign Exchange Law endorsed several benefits of the ex post facto reporting system: it would both speed up transactions and generate a crucial information flow that would allow market participants to make more informed decisions; it would provide accurate balance-of-payments statistics, useful not only to Japanese officials but also to the world community (individual investors, foreign governments, and multilateral organizations); and it would allow Japan to impose international sanctions following UN Security Council resolutions (Committee on Foreign Exchange 1997).

Politically, the hardest task for the reformers was to end the monopoly of the authorized banks over currency transactions. As previously discussed, MOF had steadfastly defended throughout the postwar period the special status of this important client group. The government-authorized FOREX banks (originally a privileged group of eleven city banks) had expanded to encompass regional, long-term, trust, and foreign banks (around 350 banks). In exchange for handling all of the country's foreign currency transactions,[10] the government had delegated to the FOREX banks some key public tasks: reporting FOREX transactions to the Bank of Japan; verifying that currency dealings met the government's legal standards; and implementing emergency restrictions on cross-border capital flows (Tanikawa 1996: 23).

The banks had not reacted favorably when the first suggestions were made in 1996 that they should lose their monopoly power and make room for other currency dealers. In the words of an industry representative: "Foreign exchange control is overseen by sophisticated professionals. This process hardly will be understood by laymen" (quoted in Choy 1997: 4). This time, though, contrary to the vigorous opposition lodged in the past against terminating the special status of FOREX banks, the banks and the ministry did not put up a strong fight. Their muted opposition reflected the troubled position of both the banking industry and MOF during the financial turmoil of the 1990s. The banks were undergoing their worst crisis in the postwar era.

The public was particularly critical of the banks' mismanagement after the 1995 *jūsen* debacle (when several housing loan subsidiaries of the banks went under owing to poor management of their loan portfolio during the bubble years). In order to keep the *jūsen* (and their creditors, the agricultural cooperatives) afloat, the government had had to inject 685 billion yen in taxpayer money (Hiwatari 2000: 115). The bailout was extremely unpopular. In addition to the *jūsen* scandal, the banks themselves were saddled with a huge number of bad loans, totaling according to some estimates as much as 28 trillion yen (Lincoln and Litan 1998). The cleanup of the bad-loan mess was intensively discussed in the Diet and the media at the time (with sharp differences of opinion among political parties over the desirable size of the rescue package and the fate of the failed financial institutions). Consequently, there was little sympathy in Japan for maintaining the monopolistic rents of a privileged group of banks over FOREX transactions (Tanikawa 1996: 22).

MOF's public standing was also at an all-time low. The onset of the banking crisis and a series of corruption scandals had discredited the ministry's ability to monitor of public financial institutions. MOF was clearly on the defensive at a time when the partition of the ministry was being discussed (the creation of a separate monitoring agency, the Financial Supervisory Agency, was first discussed in 1996 and came into being in April 1998) (Laurence 2001: 176–77). Moreover, it was hard for MOF to defend entry barriers to FOREX markets, after the move to desegment the financial industry had gained momentum through the reforms of the early 1990s and the ongoing formulation of the Big Bang liberalization package.

Given the strong representation in the Committee on Foreign Exchange of groups critical of the FOREX banks' grip on currency dealings, it is hardly surprising that all entry restrictions into the market were lifted.[11] In early deliberations, the question of which market participants should be allowed to transact foreign currency received the most attention (Tanikawa 1996: 22). In the end, the net was cast very wide, allowing both bank and nonbank market participants to engage freely in cross-border capital transactions (with appropriate monitoring of financial institutions and ex post facto reporting by the end users to the authorities).

The liberalized regime governing cross-border capital transactions imposed adjustment costs on the FOREX banks. Previously captive customers, such as the *sōgō shōsha*, moved aggressively to lower the cost of foreign currency settlements by opening in-house banking operations. In order to recoup dwindling profits from lost currency commissions, the banks quickly lowered their service fees and developed new products to attract clients. Even before the new law went into effect, FOREX banks jockeyed for position by lowering FOREX transaction fees and sometimes eliminating them altogether (Fuji Bank, for example, abolished all fees on foreign-currency-denominated transfers among group subsidiaries in Japan) (Maeda 1998: 83).

Regulations covering foreign direct investment were eased considerably with the adoption of the ex post facto reporting system.[12] In this way, MOF lost the leverage awarded by the prior notification mechanism (which had given the ministry twenty days to approve or reject a proposal).

Moreover, for the first time in the postwar period the number of restricted sectors decreased. Banking and cultured pearl and fiber manufacturing were no longer subject to the more stringent screening process. Yet, as explained by an official of MOF's International Finance Bureau, tougher monitoring of foreign direct investment (both inward and outward) in certain industries is well ingrained in government policy (Uranishi 1996: 25). Indeed, MITI continues to defend the policy of restricting FDI in some sectors in order to avoid a "boomerang effect" (surges of reverse imports), regional deindustrialization, and bankruptcy of subsidiaries and other *keiretsu* firms.[13] In sensitive sectors, therefore, the government continues to endorse its role as gatekeeper for FDI projects.

Just as the case of FDI regulation exemplifies, the liberalization of cross-border capital movement embodied in the new Foreign Exchange Law is less than complete. Several observers have pointed to the limits of the deregulation effort and the reimposition of constraints in areas the government deems sensitive (Nakaoka 1998: 29). Beyond emergency exchange controls, the government will continue to regulate the net foreign currency position of financial institutions to avoid instability of the yen. This is a unique Japanese practice among industrialized nations, and one that the government has been unwilling to abandon despite the liberalization campaign (Masunaga 1997: 4).

With the stated goal of avoiding money laundering or tax evasion the government also quickly reimposed stricter reporting requirements for remittances abroad (Lincoln and Litan 1998: 6). MOF originally had anticipated applying the notification system to remittances over 1 million yen. The banking industry estimated that this low ceiling would subject half of all money transfers out of the country to the special reporting requirement and successfully lobbied MOF to raise the ceiling to 2 million yen (around $18,000) ("Gaitamehō Kaiseigō no Hōkoku Gyōmu wa nihyaku man en chō ni": 35).

These examples illustrate that even as the Japanese government embarked on the most thorough deregulation of its financial markets, its inclination to closely monitor international financial transactions did not die.

A RECAP OF PROTRACTED FDI LIBERALIZATION IN JAPAN

The efforts of the Japanese state to preserve far-reaching screening powers over FDI, amid liberalization pressures, indicate how crucial it deemed retaining the discretion to deter "undesirable" overseas investments by Japanese firms. Table 3.1 summarizes the protracted process of liberalizing capital outflow in Japan.

Equipped with ample powers in the FECL to monitor international capital transactions, the Japanese government eagerly played the role of gatekeeper, approving every outward FDI project until the late 1960s. Because of weakness in the balance of payments, the government expected Japanese firms to carry out overseas investments compatible with the larger industrial policy goals of export promotion, industrial restructuring, and raw materials procurement. Japan's membership in the IMF and OECD together with marked improvement in the balance of payments, however, intensified international pressure on Japan to loosen its strict controls on capital mobility. The Japanese government complied only on the surface, with five different rounds of piecemeal deregulation. Automatic approval for smaller FDI projects was gradually expanded, but restrictions were quickly reinstated with the deterioration in the capital account after the first oil shock.

It took more than three decades for Japan to reform the Foreign Exchange Control Law. Although the establishment in principle of freedom to conduct any international capital transaction was a major breakthrough in the Japanese regulatory regime, de facto government discretion over capital outflows remained largely intact. MOF preserved its broad authority to interdict outbound FDI projects that it deemed would have deleterious effects on the economy; the government-authorized banks continued to monopolize foreign exchange transactions; and the more stringent rules on outward FDI for several special sectors still applied.

It was only in the context of the most thorough deregulation of the Japanese financial system (encapsulated in the Big Bang program) that a major breakthrough in the capital outflow regulatory regime took place. The new Foreign Exchange Law of 1998 finally broke the bank monopoly over currency transactions, established an ex post facto reporting system on FDI (diminishing the government's opportunity to deter overseas investment projects), and for the first time significantly reduced the number of special sectors subject to more strict FDI regulation.

Consequently, at the turn of the twenty-first century Japan looked much more like its counterpart home governments in the regulation of FDI outflows. As noted in Chapter 1, most countries (including Japan) that in the past thoroughly screened outbound FDI projects have relaxed their monitoring mechanisms. Ex post facto notification of direct investments overseas, mostly

TABLE 3.1

A Chronology of Capital Outflow Liberalization in Japan, 1949–1998

1949	Foreign Exchange and Foreign Trade Control Law	Prohibition in principle of all capital outflows, unless explicitly authorized; currency transactions carried out only by authorized FOREX banks; government approval required for each FDI project.
October 1969	Liberalization round 1	Automatic approval for FDI projects under $200,000; case-by-case screening of FDI projects in restricted sectors.
September 1970	Liberalization round 2	Automatic approval for FDI projects under $1 million; case-by-case screening of FDI projects in restricted sectors (tighter restrictions on textiles).
July 1971	Liberalization round 3	Elimination of the lower ceiling for automatic approval; in its place a system of prior notification; case-by-case screening of FDI projects in restricted sectors.
July 1972	Liberalization round 4	Investments in foreign corporations where Japanese firms held less than 25 percent of shares but had long-term business relations could now qualify for automatic approval; case-by-case screening of FDI projects in restricted sectors.
January 1974	Capital controls reimposed	MOF restrains all overseas investment projects except those deemed strategic (natural resource procurement).
April 1978	Liberalization round 5	Prior notification system reinstated; case-by-case screening of FDI projects in restricted sectors.
December 1980	Amended Foreign Exchange and Trade Control Law	Freedom in principle of all capital outflows, unless explicitly forbidden; currency transactions carried out only by authorized FOREX banks; prior notifications system for FDI projects; case-by-case screening of FDI projects in restricted sectors.
April 1998	New Foreign Exchange Law	Freedom in principle of all capital outflows, unless explicitly forbidden; elimination of the foreign exchange bank system; introduction of an ex post facto notification system for FDI projects; reduction of special sectors subject to case-by-case screening.

SOURCES: Safarian 1993; Bailey, Harte, and Sugden 1994; MITI 1993; Committee on Foreign Exchange 1997.

to compile balance-of-payments statistics, has become common practice in advanced capitalist economies. This policy convergence is evident in the substantial elimination of capital controls (both short and long term) in the industrialized world. Goodman and Pauly (1993) argue that the globalization of production and finance enabled firms to avoid controls over short-term capital transactions, and so governments eventually abandoned them.

Obviously, the ability of Japanese MNCs to raise capital in local markets or expand their operations through reinvestment is inversely correlated with the ability of the Japanese government to control FDI through domestic capital controls. Yet Japanese MNCs stand out for their strong reliance on domestic sources of capital (a parent company's retained earnings or loans from Japanese private and public financial institutions) to pay for their overseas investment projects. For example, a 1993 MITI survey revealed that more than 65 percent of all capital for Japanese FDI projects was raised in Japan, and that host financial institutions supplied only 13 percent of the funds for Japanese projects (MITI 1994c). The internationalization of finance and production therefore seems insufficient to explain Japan's move toward capital liberalization.

Another common explanation of the Japanese government's willingness to liberalize the regime governing capital outflows is pressure from the international community: the IMF, the OECD, and the United States. While recognizing the importance of these international factors (the globalization of finance and *gaiatsu*), I believe the domestic politics of deregulation better explains the timing and the manner in which controls on capital outflows were lifted in Japan.

Bureaucratic clashes and the protection of client interests decisively shaped the deregulation of cross-border financial transactions at several crucial junctures. The attempts of MOF and MITI to use reform of the FECL to expand their own jurisdiction at the expense of the other effectively derailed the reform efforts in 1959 and 1963. A severe balance-of-payments crisis in 1974 also produced a major bureaucratic clash when MITI boldly tried to gain extraordinary powers over FDI monitoring and financing.

The first reform of the Foreign Exchange Control Law in 1980 was possible only after both ministries agreed to uphold the status quo on jurisdictional lines and to maintain the privileges of the foreign exchange banks. Although the desire to restore the international competitiveness of the Japanese financial system was a major motivation behind the 1998 implementation of the New Foreign Exchange Law, the breakup of the bank monopoly over foreign currency transactions was possible only at a time of extraordinary weakness of both MOF and the banking community.

Consistently then, political bargaining between the supervising ministries decisively influenced the evolution of the regulatory regime governing capital outflows.[14] The outcome of this political negotiation has been greater Japanese convergence toward international rules on capital mobility. However, the other pillar of the Japanese state's FDI policy—preferential financing—has proved far more resilient. The Japanese government continues to be the world's largest public banker to multinational corporations.

CHAPTER 4

Public FDI Credit and the Expansion of Japanese Multinational Corporations

FOR MOST OF THE postwar period, the Japanese government zealously guarded its prerogative to interdict FDI projects that it deemed ran counter to its industrial policy goals. The flipside to this policy of control was generous financial support to overseas investments that helped ease natural resource procurement or industrial restructuring. The government's willingness to bank on multinationals was also a response to lobbying for FDI subsidies from politically powerful interest groups in economic distress.

This chapter discusses the domestic politics informing the largest government FDI financing program in the world. It lays out the motivations behind Japan's remarkable commitment of public resources to its firms' overseas expansion. And it takes on the single most divisive issue concerning public FDI financing: unequal rates of subsidization for different producer groups.

Ever since Japan launched its FDI loan program in the 1950s, politicians from the ruling party and Treasury bureaucrats have clashed over control of soft FDI credit. Their disagreements have had important implications for the evolution of the institutional framework of Japanese FDI financing. Ruling-party politicians have consistently pressed for the establishment of public financial agencies that would serve their core constituencies, and more important, they have battled with Treasury bureaucrats over the budgetary design of these FDI-financing institutions.

In this political story, budgetary rules emerge as the key focal point in the contest between bureaucrats and politicians to use public loans as a tool to subsidize interest groups. Budgetary design influences the quality of government lending in the sense that public institutions that enjoy generous transfers from the general account (approved by the politicians) can soften the terms of their FDI credit, whereas agencies that borrow (from the Treasury and through bond issues) or generate their own resources will be less inclined to subsidize their loans.

For most of the postwar period, the bureaucrats prevailed in guarding the financial discipline of the largest public agency financing FDI. However, over time and especially during the early 1990s, political activism has led to more subsidized credit at the expense of bureaucratic authority.

The Politics of Japanese Financial Industrial Policy

Japan's systematic attempts to improve its position in the international division of labor through a proactive industrial policy have been at the core of the developmental state model of Japanese political economy. Chalmers Johnson's pioneering work (1982) portrayed an elite pilot agency (MITI) determined to challenge classical comparative advantage law that would have limited Japan to the production of labor-intensive, low-value-added products. The talented industrial policy bureaucrats boldly attempted to upgrade the country's industrial structure by nurturing infant industries and promoting higher value added exports. In the very first years of the postwar period, MITI artfully put together an impressive array of policy tools to promote high growth: it controlled the access of foreign exchange, firms, goods, and technology to the Japanese market; it was capable of marshaling substantial resources to selected industries in the form of discounted loans, subsidies, and tax breaks; and it could sanction cartels to combat the problems of excessive competition and redundant capacity during economic downturns (Johnson 1982: 199).[1]

However, this extraordinary concentration of formal powers in the hands of the economic bureaucracy to directly intervene in the market was short-lived. Through its membership in multilateral economic organizations such as the International Monetary Fund and the General Agreement on Tariffs and Trade (GATT), Japan acquired commitments to liberalize its tight regulatory regime over international transactions. As discussed in Chapter 3, in 1964 MITI lost one of its most potent tools of industrial policy, the foreign exchange budget that had allowed the ministry to allocate scarce foreign exchange to Japanese producers. MITI's failure to ratify new formal powers of bureaucratic intervention in the economy—in the form of a Special Measures Law for the Promotion of Designated Industries—gave saliency to one of the most discussed traits of Japanese industrial policy: the practice of administrative guidance: "the authority of the government, contained in the laws establishing the various ministries, to issue directives, requests, warning, suggestions, and encouragements to the enterprises or clients within a particular ministry's jurisdiction" (Johnson 1982: 265).

Whether administrative guidance is the product of bureaucratic strength or weakness has generated considerable debate. Upham (1987), for example, points to the benefits of extralegal admonitions in sheltering the bureaucracy from judicial review (that is, the use the court system to challenge bureaucratic policies). In contrast, others note that MITI's first choice was always direct control, but in the face of resistance from the private sector or rival bureaucracies it had to content itself with indirect intervention (Reed 1993; Samuels 1987). Instead of a top-down economic policymaking process, economic bureaucrats enticed business cooperation through extensive information-sharing, joint discussion of policies, and economic inducements. The end result according to Haley was "governance by negotiation" (1987: 89).[2]

These disagreements aside, Japan scholars concur that a market-conforming industrial policy was essential to Japan's successful growth experience (Johnson 1982; Samuels 1987; P. A. Hall 1995; Pempel 1998). Instead of displacing market competition—by, for example, artificially fixing prices or creating state monopolies—the genius of the Japanese government was to affect investment patterns with informal guidance and economic incentives.

Despite the accomplishments of economic bureaucrats and industrialists in generating high-speed growth in the first half of the postwar period, there are many instances of pork-barrel and compensatory policies that point toward more politicization of economic policymaking than has been recognized by the developmental state model. Two positions on the influence of political pressure on economic policy deserve attention. On the one hand, Johnson (1982), who famously observed that "politicians reign but bureaucrats rule," has argued that politicians are shields who deflect interest group pressure in order to preserve the autonomy of the bureaucracy. On the other hand, Ramseyer and Rosenbluth (1993) argue that bureaucrats are merely agents of the politicians who have devised effective strategies to minimize agency slack.

Neither of these polar interpretations is entirely convincing, though. Ramseyer and Rosenbluth provide very modest empirical evidence to back up their claim that politicians successfully rein in bureaucrats (for instance, evidence of how and how frequently politicians actually influenced the placement of retired bureaucrats—*amakudari*—in order to discipline their actions). But Johnson's claim that the politicians' role is limited to protecting bureaucratic autonomy from interest group lobbying is also not credible. Revealingly, public policy in postwar Japan has exhibited a strong materialistic bias, with politically influential low-productivity sectors, such as agriculture and small-scale establishments receiving generous budgetary allocations (Calder 1988). In fact, statistical tests buttress the conclusion that politicians from the ruling Liberal Democratic Party (LDP) reallocated financial aid to small firms when they feared the defection of this support group to the opposition (Patterson 1994).

Both Calder and Patterson demonstrate that increased financial assistance to low-productivity sectors in the Japanese political economy is not only a reflection of a larger pool of financial resources in a more affluent Japan, but also a consequence of electoral politics. During periods of political crisis, the growth of general account budget allocations far surpassed rates of GNP growth, a pattern not observed during periods of electoral stability (Calder 1988: 176). And controlling for incremental growth in public loans to small enterprises, Patterson still found a statistically significant relationship between decreased LDP support and preferential financing for the small-firm lobby.

Further attesting to the importance of politics in Japanese economic policy are the sharply divergent patterns of politicization among Japanese bureaucracies, with some ministries more immune to political pressure from politicians and private sector lobbies (MITI, MOF), and others blatantly colonized by interest groups (agriculture, construction). The uneven pattern of political interference in bureaucratic agencies reflects variation in the type of political exchange established between ruling-party politicians and interest groups (Okimoto 1988: 323–25). Noncompetitive sectors that depend on public assistance to stay afloat will use their political connections more intensively to maintain the bureaucratic mantle of protection. And they will be most successful in mobilizing politicians on their behalf if they can offer clientelistic votes or financial contributions.

If anything, politicization seems to be a growing trend in the Japanese political economy. The 1990s recession exacerbated distributive conflicts in Japan and produced for the first time a major setback to conservative rule (in 1993 the LDP was ousted from power, although the party made a comeback ten months later as a member of the coalition government). In the past, rapid economic growth had allowed politicians to compensate low-productivity sectors, but the economic recession, budgetary deficits, and LDP electoral vulnerability could make this policy of "no losers" unsustainable (Pempel 1999). Zero-sum conflicts over the distribution of scarce public resources, renewed political pressure from inefficient sectors increasingly exposed to international competition, and the conservative politicians' concern with electoral instability could in fact further politicize economic policymaking.

The Japanese state has played a very active role in economic development. Yet the bureaucracy has had to negotiate its industrial policy with the private sector and therefore, has relied heavily on economic inducements (such as discounted loans and subsidies) to affect business investment patterns. Politicians too have been interested in controlling the administration of many of these economic promotion programs as part of their electoral strategies. Under what conditions preferential financing can be a powerful tool of industrial policy to achieve bureaucratic goals of industrial restructuring, and under what circumstances politicians can distort the allocation of public loans to feed clientelistic networks are among the most pressing questions in Japanese economic development.

THE ROLE OF GOVERNMENT INDUSTRIAL FINANCING

Preferential financing is the lifeblood of a market-conforming industrial policy. By providing low-cost loans the government can encourage private sector investment in priority areas. In other words, preferential financing allows the bureaucracy to send signals and incentives to guide private sector behavior without foreclosing market competition through more obtrusive forms of intervention.

The role of public financing in Japanese economic growth has been the subject of increased examination.[3] Those who favor active public credit programs point to its many advantages over other industrial policy tools: loan guarantees to private financial institutions to encourage lending create a "moral hazard," since a public commitment for bailout will relax credit discipline; tax breaks and special depreciation schemes spur investment expenditure, but they depend on the availability of sufficient tax revenue and are not fine-tuning instruments to aid specific projects; and subsidies cannot be targeted to individual projects without raising equity concerns, and they often result in lax policy implementation. In contrast, public financing is much more flexible and effective: it can target individual projects, and its requirement for repayment results in much more efficient project identification and implementation (Kato et al. 1994: 50, 88).

Public credit is deemed a powerful tool of industrial policy for its multiple functions (ibid.: 49). Government financial institutions are praised for carrying out the key tasks of *risk-compensation*, through participation in projects with high technical or market risk; *long-term financing*, by supplying stable funds to projects with long periods of investment recovery; *income complementation* through the provision of loans at low interest rates; and *signaling and pump-priming*, by disseminating information about borrowers to private sector financial institutions and guaranteeing protection or favorable treatment to an industry or project. In other words, public financing is regarded as an essential supplement to commercial lending because it offers long-term funds with fixed and low interest rates to high-risk projects where private financing would not occur in the absence of state indicative credit (that is, in instances of market failure).[4]

The attractiveness of public industrial credit programs can be gauged by the high ratio of public loans to total loans contracted by the Japanese private sector. Between 1970 and 1990 the share of outstanding public loans hovered around 12 percent for manufacturing, and was 26–30 percent for mining. Within manufacturing, heavy and declining industries strongly depended on public credit: nonferrous metals (16 percent), iron and steel (12.4 percent), metal products (14 percent), and textiles (12.1 percent) (Bank of Japan, *Economic Statistics Annual*, several issues).

During the gradual process of financial market liberalization, Japanese firms have moved away from indirect financing (commercial and public loans) and relied more on capital markets (bonds, stocks, and other securities) to meet their financial needs. For instance, the share of bank lending in total corporate funding decreased by about 10 percent (from 87 percent to 77 percent) between 1970 and 1990; yet not all Japanese industries or firms were equally capable of securitizing their corporate financing (Hoshi and Kashyap 2001: 245). The shift away from indirect financing was far more acute among large enterprises (with a 24 percentage point reduction in the ratio of bank debt to total assets between 1970 and 1997) than for smaller firms. Moreover, stagnant industries have remained far more dependent on bank credit. In 1998 the average ratio of bank loans to total assets for the manufacturing sector was 20 percent. Industries that reported a much higher dependence on bank loans included textiles (24.6 percent), pulp and paper (35.5 percent), petroleum and coal (41.6 percent), iron and steel (26.4 percent), and nonferrous metals (35.9 percent) (Hoshi and Kashyap 2001: 315).

These statistics demonstrate that the benefits of public financing are especially important for firms without easy access to private loans and capital markets because they operate in stagnant industries or are very small (that is, they lack sufficient collateral or face higher risks of bankruptcy). This is especially true when they are considering overseas investment (as a last-ditch effort to survive in a lower-cost location), since private banks may be reluctant to absorb the additional risk of such projects. Indeed, one of the most important benefits of public FDI financing is that it can lower the political risk of investing in foreign countries with forced disinvestment or more stringent performance requirements.[5] IPE scholars have long identified the high-risk areas: raw materials investments and large-scale manufacturing/infrastructural projects where multinational corporations face large sunk costs and thus lose bargaining power with their host governments (see Vernon 1971; Moran 1985; Shafer 1985). For these multinational corporations facing a deteriorating and "obsolescing bargain" (to use Vernon's influential term), enlisting their home government as creditor to the overseas project may be an effective strategy for increasing their leverage with local authorities.

In the best of all worlds, Japanese public financial institutions are expected to contribute to economic development by lowering market and political risk, encouraging private investment, and reducing the cost of capital. And yet an activist financial industrial policy is not without its perils. Funding large-scale public loan programs without eating up tax revenues, exacerbating government indebtedness, and fueling inflationary pressures may be a daunting task. Moreover, instilling discipline in public financial institutions to ensure efficient loan allocation, and to avoid a spiral of nonperforming loans requiring expensive bail-out packages, is also a tall order.

Japanese public credit agencies have a mixed record, with some disciplined institutions uneasily coexisting with heavily politicized banks. The politics of budgetary negotiation is an essential ingredient in producing the uneven pattern of strategic credit allocation and pork-barrel financing in Japan.

THE BUDGETARY FOUNDATIONS OF JAPANESE FINANCIAL INDUSTRIAL POLICY

Budgets loom large in Japanese financial industrial policy. The ability of the state to affect private investment patterns through indicative credit hinges on the government's capacity to pool sufficient financial resources at reasonable cost. Japan developed an ingenious mechanism for funding its public policies. The Fiscal Investment and Loan Program (FILP), frequently referred to as the "second budget," gave the Japanese state access to a vast pool of financial resources in the form of public pensions, postal life insurance, and especially postal savings—representing 46 percent of all private deposits channeled into the second budget in the postwar period (MOF 2001: 7). The sheer financial dimensions of the second budget are staggering: annual FILP plans grew from 323 billion yen in 1953 to 43,676 billion yen in 2000. By the early twenty-first century, cumulative FILP funds had reached the unprecedented figure of 418 trillion yen. Revealingly, the second budget has expanded more quickly than the general account budget. FILP's share of the general account budget grew from 33 percent in 1953 to 51 percent in 2000 (Ishi 1986: 84; MOF 2001). A rapidly expanding second budget, therefore, has allowed the Japanese government to exceed the limits of its income from taxation to finance its industrial policies.

The Ministry of Finance has played a key role in the allocation of the plentiful second budget. Private sector deposits in FILP are distributed among four different funds, but the lion's share goes to the Trust Fund Bureau (TFB) in the Ministry of Finance; in 2000 it received 84 percent of all FILP deposits (MOF 2001).[6] MOF bureaucrats in the Financial Bureau are responsible for allocating these monies to the network of public financial institutions and special corporations that depend on FILP loans to carry out their operations—their appellation as FILP agencies is no misnomer. These public financial institutions in turn are expected to provide low-cost loans to the private sector in priority areas.

The system of public industrial financing, with FILP at its core, is justified by bureaucrats on two scores. First, it allows the government to perform some essential functions: to solve market failure by financing welfare-enhancing projects neglected by commercial lenders; and to regulate the level of economic activity by injecting resources into the market and stimulating private investment. Second, because all postal savers must be paid back with interest, government credit institutions borrowing FILP money must be disciplined in their project selection and implementation.

The Political Contest over the Second Budget

Over time, however, bureaucratic autonomy to administer the second budget eroded. The vast amounts concentrated in FILP, and the desire to influence allocation patterns in favor of support groups, have long motivated LDP politicians to gain greater sway over FILP money. In the first twenty-five years after World War II, MOF prevailed over politicians in exerting control over FILP. The Treasury bureaucrats effectively defended the principle of "integrated management." In other words, postal savings and public pensions were not administered by the ministries in charge of collecting them (the Ministry of Posts and Telecommunications, MOPT; and the Ministry of Health and Welfare, MHW), but were automatically deposited in MOF's Trust Fund Bureau. Moreover, until 1973 legislative oversight of the FILP was very weak. Diet approval was mandatory only for the funding of the Industrial Investment and Government Bonds accounts. The core of the FILP—the Trust Fund Bureau—was excluded (Y. Suzuki 1987; Noguchi 1995: 263, 267).

Gradually, politicians began to exert more influence over the second budget. Since 1973 the Diet has voted to approve the disbursement of FILP's four funds into every FILP agency.[7] A marked reorientation in FILP priorities ensued. Whereas in the early postwar period the bulk of FILP resources targeted industrial promotion programs, in subsequent decades projects geared toward social infrastructure and support for low-productivity sectors gained prominence. For instance, in the 1950s almost a quarter of all FILP loans went to support industry, trade, and economic cooperation; in the year 2000 loans for these activities had shrunk to 6.7 percent. FILP financing for housing, the environment, welfare, education, small business, agriculture, forestry, and fisheries grew steadily during these years: from 45 to 77 percent of all second budget loans (Kato et al. 1994: 16; MOF 2001: 15). Prominent among the recipients of FILP discounted loans are support groups that provide LDP politicians with much-needed votes (farmers, small businesses) and financial contributions (mega-construction companies).

One of the most important areas of leverage politicians have over industrial financial policy is their control over first budget subsidies. In their allocation of these general account transfers to different government credit institutions, politicians have in fact relaxed the constraints on soft financing. The distribution of first budget subsidies reflects the same political criteria in that bastions of LDP support have captured the lion's share of these general account transfers: housing and small-business financial institutions received 92 percent of these subsidies in the mid-1980s (Calder 1993: 60–61). These subsidies allow politicized public financial institutions to lower their interest rates (that is, engage in soft financing) and avoid the consequences of poor lending decisions (to stay afloat despite substantial nonperforming loans).

Public financial institutions recording the highest levels of nonperforming loans also rely most heavily on first budget subsidies. In 1999 the institutions with the largest percentage of insolvent loans included the Hokkaido-Tohoku Development Finance Corporation (15.8 percent); the Agriculture, Forestry, and Fisheries Finance Corporation (5.5 percent); the Japan Small Business Finance Corporation (5.1 percent); and the Overseas Economic Cooperation Fund (3.84 percent). Many of these institutions needed budget subsidies to carry out their operations.

In 1998 public financial institutions with the largest ratio of general account transfers to FILP loans included the Overseas Economic Cooperation Fund (66 percent); the Agriculture, Forestry, and Fisheries Finance Corporation (38 percent); the Hokkaido-Tohoku Development Finance Corporation (8.4 percent); the Housing Loan Corporation (10.1 percent); and the Japan Finance Corporation for Small Business (9.4 percent).[8] In contrast, the two public banks in charge of industrial promotion operate under the principle of self-sustainability and must fund their lending programs through earnings, bond issues, and FILP loans. The Japan Development Bank (JDB) and the Japan Eximbank have recorded the lowest levels of nonperforming loans among public financial institutions (0.8 percent and 0.6 percent, respectively, in 1999).

The sharp differences in the lending discipline of public financial institutions closely resemble the uneven politicization of Japanese bureaucratic agencies (see Okimoto 1988). Some ministries and public financial institutions remain relatively immune to interest group influence, while others readily cater to the demands of needy constituencies. But what kinds of institutional safeguards are responsible for this mixed pattern of economic targeting and political compensation in Japanese public policy?

I believe that budgetary design is a key influence on whether pork-barrel practices emerge in public financing. The analysis here of the political battles to determine the mandate and budgetary structure of public FDI financing institutions reveals a clear pattern: MOF bureaucrats pushed for stiff budgetary constraints on public credit agencies, but politicians managed to implement soft budgetary rules for the public financial institutions that service important electoral constituencies.

The Japanese state actively banked on its own multinationals, but did not subsidize FDI evenly across producer groups. The bulk of the FDI credit program was administered by the more disciplined Japan Eximbank. But structurally depressed heavy industry and distressed small establishments were able to obtain much more subsidized FDI financing from other government financial agencies. Thus did domestic politics affect the manner in which the Japanese government ran the world's largest loan program to promote the expansion of multinational corporations.

The Division of Labor in Public FDI Financing

In the aftermath of World War II, US occupation authorities and Japanese bureaucrats quickly identified trade promotion as crucial to the task of economic reconstruction. One of the biggest obstacles to restarting the economy was the shortage of foreign exchange needed to import essential foodstuffs, raw materials, and equipment. In order to promote export earnings in hard currency, therefore, the Japanese government established the Export Bank of Japan in December 1950. The mandate of the newly created bank and the budgetary rules affecting its lending behavior were shaped by two factors: the failure of the Reconstruction Finance Bank, and the US attempt to use the American Eximbank as a model for the new Japanese public institution.

The 1947 establishment of the Reconstruction Finance Bank had been the first postwar attempt of the Japanese state to use preferential financing as a tool of industrial policy. This experiment, however, did not go well. The Reconstruction Finance Bank contributed to an inflation spiral by financing its credit operations with government bonds and transfers from the general account, and it was abolished just two years after its creation. It was the first casualty of the strict deflationary policy recommended by the economic adviser Joseph Dodge to American occupation authorities in 1949. Japanese policymakers learned a hard lesson from the dramatic failure of the Reconstruction Finance Bank: government banks that strain public finances (by worsening public debt and generating inflationary pressures) are not sustainable. Stricter fund procurement rules were in order.

THE JAPAN EXIMBANK: FROM EXPORT CREDIT TO FDI FINANCING

The new emphasis on disciplined public credit institutions meshed well with the view of American officials, who openly pushed for the adoption of the US Eximbank model in Japan. Mirroring US practices, the Export Bank of Japan was established as a self-reliant public institution guided by the principles of sound and supplementary financing. This time the government refrained from capitalizing the new bank through government bonds or general account transfers and relied instead on the Industrial Investment Special Account, and after 1952 on FILP loans.[9]

The choice of a bureaucratic monitor for the bank further reflected concerns about its financial soundness. The bank was placed under the supervision of the Ministry of Finance (the guardian of national finances), and not MITI (the industrial policy strategist). In addition, the bank was instructed to extend loans only when there was certainty of payment and to avoid crowding out the market by operating as a lender of last resort. In other words, the bank was to "supplement and encourage financing by commercial banks" through the practice of syndicated lending to fund domestic exporters' activities (Japan Eximbank 1994: 1). And following US practice, the Japan Eximbank was originally established as a sunset agency to be phased out once it had served its mission.[10]

Soon after Japan regained independence, government officials made several changes of consequence to the bank's charter. First they eliminated the sunset clause in order to ensure the long-term sustainability of the Bank (Japan Eximbank 1983: 42). Moreover, Japanese public officials acquiesced to a long-standing demand from the private sector that they receive preferential loans for the importation of vital resources. The bank changed its name in 1952 to the Japan Export-Import Bank, and in 1953 it broke new ground for a public international credit agency by inaugurating a program to finance the overseas investment projects of Japanese private enterprises. In the Japan Eximbank's own words: "The use of public funds for the financing of private overseas investments is a very special Japanese system with almost no examples in other countries" (ibid.: 40). This policy innovation responded to the conviction of public officials that neither domestic corporations nor commercial banks had the capital to finance riskier investment projects abroad. The bank justified the new FDI loans by emphasizing their trade impact: these projects would secure the import of key raw materials and promote the export of Japanese equipment.

Tight strings were attached to the purse of public FDI credit, though. After the difficult balance-of-payments situation in the early 1950s, the government proceeded cautiously in approving FDI projects. The Japan Eximbank stipulated that government-supported FDI ventures should lead to export promotion or improved import contracts for industrial inputs. However, concern over natural resource procurement led to further expansion of the Japan Eximbank's FDI banking role.

In 1957 the bank relaxed some of the tight conditions on overseas investment credit. The purpose of FDI financing was expanded from export promotion to include the improvement of international economic exchange. FDI financing was extended to Japanese consortiums that specialized in foreign direct investment; it was made available for long-term financing as well as equity acquisition; and it was extended to foreign governments participating in joint ventures (Japan Eximbank 1983: 94–96). In this way, the Japan Eximbank emerged better suited to finance both the exploitation of natural resources abroad and the relocation of heavy industry, projects that, because of their enormous capital requirements, are often conducted as joint ventures between consortiums of Japanese firms in cooperation with the host government.

The latest wave of innovation in FDI financing took place in the 1980s, in the context of yen appreciation, structural adjustment, and accelerated investment abroad. In 1986 the Japan Eximbank first used the "project finance" formula and became the first export-import bank to establish a specialized department in this area two years later.[11] The Japan Eximbank's project finance chiefly targeted natural resource development, including liquefied natural gas, petrochemicals, and copper mining. Because these operations were high-risk and expensive, the Japan Eximbank approved only ten such projects between 1986 and 1996. Moreover, only a few were financed through overseas investment loans; the rest were covered with buyer credit (Japan Eximbank 1996: 10).[12]

Moreover, in 1989 the government authorized the Japan Eximbank to make equity investments in FDI projects ("Sengō Gojūnen," 1995: 107). However, the Japan Eximbank rarely relied on this new instrument: only in 1993 did it invest 1.5 billion yen for an airport terminal in Los Angeles. The reluctance of the Japan Eximbank to use equity investments to fund overseas projects was the result of the higher risks of direct ownership and the longer time it would take to recover the initial investment capital. Although ready to experiment with new financing techniques to aid the internationalization of Japanese industry, the Japan Eximbank still promoted multinationalism mostly through the more traditional tool of FDI credit.

Shifting Priorities in Japan Eximbank Financing

In the half century after its creation, the Japan Eximbank transformed itself from a traditional export promotion agency to a more complex public financial institution supporting the overseas expansion of Japanese corporations and the main international economic initiatives of the Japanese government (including debt relief, capital recycling, and market transition in Eastern Europe). The transformation of the Japan Eximbank's mandate is reflected in the shifting composition of its loan portfolio (see Figure 4.1).

In its first decades, export credit and bilateral government loans were its mainstays, but not anymore. Bilateral government-based loans were the first area that the Japan Eximbank relinquished. These loans had represented 4–15 percent of the bank's financing during the 1950s and 1960s, but after 1975 they became the responsibility of the Overseas Economic Cooperation Fund (OECF), the Japanese aid agency. Trade financing also ceased to be a central mission. Export promotion was its driving goal for three decades (representing 60–90 percent of all loans). After the 1980s, however, export financing receded in importance, and from 1991 to 2000 export credit represented only 14 percent of total financing. In contrast, import loans first surged in 1972–73 as a result of special import promotion programs to ease revaluatory pressure on the yen. Owing to greater international pressure on Japan to reduce its soaring trade surplus, import loans represented 13 percent of total lending during the 1980s. Then during the 1990s the share of import loans in total financing decreased to single digits.

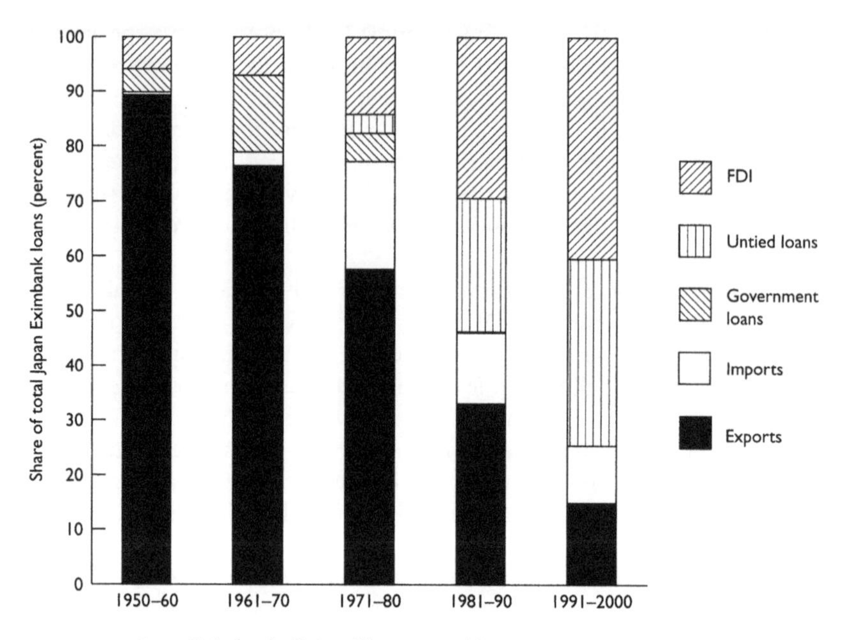

SOURCE: Japan Eximbank, *Gyōmu Binran*, several issues.

Figure 4.1 Shifting Priorities in Japan Eximbank Financing, 1950–2000

The Japan Eximbank's modern mandate revolved around the provision of untied loans (loans without a requirement to procure Japanese products) and FDI financing. The bank launched untied loans in 1973, but this program took off only in the second half of the 1980s when the Japanese government used it to disburse the $65 billion committed under the capital recycling initiative to alleviate the third world crisis (Kinoshita Toshihiko 1992: 204). In the 1990s, untied loans represented 35 percent of all finance and were used mostly as bridge loans to countries facing a currency crisis or as adjustment loans to facilitate market transition reforms (see Figure 4.1).

Gradually, multinational investment support became the defining mission of the Japan Eximbank. Throughout the 1950s and 1960s outward investment credit remained a small part of the bank's lending (6–7 percent). During the 1970s, it rose to 14 percent and increased dramatically in the following decade to represent close to 30 percent of all lending. During the 1990s, FDI loans were the single most important lending activity of the Japan Eximbank, averaging close to 40 percent of total financing during the decade. In sum, the lending portfolio of the bank moved away from traditional export financing to fully embrace the role of banker to Japanese multinational corporations.

The Goals of FDI Financing

In the fifty-year period between 1950 and 2000, the Japan Eximbank extended close to $70 billion in FDI credit to overcome financial market failure in resource procurement and industrial adjustment. Those two goals were clearly reflected in its allocation of overseas investment loans. The primary sector (agriculture, forestry, fishery, and mining) received 34 percent of all FDI loans between 1953 and 1984, and only between 1985 and 1999 did this sector recede in importance (receiving only 12 percent of total FDI loans). Manufacturing remained at the core of the FDI loan program, capturing throughout the postwar period 65 percent of all FDI credit.

The composition of manufacturing FDI loans reveals strong backing for downstream sectors processing raw materials, for industries with eroding export competitiveness (due to wage increases or currency realignments), and for heavy industries undergoing structural decline due to rising energy costs (see Table 4.1). In its first twenty years of providing FDI loans, the Japan Eximbank generously financed natural resource extraction projects abroad to feed processing plants back home (lumber and pulp received 29.5 percent of all credit, iron and steel and nonferrous metals 23 percent).

Japan's support for troubled manufacturing sectors began with the textile industry as it entered a structural process of decline in the mid-1960s due to wage hikes (21.5 percent of manufacturing FDI credit between 1953 and 1970). Next, the Japanese government lent its financial muscle to heavy industries dependent on cheap energy (iron foundries, copper smelting, aluminum refining, petrochemical complexes, and others) when they abruptly lost competitiveness in the post–oil shock years (chemicals, iron and steel, and nonferrous metals received 68 percent of the bank's FDI loans between 1971 and 1984). In more recent times, Japan financed more assembly-intensive export industries (automobiles and electronics) threatened with loss of market share due to yen appreciation (the bank's FDI loans to the electronics and automobile industries jumped dramatically between 1985 and 1989, from 2 and 12 percent, respectively, to 22 percent).

The sectoral breakdown of Japanese public credit for overseas investment closely mirrors the evolution of the industrial composition of Japanese FDI. As noted in Chapter 2, the first wave of Japanese industrial FDI centered on textiles and sectors devoted mostly to the processing of natural resources (lumber and pulp, iron and steel, and nonferrous metals). In the second wave of Japanese overseas investment (1971–84), energy-intensive industries such as iron and steel, nonferrous metals, and chemicals were the most active overseas investors. In its latest phase, Japanese FDI flows were heavily dominated by assembly industries such as electronics and automobile machinery. Electronics FDI alone represented 30 percent of all manufacturing overseas investment in this period of rapid growth in Japanese FDI.

TABLE 4.1

Allocating Public Credit for Multinational Production: Distribution of the Japan Eximbank's Overseas Investment Loans in Manufacturing, 1953–1999 (percent)

	Food	Textiles	Lumber, pulp, paper	Chemicals	Iron and steel; nonferrous metals	General machinery	Electrical machinery	Transport machinery	Manufacturing total (million US$)
First period (1953–70)	3.8	21.5	29.5	1.9	23.0	4.2	3.5	8.6	282.4
Second period (1971–84)	1.3	5.9	5.1	19.1	48.8	1.8	1.9	11.9	5,459.2
Third period (1985–99)	1.0	3.3	1.1	18.4	22.6	2.2	22.2	22.5	40,436.8
Total	1.1	4.1	2.3	18.3	28.0	2.1	17.7	20.1	46,178.4

SOURCE: Estimated by the author with data provided by the Japan Eximbank.

TABLE 4.2

Relying on the State to Multinationalize Production: Ratio of the Japan Eximbank's Overseas Investment Loans to Approved/Notified FDI Flows, 1953–1999 (percent)

	Food	Textiles	Lumber, pulp, paper	Chemicals	Iron and steel; nonferrous metals	General machinery	Electrical machinery	Transport machinery	Manufacturing
First period (1953–70)	18.0	31.9	42.4	10.5	47.5	18.1	14.0	24.9	30.4
Second period (1971–84)	7.2	16.1	29.5	27.6	58.5	6.5	3.3	24.9	25.9
Third period (1985–99)	1.8	18.5	8.2	28.7	53.2	4.8	14.2	30.9	18.8
Total	2.3	18.3	15.9	28.4	54.9	5.2	13.2	29.9	20.0

SOURCE: Estimated by the author with data provided by the Japan Eximbank and FDI statistics from the MOF.

This close correspondence between the sectoral distribution of manufacturing FDI loans and the industrial composition of overseas investment is not surprising, given the extraordinary reliance of structurally depressed industries on government loans to finance their FDI projects (see Table 4.2). Note the very high ratio of Japan Eximbank loans to FDI flows in iron and steel, nonferrous metals, chemicals, textiles, and lumber and pulp. Even sectors that traditionally self-financed their investment strategies have increased their dependence on public financing in troubled times. The share of public credit in total FDI flow increased for electronics from 1 percent in the early 1980s to 14.6 percent in the 1990s (although its dependence on state preferential financing did not approach that of the structurally depressed industries).

On average, the Japan Eximbank's loans for overseas investment represented 20 percent of all Japanese manufacturing FDI. This is a staggering figure by international standards and underscores the high priority the Japanese government has attached to the promotion of manufacturing FDI through preferential financing.

Although the Japan Eximbank enjoyed a robust mandate to promote Japanese multinationalism, its mission was profoundly shaped by the budgetary rules of self-sustainability. It had to be financially sound in order to meet its repayment obligations to the FILP, and to procure funds through bond issues in overseas markets. It did not therefore provide large quantities of soft financing. Collateral was always demanded, and the interest rates charged for FDI loans were higher than its own cost of fund procurement. Other Japanese public financial institutions did not face the same domestic institutional constraints and consequently extended more soft FDI credit.

THE OVERSEAS ECONOMIC COOPERATION FUND: THE AID AND INVESTMENT LINK

Japan has openly endorsed an unorthodox approach to economic assistance that integrates official aid with private trade and investment flows. In the first annual White Paper on Economic Cooperation published in 1958, MITI categorized economic aid "according to the content of cooperation in overseas investment, capital cooperation, technical cooperation, and trade transactions." Moreover, MITI noted that "one special point about economic cooperation is that although the role of the state is gradually expanding, it is normally private sector-based" (quoted in Arase 1995: 38).

Another early Japanese position focused on the role of economic cooperation in facilitating the relocation of Japanese sunset industries to developing nations. One influential government advisory body, the Industrial Structure Council, deemed official development assistance (ODA) and foreign direct investment to be inextricably linked. The council considered it indispensable to increase both official aid and private investment to support Japanese industrial adjustment and improve the international division of labor (Industrial Structure Council 1972: 28–29). The government early on also espoused the promotion of overseas projects with a developmental dimension through special funding considerations, risk-minimization, and tax incentives (Sakurai 1972: 183).[13]

The yen appreciation of the late 1980s once more spurred the need to use FDI to facilitate structural adjustment. In its 1987 report the Council on Foreign Economic Cooperation (1987: 10–11) called international structural adjustment the central task of economic cooperation and emphasized the vital contribution of the private sector to economic cooperation with developing countries. To further expand the role of private companies, the council argued for more loan and equity investment from the Japan Eximbank, the Overseas Economic Cooperation Fund, and the Japan International Cooperation Agency; relaxation of the tax burden; and strengthening of the loan guarantees and investment insurance systems. Backed by this understanding of the joint contribution of official economic cooperation and private overseas investment to structural adjustment at home, the main Japanese ODA agency was actively involved in FDI promotion.

The Quest for Institutional Autonomy

The creation of the Overseas Economic Cooperation Fund, and its emergence from the shadow of the Japan Eximbank, was the result of an intense process of domestic political negotiation. In 1959 the LDP championed the establishment of a special fund for economic assistance. Behind this political initiative was the feeling in some Japanese business circles that the strict requirements necessary to receive Japan Eximbank financing foreclosed public credit for corporate expansion in the more unstable Asian markets. However, MOF strongly opposed the establishment of a public institution to finance unprofitable development projects abroad. In MOF's opinion, government financial institutions relying on taxes or other public funds should work under the principle of guaranteed repayment. In instances where repayment was not assured, MOF recommended a Diet resolution before funding could go ahead (MOF 1992: 150). In the end, however, MOF agreed to the establishment in 1961 of the OECF, in order to shield the Japan Eximbank from the pressure to finance riskier projects with softer financing. The ministry had realized that longer repayment terms, lower interest rates, and less stringent collateral requirements could compromise the financial soundness of the Japan Eximbank (MOF 1992: 148).

Although the LDP initiative to establish an economic assistance agency succeeded, the OECF faced major obstacles to expanding its operations (in its first year it funded only three projects). First, under the provisions of the FECL all projects of economic cooperation were subject to individual review, and the criteria for approval were very strict. Second, heeding MOF's concerns, the OECF's charter mandated that only projects with guaranteed success should be financed. Given the uncertain economic and political environment in many developing countries, this clause effectively limited the number of potential projects. Third, the charter required borrowers to provide collateral; but many of the firms interested in OECF financing were small and medium-sized companies with few assets (OECF 1982: 43).

The biggest barrier to active lending from the fund was the overlap between the OECF and the Japan Eximbank. The OECF charter commanded the fund to extend loans or make equity investments to development projects denied financing by the Japan Eximbank. Based on this provision, the "Japan Eximbank had the right of prior consideration of all projects" (ibid.: 43). Moreover, a Japan Eximbank director served on the OECF's board and played a key role in the decision-making process. This director had the right to review decisions by the OECF staff to finance specific projects. The OECF had particular difficulty extending bilateral government loans—the core of the ODA program. Historically, the Japan Eximbank had handled this type of official financing, and at the time loans to foreign governments were justified mainly by their contribution to the growth of Japanese exports (ibid.: 45, 76). The OECF therefore chose to facilitate the participation of the Japanese private sector in economic cooperation projects in developing nations through soft loans and equity investments. Because of MOF's concern financial concerns and the Japan Eximbank's interest in protecting its own operational turf, the agency created with the specific mandate to extend economic assistance to third world governments ended up exclusively financing FDI projects of Japanese enterprises.

Nevertheless, the OECF strengthened its position in two ways during the 1960s. In 1962, in response to continued pressure from the corporate world, the four ministries responsible for economic cooperation agreed to reform the OECF charter.[14] The clause requiring guaranteed completion of a development project was scrapped in favor of allowing funding for ventures with reasonable prospects for success (OECF 1982: 44–45). More projects were thus automatically considered for OECF financing. Then in 1965 the OECF offered its first direct loans to the governments of South Korea and Taiwan, effectively bypassing the working rule that had limited its financing operations to Japanese enterprises. The OECF maintained it was filling a void in the financing of large-scale infrastructure projects, since Japan Eximbank's direct loans had primarily targeted plant exports (ibid.: 77–78). However, the inauguration of OECF direct loans to foreign governments intensified the overlap with the Japan Eximbank's activities: both public agencies were now offering bilateral government loans and credit for the international activities of Japanese enterprises.

More than a decade of difficult political negotiations between these two public agencies, their bureaucratic monitors, and LDP politicians would be necessary to finally differentiate the areas of operation of the Japan Eximbank and the OECF. LDP politicians—especially those on the Diet Financial Committee—kept pushing to expand the OECF's mandate, only to confront the stubborn resistance of MOF. However, MOF finally agreed to redraw the division of labor between these two agencies under pressure from influential Diet committees and other bureaucracies in charge of economic cooperation.

In 1975 the OECF and the Japan Eximbank reached a demarcation agreement on their respective fields of operation. ODA loans (direct credit to governments of developing countries with a grant element of 25 percent or higher) became the exclusive domain of the OECF. Just as the OECF consolidated its position as Japan's premier ODA agency, financing the international operations of Japanese private enterprises became the primary responsibility of the Japan Eximbank. Some important exceptions were made to the rule that private investors should be financed through the bank's FDI loan program. As part of the demarcation agreement, the OECF was still allowed to finance the overseas activities of Japanese firms in areas such as agriculture, forestry, fisheries, and prospective mining. OECF loans to manufacturing projects abroad were barred, but equity investments were permitted (OECF 1982: 119). Also, the 1975 agreement gave the OECF more institutional autonomy by eliminating the practice of appointing a Japan Eximbank director to the fund's board of directors.

Shareholder in Offshore Economic Cooperation Ventures

For the OECF, which emerged as the main supplier of Japanese economic assistance loans, the demarcation agreement brought about a reversal of financing priorities. After 1975 the share of private sector finance in total OECF commitments plummeted to 5 percent for the following decade, and since the mid-1980s it averaged only 1 percent of total OECF financing. This trend notwithstanding, the OECF continued to play an important role as financier to Japanese overseas investors.[15] In absolute terms, the OECF's investment finance program was very large when compared cross-nationally. At the end of 1999, its loans to the private sector totaled $2.5 billion, roughly equivalent in size to the FDI programs of Germany's KfW and South Korea's Eximbank (see Chapter 1). Also, the OECF enjoyed more autonomy over overseas financing decisions. Only the approval of the Economic Planning Agency (EPA) and MOF was required for private investment finance, whereas the four ministries in charge of economic cooperation supervised ODA loans.[16] More important, the OECF was the only FILP agency entitled to carry out equity investments in overseas projects in all industrial sectors.[17]

The OECF's equity investments concentrated on projects related to infrastructure, basic industry relocation, and exploitation of natural resources (see Table 4.3). Manufacturing—the one area where only equity investments from the OECF were permitted—received the largest share of the fund's private investment financing. Next in importance were agriculture, mining, and forestry. Within manufacturing, iron milling, aluminum smelting, and petrochemical manufacture benefited greatly from OECF involvement as a shareholder in ventures of a considerable size (see OECF 1995: 189). Most of these undertakings were very large-scale ventures that often took the form of "national projects."[18]

Many structurally depressed industries in Japan moved abroad with the Japanese government (OECF) as an investment partner. The benefits of government equity contributions were especially important for uncompetitive heavy industries facing huge relocation costs. First, the OECF's capital participation did not create the burden of loan repayment, thereby reducing the need to generate cash flow quickly. Second, the government fully shared the risks of the development project abroad, collecting dividends only if and when the project succeeded. The differences in mandate and financial principles between the Japan Eximbank and the OECF were nowhere clearer. For the Japan Eximbank, assurance of repayment and self-sustainability were mandatory, whereas for the OECF a reasonable prospect for the successful implementation of the project was sufficient, and the fund relied heavily on tax money. The OECF thus enjoyed more budgetary leeway to undertake higher-risk equity investments.

Beginning in the late 1980s, OECF equity investment moved away from large-scale ventures and increasingly into small and medium-sized projects in order to better match the shifting nature of Japanese FDI (with the larger participation of assembly industries) ("Minkatsu Jūshi Rosen" 1989: 28–29). To achieve this goal, in 1989 the OECF helped capitalize a novel Japanese company specialized in FDI, the Japan International Development Organization (JAIDO).[19]

JAIDO: FDI and Economic Cooperation Financing Cross Paths Again

In the late 1980s, facing sharp yen appreciation, the private sector pushed for the establishment of a financial institution to promote private direct investment in recessionary periods through equity contributions to projects in high-risk developing countries (MOFA 1991: 190). Keidanren responded in 1989 by creating an investment company to promote joint ventures among Japanese enterprises in the developing world.

In many ways, JAIDO was a unique organization within the Japanese institutional framework for FDI financing. First, it was a private sector effort to create a company that would handle multiple investment projects of medium

TABLE 4.3

The Aid and Investment Link: OECF Financing of Private Sector Investment, 1961–1998

Sector	Number of projects	Amount (million yen)	Share of total financing (percent)
Telecommunications	11	7,332	1.4
Irrigation and flood control	4	2,399	0.5
Electric power and gas			
Multipurpose dams	3	844	0.2
Power plants	12	7,367	1.4
Transmission lines and distribution systems	2	1,469	0.3
Gas	3	9,466	1.8
Subtotal	20	19,146	3.7
Transportation			
Roads	10	10,358	2.0
Railways	8	3,425	0.7
Airports	1	46	0.0
Ports	5	6,633	1.3
Marine transportation	5	1,753	0.3
Others	3	695	0.1
Subtotal	32	22,909	4.5
Agriculture, forestry, fishery			
Agriculture	123	68,153	13.3
Forestry	74	54,519	10.6
Fishery	60	16,005	3.1
Farming	1	280	0.1
Subtotal	258	138,957	27.0
Mining and Manufacturing			
Mining	158	56,346	11.0
Manufacturing	247	185,641	36.1
Subtotal	405	241,986	47.1
Social Services			
Water supply and sewerage	7	6,675	1.3
Health	1	3	0.0
Tourism	7	15,546	3.0
Subtotal	29	37,485	7.3
Grand total	799	514,135	100.0

SOURCE: OECF, *Annual Report*, 1999.

or small size. In this sense it differed markedly from consortia of Japanese firms and the government that financed a single, usually very large, venture abroad in the form of a national project. Furthermore, even though close to 40 percent of its capital came from the OECF, JAIDO was constituted as a joint stock company, not as a *zaidan hōjin* (private foundation).[20] Keidanren insisted on the formation of a stock company to prevent the government from controlling its budgetary allocation and to minimize public intervention in its approval and implementation decisions.[21] The cost of independence was financial sustainability; in other words, JAIDO had to finance its operations with capital from the OECF and member companies without money subscriptions from any ministry. During a period of economic contraction many Japanese firms were reluctant to pay their individual quotas, making long-term financial survival a serious concern for JAIDO.

The fund procurement problem was compounded by JAIDO's stated purpose of promoting projects that official assistance cannot easily target and that are difficult to implement under normal commercial conditions (JAIDO 1995). JAIDO had to select projects that were not profitable unless some special financing could be made available, but that had a reasonable chance for success. And it had to carefully manage its portfolio to ensure some income in the form of dividends and capital gains. In addition, JAIDO's financial contribution to a joint venture was made only through equity investments.

So that the two organizations' activities would not overlap, they agreed that JAIDO would provide small and medium-sized equity investments to industrial projects with export or job creation potential, and that the OECF would focus on FDI loans and large-scale equity investments.[22] However, JAIDO's tight financial situation made the extension of loans increasingly desirable to its officials. Loan repayments would provide faster income recovery than dividends and capital gains. For these reasons, in June 1995 JAIDO began offering loan financing. But the total amount of lending was modest since it was used only to complement the financing of projects in which an equity investment had already taken place.[23]

JAIDO's impact on Japanese foreign direct investment was constrained by its size. Its staff comprised only twenty-three people, many of who were seconded from member companies (usually the *sōgō shōsha* or banks). Limited human resources complicated the tasks of project selection and implementation. JAIDO therefore relied heavily on the expertise of its member companies (especially the *sōgō shōsha*) to identify projects and conduct feasibility studies. Moreover, JAIDO's financing of a joint venture could not exceed $860,000. In its first twelve years of operation, JAIDO funded forty-eight projects. In both number of projects and financial resources committed, JAIDO's financing of Japanese FDI was modest when compared with the OECF's and the Japan Eximbank's equity and lending programs.

SMALL-FIRM FDI FINANCING: A POLITICAL RESPONSE TO ECONOMIC CONTRACTION

Reflecting the political clout of small enterprises in Japan, several government agencies were created with the single purpose of satisfying the credit needs of SMEs.[24] In the early 1950s the government established the Japan Finance Corporation for Small Business (JFS) to appease an interest group that in the postwar recession had grown close to the leftist opposition.

The small-firm lobby had felt that its long-term financing needs for capital equipment expansion were not being adequately met: the Japan Development Bank focused mainly on basic industry, leaving little room for SME financing; the Shōkō Chūkin attended to the financial demands of cooperatives and their member firms only; and the People's Finance Corporation provided only small loans to Japan's smaller firms. LDP politicians, worried about losing support from a swing electoral group, defeated the opposition from the bureaucracy to the creation of another credit disbursing agency for small enterprises and ensured the smooth approval in the Diet of the JFS bill in 1953 (Calder 1988: 339).

In this way, the small-firm lobby early on obtained government financial assistance to promote domestic manufacturing. However, their demand for preferential financing to internationalize production went largely unanswered for more than four decades. Before the *endaka* (yen appreciation) crisis of the late 1980s forced a reevaluation of government SME policy, only one Japanese public institution provided FDI loans for the small-business sector in Japan: the Japan Overseas Development Corporation (JODC).

MITI established the JODC in 1970 as a *zaidan hōjin* to facilitate imports of natural and energy resources from Asia. Interestingly, in 1973 MITI decided to fund pet FDI projects in the developing world through JODC. Overseas investment credit for small businesses was initially offered at very attractive terms: no interest rate (though there was a 0.75 percent fee), and long-term repayment (twenty years). Eventually, though, this subsidy strained the foundation's financial resources and it began charging interest (Oishi 1994: 21). Overall lending volumes have been very low, however: between 1973 and 1998, JODC financed 180 SME overseas projects for a total $91.2 million.[25]

Why did Japanese SMEs resort so infrequently to the soft financing of JODC? First, JODC's decision-making structure did not facilitate rapid selection and implementation of projects; a committee that met three times a year had to approve each venture.[26] Second, a fade-out clause (in place until 1984) discouraged Japanese SMEs from turning to JODC, since they were obligated to eventually transfer ownership to the local partner (Oishi 1994: 17). Therefore, while it is true that JODC "subsidizes foreign direct investments by Japanese manufacturers" (Arase 1995: 132), its impact on Japanese FDI should not be overstated. JODC's financing was available only to small businesses, the subsidy element decreased markedly over time, and total FDI financing was very modest.

Consequently, the small-firm lobby remained dissatisfied with the availability of loans to support overseas investment. Bowing to the demands of this pressure group, in 1976 the Diet passed a resolution calling for increased Japan Eximbank support of SME operations. To comply nominally, the Japan Eximbank opened up an investment consulting service, strengthened its links to government banks that focused on SME financing, and attached preferential conditions to its SME loans (Japan Eximbank 1983: 321). But the bank's stringent lending requirements (acceptable collateral, and loans with interest rates close to market levels) effectively preserved the role of the Japan Eximbank as banker to large multinational firms. Small enterprises were clearly disappointed. In a 1979 survey, SMEs ranked as one of the main problems with government policy the lack of long-term low-cost financing for FDI projects (Takisawa 1982: 69–71).

The Japanese government did not begin financing small-firm investments abroad until small enterprises faced a severe adjustment crisis in the late 1980s. As part of its broader package to promote industrial restructuring, the government established a special FDI loan program in 1987 in the three main public financial institutions for small enterprises.[27]

The 1993 Restructuring Law aimed to assist small enterprises with industrial diversification and overseas investment.[28] Only firms in manufacturing, publishing, software, and information services could apply for the FDI loans. These enterprises had been particularly hard hit by the yen appreciation and wave of overseas investment by large enterprises.[29] To qualify for these soft loans, Japanese companies had to have experienced in the previous three years a decrease in production of more than 10 percent for three consecutive months. Exporters and subcontractors received special treatment since they needed to demonstrate only a 5 percent production cut over the same period (MITI 1993a).

Reforms to the Restructuring Law in the spring of 1995 further eased access to preferential FDI loans. All SMEs were now entitled to soft public loans if they had experienced a 5 percent cut in production for three months in the previous three years; their loan application also had to include a plan to manufacture a slightly different product or to carry out a feasibility study of foreign production (MITI 1995). The most noteworthy reform was the introduction of loans from the Association for Small and Medium-Sized Businesses. The association was well known for its heavily discounted loans with a fifteen- to twenty-year repayment period, low and fixed interest rates, and in special circumstances no interest at all.[30]

The subsidization of small-firm FDI intensified with the Asian financial crisis. In order to help Japanese SMEs operating in Asia resist the local credit crunch, the three SME public financial institutions adopted a new FDI financing scheme in December 1998.[31] Subsidiaries of Japanese SMEs in Asia could now obtain soft loans to finance their working capital needs (previous FDI loans were used exclusively for equipment investments). Moreover, if companies applying for these new loans did not have sufficient collateral, they could rely instead on no-collateral guarantees issued by the Association for Credit Guarantees.[32]

Through this soft credit, public SME financial institutions supported the overseas expansion of smaller Japanese enterprises (see Table 4.4). One institution alone, JFS, extended $631.4 million in FDI credit for 923 projects, which represented 9.4 percent of overseas investment by Japanese SMEs between 1987 and 1999. By the mid-1990s, JFS overseas investment loans were concentrated in manufacturing (93 percent), primarily in three sectors: electric equipment, general machinery, and textiles.[33] Because they were classified as "policy loans," they carried a lower interest rate than general purpose loans. Throughout 1999 the general loan interest rate ranged between 2.3 and 2.9 percent, and the FDI loan interest rate fluctuated between 1.8 and 2.2 percent.

And yet the impact of the special FDI financing program on SME industrial adjustment is questionable. Far from targeting firms with a high potential contribution to adjustment, the entry conditions permit broad access. During the multiyear economic contraction, most firms recorded a decrease in production that would qualify them as participants. Furthermore, the industrial upgrading goals promoted through preferential credit were very modest. A company's smallest transformation of the product under the Japanese industrial code, the use of a different material or machine, or targeting a different market was enough diversification to qualify.[34] The government did not even attempt to check that the industrial adjustment goals of the special lending program were met. There was no systematic effort to collect and analyze data on the performance of the credit recipients despite the fact that such information could be obtained from the prefectural authorities or from the public financial institutions serving SMEs.[35]

The public subsidization of small enterprises intensified with the prolonged recession. Some FDI loans charged no interest, and credit was made available to firms without sufficient collateral. In addition, a lower interest rate was charged for projects sanctioned by politically conservative local chambers of commerce (MITI 1993a). Economically, there was no justification for giving such projects preferential treatment, but the chamber's recommendations allowed LDP politicians to serve their constituencies. As noted earlier, local chambers of commerce had also administered no-collateral loans approved by the LDP in the 1970s to rob the opposition of one of its most popular banners (Calder 1988: 346).

TABLE 4.4
Public Financing of Small-Firm Multinationals, 1987–1999

	Japan Finance Corporation for Small Business (JFS)		All SME financial agencies[a]	
	Number of projects	Amount (million US$)	Number of projects	Amount (million US$)
1987	36	18.6	39	19.9
1988	85	48.0	91	53.0
1989	164	110.4	176	119.8
1990	112	58.4	121	64.6
1991	75	31.1	82	35.6
1992	49	29.7	56	30.9
1993	11	10.3	n.a.	13.8
1994	115	100.4	n.a.	135.1
1995	95	88.4	n.a.	103.9
1996	60	51.0	n.a.	62.6
1997	35	22.6	n.a.	33.6
1998[b]	49	29.2	n.a.	n.a.
1999	37	33.3	n.a.	n.a.
Total	923	631.4		

[a] Includes the Japan Finance Corporation for Small Business, Shōko Chūkin, and the People's Finance Corporation (now the National Life Finance Corporation).

[b] The figures for 1998 include the special "Asia crisis loans." JFS extended fourteen such loans for a total of $7.2 million.

n.a. = not available.

SOURCE: Compiled by the author with data provided by MITI's Small and Medium-Sized Enterprise Agency, the Japan Finance Corporation for Small Businesses, and MOF's *Zaisei Toyūshi Tokkei Geppo*.

Given the political clout of the small-business sector, FDI credit for small enterprises was more overtly subsidized than the FDI loans received by large enterprises through the Japan Eximbank. The politics of Japanese industrial financing surfaced once more: economic sectors in distress, essential to keep the conservative politicians in power, have benefited disproportionately from public subsidies.

Budgetary Design and Soft FDI Financing

Japanese bureaucrats launched an unprecedented FDI loan program out of concern over natural resource procurement and industrial adjustment, but could not completely fend off politicians' attempts to open soft FDI financing windows by relaxing loan approval requirements and injecting tax money into selected public financial institutions. A comparison of the Japan Eximbank and the OECF illustrates how a political compromise influenced the allocation of FDI subsidies to different producer groups.

Shielded by MOF, and subject to stricter fund procurement rules, the Japan Eximbank administered a more disciplined FDI loan program. Table 4.5 shows that the bank received very modest subsidies from the general account and relied instead on public resources from the second budget: the Industrial Investment Special account and FILP loans.

Obviously, Treasury capitalization of the Japan Eximbank relieved its loan repayment burden, but did not pave the way for soft FDI financing for several reasons. Capital injections from the Industrial Investment Special Account were only important in the first two decades of Japan Eximbank operations and never exceeded 11 percent of funds. After the 1980s they were of minor importance (representing between 0.1 percent and 3 percent of the bank's total funding). Consequently, most government capitalization took place while the Japan Eximbank was competing internationally with other export credit agencies to lower the cost of trade credit; even then its relative share of total funds was very moderate, and eventually became insignificant.

The Japan Eximbank maintained healthy annual profits and yearly dividend payments to MOF (annual payments averaged $181 million during the 1990s). Financial soundness was essential for the bank in order to meet its repayment obligations to FILP, but also to successfully sell bonds in overseas markets. FILP loans and bond issues weighed heavily in the bank's fund procurement strategy: bonds contributed 77 percent of all funds secured during the 1990s (see Table 4.5). Given its substantial repayment obligations, the Japan Eximbank cautiously managed its FDI credit allocation: it carefully examined each project's feasibility, always demanded collateral, and charged interest that was close to market rates and never below the cost of fund procurement (the Trust Fund Bureau rate charged on FILP loans to government institutions).

The bank's experience with equity investments illustrates the limits on subsidization imposed by budgetary rules. As mentioned before, in 1989 the Japan Eximbank introduced equity financing for FDI projects, but only one project was selected. The higher risks of equity financing and the very long time horizon for receiving dividends from an overseas investment project made the bank reluctant to use equity injections to support the overseas expansion of Japanese MNCs. But the OECF enjoyed more budgetary flexibility to engage in the most risky option: becoming a shareholder in huge projects overseas for the exploitation of natural resources or the relocation of Japanese heavy industry.

TABLE 4.5

Budgetary Design and Public FDI Financing in Japan, 1950–1999 (million US$)

	First budget transfers			Second budget funds			Self-generated funds		
	Equity	Grants	Share (%)	Investments[a]	Trust Fund Bureau (TFB) loans	Share (%)	Amount	Share (%)	FDI financing terms
Japan Eximbank									
1950–60	0	0	0.0	161.9	254.4	28	822.1	56	TFB interest rate; up
1961–70	0	12.8	0.1	1,289.2	4,987.9	56	4,655.5	41	to 15-year maturity;
1971–80	0	91.1	0.2	1,746.6	18,904.7	39	25,704.1	49	up to 70 percent of
1981–90			0.0	128.2	41,289.3	70	16,299.6	28	total investment
1991–99	0	0	0.0	153.0	90,474.7	70	29,952.3	23	
OECF									
1960–70	255.1	0	33.1	0	170.3	22.1	345.2	44.8	Equity investments; up
1971–80	2,975.6	0	32.2	0	4,131.1	44.7	2,036.0	22.0	to 50 percent of paid-in
1981–90	10,926.4	1,461.2	23.9	0	26,367.2	51.0	12,707.6	24.6	capital of Japanese
1991–99	21,837.3	1,619.1	29.3	0	33,777.7	42.2	24,778.9	30.9	investment consortia

[a]Investments made from the Industrial Investment Special Account of FILP.

SOURCES: JBIC, *Annual Report*, 2000; MOF, *FILP Report*, several issues; MOF, *Zaisei Kinyū Tokkei Geppo*, several issues; OECF, *Annual Report*, several years; MOF, FDI statistics.

Fewer constraints on its domestic fund procurement allowed the OECF to become a major shareholder in enormous overseas projects. The OECF relied heavily on annual equity injections and subsidies from the first budget to finance its operations: these transfers typically represented 30 percent of all sources of income. Since the OECF offers concessional loans to developing countries—with a lower interest rate than the one at it which it procured its own funds—and *because it extended very soft financing to investment projects abroad with only a reasonable chance of success,* this agency frequently reported a deficit.[36] In other words, tax money allowed the OECF to manage the substantial official development assistance program, but also to act as equity investor in Japanese offshore investment projects in the developing world, effectively sharing all the project's risks.

Table 4.6 shows the impact of budgetary rules on FDI subsidization rates. This table estimates the alleviation in the interest burden that Japanese multinationals enjoyed through public loans or equity investments. More concretely, the table compares the preferential interest rates offered by commercial banks (the long-term prime rate), the Japan Eximbank (Trust Fund Bureau rate), and the OECF (equity injection with no interest). It estimates the "open subsidy" supplied through government FDI by tracing the disparity in the cost of capital due to the differential in posted interest rates by commercial banks and public financial institutions.[37]

OECF subsidized manufacturing overseas investment much more heavily than the Japan Eximbank (approximately 7 percent for the former and 0.5 percent for the latter during the 1990s). However, it is important to keep in mind that the total amounts of manufacturing FDI credit issued by the OECF were much lower than those from the Japan Eximbank.

The subsidy benefits of public FDI financing have decreased over time because of the smaller gap between public and private interest rates. But government FDI financing has not lost its attractiveness. Only the largest and most profitable Japanese enterprises qualify for the preferential prime rate offered by commercial banks. For enterprises struggling in stagnant industries and for smaller firms there is still a substantial benefit in securing public FDI loans. Second, a smaller cost of capital is only one benefit of public financing. Another important advantage is the supply of long-term funds, which are particularly important for projects with long time horizons for generating cash flow. Moreover, through cooperative financing, the public FDI credit agencies have been able to augment the amount of funds channeled to overseas projects. This "pump-priming" or generation of information about the borrower creates a public commitment to the success of the venture that encourages private banks to participate in cofinancing. Finally, public FDI credit minimizes the political risk of overseas investment. Revealingly, much public FDI financing has been concentrated in the areas where multinational corpora-

TABLE 4.6

Public Subsidization of Private Overseas Investment, 1953–1999 (million US$)

	FDI financing in manufacturing		Open subsidy amount		Open subsidy as a percentage of FDI financing in manufacturing		Open subsidy as a percentage of manufacturing FDI	
	Japan Eximbank	OECF	Japan Eximbank	OECF	Japan Eximbank	OECF	Japan Eximbank	OECF
1953–75	1,453.4	n.a.	27.0	n.a.	1.86	n.a.	0.5	n.a.
1976–90	14,816.7	629	138.1	48.5	0.93	7.7	0.2	0.06
1991–99	29,908.2	142	146.4	9.4	0.49	6.7	0.1	0.01

n.a. = not available.

SOURCES: Japan Eximbank, *Gyōmu Binran*, several issues; OECF, *Annual Report*, several years; Bank of Japan, *Economic Statistics Annual*, several years; MOF, *Zaisei Kinyū Tokkei Geppo*, several issues; MOF's FDI statistics.

tions are highly vulnerable owing to the hostage effect of fixed assets: raw materials processing and large scale infrastructure projects.

Because of the varied benefits of public FDI loans, many Japanese multinationals are still keen clients of government banks—at the end of the twentieth century, public FDI loans from the Japan Eximbank represented 20 percent of all Japanese offshore investment in manufacturing, and as noted before this figure is much higher for the usual suspects: iron and steel, nonferrous metals, transportation equipment, and chemicals (see Table 4.2). Yet the administration of public loans changed substantially during the 1990s as the result of renewed political meddling in the FDI institutional framework.

The Forces of Change in Japanese Public FDI Financing

In recessionary Japan, conservative politicians have become ever more assertive in shaping the future of public loan programs. Two developments are of particular significance: the political initiative to merge the Japan Eximbank and the OECF in the 1990s, and the structural changes introduced into the FILP system itself in 2001.

The movement for administrative reform—which would eventually decide the fate of the Japan Eximbank and the OECF—acquired new life after the collapse of the financial bubble in the early 1990s. A sense of impending fiscal crisis, as Japan's public debt exceeded that of all other industrialized countries, fueled the reform movement. The calls for administrative reform also intensified with the public's disenchantment with the government's failure to rationalize public corporations and agencies, and because of widening mistrust of MOF's supervisory skills after the banking crisis.

Realignments in the party system also influenced the campaign for administrative reform. In August 1993 the period of unbroken conservative rule ended when the LDP lost its Diet majority and the era of coalition government dawned in Japan. The LDP was able to engineer a quick comeback in June 1994 through an alliance with two other parties—the Social Democrats and the Harbinger Party (Sakigake). This coalition, though, was possible only after the LDP agreed to implement the administrative reform agenda that these parties had helped draft as members of the previous government (Carlile 1998: 97). The new coalition in public office sought to deliver on its promise to rationalize the bureaucracy by streamlining public financial organizations. Agencies dealing with international financing were deemed an easier target than those extending credit to vocal domestic constituencies (small-firm financial corporations and regional development banks).

Ironically, the campaign to restructure inefficient public corporations first targeted the Japan Eximbank, a profit-generating public financial institution that received no budget subsidies. Three proposals were considered: (1) its dismemberment by allocating import financing to the JDB and untied and bank loans to the OECF; (2) integrating the JDB with the Japan Eximbank; and (3) merging the OECF and the Japan Eximbank. The Diet committee in charge of this matter finally decided on the third alternative, integrating two public institutions that operated under fundamentally different principles: one a self-sustaining government bank and the other a concessional financing agency ("Yugin to OECF," 1995: 12).

RELUCTANT PARTNERS: THE JAPAN EXIMBANK AND THE OECF BECOME THE NEW JAPAN BANK FOR INTERNATIONAL COOPERATION

The Japan Eximbank–OECF merger presented public officials with four formidable challenges. First, it was important to keep ODA and the trade/investment loan program separate in order to avoid criticism abroad that Japan was using its economic assistance program to benefit its own industrial interests. Second, it was important to prevent balance sheet consolidation from negatively affecting bond issues in the Euromarket. Third, it was necessary to settle the question of bureaucratic oversight since the Japan Eximbank had enjoyed much more autonomy in its daily business operations consulting only with MOF, whereas four ministries monitored all of the OECF's government loans. And fourth, it was necessary to determine how to integrate previously separate programs of private sector investment financing.[38]

In the face of these obstacles, it is perhaps not surprising that the brand new Japan Bank for International Cooperation (JBIC began operating in October 1999) exhibited very minor integration of the former two agencies. The new bank worked with two strictly separate accounts. The international financial activities account (the former Japan Eximbank activities of trade, FDI, and untied loans) is funded through second budget loans, bonds, and internal funds. The overseas economic cooperation operations account covers all the areas of operation of the former OECF (ODA and private sector investment financing in developing countries) and is funded as in the past through first budget transfers, second budget loans, and internal funds. In other words, although public international financing has been nominally integrated under one institutional roof, distinct budgetary constraints are imposed on the two accounts, *as was true before the merger.*[39] The major consequence of the merger, therefore, seems to be political: MOF has been deprived of an important *amakudari* position.[40]

THE POLITICAL CONTEST OVER THE SECOND BUDGET

The debate over the merits and disadvantages of FILP intensified during the economic downturn of the 1990s. To some observers, FILP continued to help the Japanese government overcome the limits of tax revenue in funding its industrial policy, while at the same time instilling discipline in credit allocation through repayable funds (Kato et al. 1994: 19). But critics of FILP pointed to a bloated system that was not flexible enough to price public loans according to market trends. The Japanese banking sector became increasingly vocal in its criticism of FILP as an example of unfair government competition. Banks complained that while they were responsible for the overhead costs in their branch operations, the postal system had an extensive network of public post offices across the country that no commercial bank could hope to replicate. Moreover, postal savings accounts were particularly attractive because until 1988 the interest paid on these accounts was tax free. Postal savings accounts were so popular (for their convenient location and tax-free treatment) that formally the government limited their use to one account per person (of up to 3 million yen). Yet critics of the postal savings system were quick to point out that the government tolerated multiple accounts. In 1979, for example, the number of postal savings accounts (236 million) was roughly twice the size of the Japanese population (Calder 1990).

The financial soundness of the FILP also emerged as a serious concern. An analysis of FILP finances by Doi and Hoshi (2002), for example, revealed that the costs to Japanese taxpayers of keeping failed public corporations on shore, covering defaults in local government debt, and clearing the Japan National Railway debt could reach the staggering figure of 78.3 trillion yen. They reassessed the financial condition of FILP agencies by factoring in under-reserving, asset overvaluation, capitalization levels, and the cost of expected future losses. In their estimation, twenty FILP agencies were insolvent, among them the JFS. The two institutions with the tightest budgetary rules—the Development Bank of Japan and JBIC—were in the best financial health in the Doi-Hoshi estimate, despite the fact that each of these government banks had recently absorbed a much less profitable public financial institution (Doi and Hoshi 2002: 14, 5–9).

FILP has also been attacked for rigidly determining interest rates and protecting special interests. Looking after its main constituency, MOPT resisted lowering the interest rate on postal savings (which directly affects the cost of public financing since it is the rate at which the Trust Fund Bureau in turn lends money to FILP agencies) (Ishi 1986: 98; Miyawaki 1995: 32).[41] And as noted before, the past few years witnessed a reversal of interest rates, with the TFB interest rate moving much more slowly downward than the LTPR. Inflexible interest rates guided by political considerations rather than market trends loomed as a serious threat to the competitiveness of public loan programs.

The reform of FILP gathered political momentum, and once more LDP politicians and MOF bureaucrats vied for control of the restructuring process. The LDP offered two proposals that would greatly affect the future of financial industrial policy in Japan: eliminating the compulsory deposit of postal savings and public pensions in the Trust Fund Bureau, and the future funding of FILP institutions through market-based bond issues. MOF fiercely opposed losing its allocation powers over the bountiful FILP resources and countered with a sharply different prescription for increasing the efficiency of FILP agencies: discipline public corporations by disclosing the subsidy cost of their operations (Tomita 2000: 5). In other words, MOF's plan was to highlight the burden imposed on taxpayers from substantial first budget transfers approved by politicians to inefficient public entities.

The spirit of the LDP proposal prevailed, however. In April 2001, MOF lost automatic access to the lifeblood of FILP (public pensions and postal savings). The Ministry of Health and Welfare and MOPT assumed total control over the management of those vast financial resources. After a seven-year transition period, FILP agencies will have to finance their operations mostly by issuing bonds (FILP agency bonds) that do not have a government guarantee. It is expected that the market will effectively discipline inefficient FILP institutions by imposing a premium on their bond issues. However, the law did contemplate supplementary financing for FILP institutions that are not able to procure funds at a reasonable cost. In these cases, government-backed bonds issued by the Fiscal Loan Fund (successor to the TFB), and first budget subsidies will be available. The only area where MOF's view prevailed was in the new requirement to disclose subsidy cost analyses for the public agencies benefiting from first budget transfers.[42]

In principle, these FILP reforms seem to promote efficiency by introducing market prices into the fund procurement practices of public financial institutions. However, there are good reasons to remain concerned about the future of Japanese financial industrial policy. First, it is unclear how public financial institutions will be able to use preferential financing to overcome market failure if they must procure their funds at market rates. Second, markets may not penalize bonds from inefficient public corporations if they expect a government bailout to keep these institutions afloat (that is, if "implicit guarantees" are at work) (Tomita 2000: 14–15). Third, and more fundamental, the reform does not really attack the source of pork-barrel financing in Japan by which politically captured banks receive large subsidies that allow them to offer cheap and poorly monitored credit. A potential perverse effect cannot be ruled out: competent FILP institutions will be financially self-sufficient, while government resources will be ever more concentrated in inefficient (and politically useful) institutions that will capture the bulk of first budget subsidies and FILP bonds.[43]

The first subsidy costs analysis of public corporations provides more data with which to judge the impact of budgetary rules on the quality of public industrial loan programs. Since the fiscal year 2000, the government has also required public corporations to publish balance sheets and income statements that follow corporate accounting rules. The result is to make cumulative losses far more transparent. In 2000 the JFS recorded 217.4 billion yen in cumulative losses, and JBIC posted a 302.4 billion yen cumulative deficit. Revealingly, 90 percent of JBIC's losses originated in the overseas economic cooperation account (the former OECF).

The new accounting rules also force public financial institutions to reveal their entire portfolio of risk-management loans (bankrupt, nonaccrual, past due, and restructured). In 2000 their share of total loans was 5.7 percent for JFS, 3.85 percent for the overseas economic cooperation account of JBIC, and 3.62 percent for the international financial account (JBIC 2002). The rather high figure in the international financial account is mostly due to restructured loans, whereas in the overseas economic account it mostly reflects already insolvent loans.

The expected future losses for these FDI financing agencies are estimated in a new policy cost analysis of the present value of future subsidies to keep these agencies running. The government estimated the subsidy cost for Japanese taxpayers at a high 634.2 billion yen in 2001 for the former OECF (JBIC's overseas economic cooperation account). The policy costs of the international financial account were noticeably lower at 88.9 billion. It is important to note that these policy costs were due only to the opportunity costs of capital investments, and that no additional fiscal spending (subsidies from the first budget) is expected. In 2001 the JFS policy costs were estimated at 88.7 billion yen with annual subsidies from the government at 62.6 billion yen, its financial condition looks precarious (MOF 2002; Doi and Hoshi 2002).

The latest round of FILP reform once more underscores the manner in which politicians have maneuvered the open soft finance windows in national credit programs. Indeed, the uneven rates of FDI subsidization are more evidence of the politics of preferential financing discussed in other studies (Calder 1988; Patterson 1994). It is not simply that government banks awash with FILP funds push loans on any potential client. Whether *some* public financial institutions can accept any client (and not worry about the risks of default) reflected a prior political decision: lax budgetary rules that allow the government bank in question to subsidize its credit and carry nonperforming loans.

PART THREE

Case Studies of Industrial Adjustment and Foreign Direct Investment

CHAPTER 5

Textiles: Public Support for the Exodus of a Declining Industry

THE INTERNATIONAL relocation of Japanese textiles challenges the conventional understanding of the adjustment options open to mature and standardized industries. Lacking the economic capability to invest abroad, textile industries have typically responded to structural decline by lobbying for trade protection. The Japanese textile industry's management of decline is remarkable in that it has introduced an international dimension: it has embarked on substantial foreign direct investment at all stages of textile manufacturing. This creation of a multinational industry was largely made possible by government FDI financing. By discouraging reverse imports and avoiding massive layoffs the move generated little opposition at home. Parts of this old consensus, however, collapsed because the more recent boom in offshore investment deliberately targeted the home market. Therefore, the new challenge to the FDI strategy did not arise from organized labor, but from the besieged producers coping with the avalanche of reverse imports. This battle for trade protection has politicized to unprecedented heights the multinationalization of textile production.

Stability and Change in the Textile Adjustment Experience

Despite several decades of accelerated change in the Japanese textile industry, key organizational features have remained fixed. Indeed, it is this mix of transformation and endurance that makes the industry's adjustment experience so intriguing. Its most lasting trait is the divide between a highly concentrated upstream industry and fragmented mid- and downstream sectors.[1] In 1998, for example, there were 104 firms producing man-made fibers (19,449 employees) and 544 companies in the spinning business (35,952 employees); in contrast to 17,560 weaving establishments (75,557 employees) and 53,595 apparel makers (543,692 employees) (Nihon Kagaku Sen'i Kyōkai 2001).

An additional sign of stability amid change is the fact that none of the major upstream firms lost its leading position, despite significant reductions in domestic equipment and the growing threat of foreign competitors. Only two amalgamations of significance took place (Tōyōbō's purchase of Kureha in 1966 and the merger between Nihon Bōseki with Nippon Rayon in 1969), and none of the large upstream firms declared bankruptcy. The Big Ten spinning firms and Big Nine synthetic companies remained at the apex of the industry despite the efforts of maverick firms (Tsuzuki Spinning and Kondo Spinning) to ascend the industrial ladder by disregarding the industrywide consensus that capacity should be reduced (McNamara 1995: 11).[2]

And yet industrial change and dwindling international competitiveness have rocked the textile industry. The sector lost its position as a leading force in Japanese industrialization. The Japanese cotton spinning industry recovered quickly after World War II, when the government lifted controls on equipment expansion, and the Korean War produced a boom in demand. Nevertheless, structural decline soon set in. Beginning in the mid-1950s, the cotton spinning industry was plagued by excess capacity, rising labor costs, and protectionism abroad. In 1955, textiles represented 16 percent of total manufacturing production, but this share decreased in twenty years to 5 percent, and in the early twenty-first century is less than 3 percent. Textiles was of paramount importance to Japanese exports in the mid-1950s (32 percent of total exports), but mirroring the contraction in production, its export share fell to 6 percent in 1975 and to close to 2 percent in 1999. The drop in textile employment was less dramatic, but still significant (from 20 percent in 1955 to 13 percent in 1975 and 8 percent in 1998) (*Japan Statistical Yearbook*, several years; Nihon Kagaku Sen'i Kyōkai 2001).

These figures do not tell the whole story of industrial change in the industry, where some traditional sectors contracted (such as natural yarns) and others were added (synthetic fibers). This turnaround took place in the 1960s as synthetic textiles overtook natural textiles in production and exports. Manufacture of man-made fibers first surpassed that of natural yarns in 1964, and by 1970 the amount of synthetic fibers produced (1.6 million tons) was twice that of natural threads (0.8 million tons). The export drive came to rest in the man-made fiber area, and once more the mid-1960s were the turning point. In 1965 synthetic fibers accounted for 51 percent of textile exports, and in 1970 for three-quarters of total industry exports (T. Suzuki 1991: 388–91).

Difficulty sustaining natural yarn production and the opening of entry opportunities in synthetics explain the rapid reconfiguration of the Japanese textile industry. Profitable growth in cotton spinning was increasingly compromised by the relentless rise in Japanese wages, the consolidation of rival spinning industries in the developing world, and the closure of export markets due to trade friction. At the same time, access to the promising field of man-made fiber manufacturing was made possible by the expiration of patents that had locked the three main synthetic fibers into monopoly or duopoly structures (M. Fujii 1971: 73–75). The "synthetic rush" produced a dramatic increase in the industry's stock of equipment as an intense rivalry developed between established producers and new entrants (T. Suzuki 1991: 399). The wisdom of vertiginously building up supply capability in synthetics was soon called into question in the eventful 1970s.

The setbacks of the 1970s irreparably damaged the optimism that had surrounded the development of the Japanese synthetic textile industry. In 1971, Japanese textiles were served a one-two punch with the revaluation of the yen and a US-Japanese textile agreement that extended export limits to man-made fibers. The plight of Japanese synthetics worsened with the two oil shocks of the 1970s, due to the industry's heavy dependence on imported oil for petrochemical inputs and for factory operation. The export drive also faltered, given the higher yen-denominated export prices and quotas imposed in main destination markets (Yamazawa 1980: 445).

Despite these setbacks, synthetic fiber companies managed to curtail capacity, increase productivity, and move into higher-value-added production. The export performance of synthetic textiles improved as well, and by 1980 exports of synthetic yarn had risen to 243,000 tons. In that same year, synthetic textile goods amounted to 1.4 trillion yen or 75 percent of all Japanese textile good exports. Therefore, the remaining international competitiveness of Japanese man-made fibers was responsible for the maintenance of a positive trade balance for the whole of the textile industry. To many observers, the key factor behind the puzzling ability of a troubled textile industry to keep cheap imports at bay and maintain relatively low import penetration ratios (in the absence of overt protectionism) was the lingering comparative advantage in synthetics (see Dore 1986; Yamawaki 1992).

However, this advantage had faded by the 1990s, and the country became a net textile importer. The relentless appreciation of the yen after the international agreement on exchange rates in 1985 (known as the Plaza Accord) and the growing competitiveness of Asian countries was a blow to Japanese firms producing lower-value-added goods with natural yarns. Pockets of export strength were no longer enough to offset the avalanche of imports, especially in clothing (see Table 5.1). Indeed, the largest contributing factor to the trade deficit was the explosive growth of apparel imports between 1985 and 1998. Other sectors that have added to the negative trade balance are nonsynthetic fibers and cotton yarns. In less than twenty years (1980–98), the

TABLE 5.1

Japanese Textiles Competing in the International Market, 1980–1998 (million US$)

	Balance of trade				
	1980	1985	1990	1993	1998
Fibers	−1,638.5	−1,405.8	−1,643.0	−497.3	−1.5
Synthetic fibers	395.0	399.1	437.2	585.9	696.4
Textile yarn and fabrics	3,401.2	2,927.9	1,474.6	2,529.7	1,342.0
Apparel	−1,049.1	−1,301.7	−8,211.0	−11,973.5	−14,543.4
All textile products	713.6	220.4	−8,379.4	−9,941.1	−13,203.0

SOURCE: UN, *International Trade Statistics Yearbook*, several years.

Japanese textile industry transitioned from a trade surplus of $713 million to a deficit of $13 billion. Import penetration complicated the task of adjustment for the Japanese textile industry in recent years.

The interplay between stability and change captures the essence of Japanese textile restructuring. During the far-reaching industrial transformation of the postwar period, the textile industry lost its preeminent place in the Japanese economy. It switched from natural to synthetic textiles, struggled in the export market, and more recently lost ground in the domestic arena to foreign producers. Despite this turbulence, no sector of the Japanese textile industry completely disappeared, and a few spinners and synthetic fiber makers stubbornly maintained their place at the apex of the industry. This paradox can be explained by the lobbying efforts of industrialists in favor of an "orderly transition" and their success (or lack thereof) in obtaining the endorsement of politicians and bureaucrats.

DOWNSIZING A DECLINING INDUSTRY

Oversupply in textile production plagued the industry for most of the postwar period, making orderly disposal of excess equipment the dominant policy prescription for domestic adjustment. Problems of excess capacity first occurred in the 1950s when demand collapsed after the Korean War (J. Hashimoto 1990: 643). After industry attempts to enforce production restrictions failed, the Japan Spinners Association (JSA) lobbied for MITI's help in regulating textile supply (Uriu 1996: 49–53). MITI decided to intervene in the spring of 1952 through informal means by recommending operational cuts (*kankoku sotan*) equivalent to 40 percent of textile output. MITI relied on administrative guidance because the original Antitrust Law stipulations ruled out formal cartels (J. Hashimoto 1990: 644). Although MITI chose informal means to bring order to textile production, it threatened noncompliant firms with its control over foreign exchange. The textile industry was a massive consumer of foreign currency: its imports of cotton represented 45.5 percent of all raw materials imports between 1951 and 1955 (Yamazawa 1984: 72). Losing favor with MITI bureaucrats, therefore, carried heavy penalties in the early 1950s.

The 1956 Temporary Law Governing Textile Equipment (the Old Textile Law), which formalized government intervention in textile adjustment, was a landmark success for the spinning industry. It ratified the industry's view that government support was necessary to solve the structural problem of excess capacity (Uriu 1996: 55). In fact, MITI accepted many of the industry's demands in exchange for its cooperation on trade negotiations with the United States (Dore 1986: 222). In 1955, bilateral trade friction escalated owing to the rapid increase in Japanese exports of cotton fabric and clothing (such as one-dollar blouses). The Japanese government agreed to voluntary export restrictions, but back home cotton spinners intensified their pressure on the government for compensation. The cabinet approved the formation of a public-private deliberation council on textile policy that swiftly drafted a textile bill. The Old Textile Law introduced a registration system for existing spindles and looms (in order to check the unregulated expansion of capacity), mandated MITI approval for the addition of new equipment, and provided public financial assistance through JDB loans to buy and scrap excess capacity (Uriu 1996: 58–59; Ike 1980: 539; McNamara 1995: 80).[3]

In the early 1960s, the age of trade liberalization dawned in Japan, forcing a revision of the legislative framework to regulate competition in the textile industry. MITI took up the banner of economic opening to push for the deregulation of textiles. In 1963 a four-member deliberation committee without direct ties to the textile industry recommended abolishing the registration system, excluding synthetic firms from capacity regulations, and initiating a scrap-and-build system. But textile industrialists vehemently opposed the market-driven blueprint for textile adjustment. All firms in the industry deplored the absence of financial support for rationalization programs, and small firms were particularly angered by the proposed abolition of the registration system. More vulnerable to the vagaries of the market, small textile firms needed to hold on to their registered spindles and looms to ensure their survival. The high stakes involved in the reformulation of the textile law prompted the JSA to actively lobby in MITI offices and Diet committees (Uriu 1996: 69–72).

Politicization of the issue forced MITI to back down and accommodate some of the industry's favorite proposals. The 1964 Temporary Law Governing Textile Equipment (the New Textile Law) preserved the registration system, provided financial support for the downsizing of the industry, and incorporated the scrap-and-build system that the industry had found acceptable. However, the cotton spinning industry did not win on all fronts. Pressure from the Japan Chemical Fiber Association (JCFA) helped restore autonomy in capacity adjustment to synthetics, and only in one kind of synthetic textile (spun yarn from synthetic staple) did the registration system apply (T. Suzuki 1991: 404).

The severity of the 1965 recession set the stage for a reformulation of textile legislation soon after the passage of the New Textile Law. The Temporary Law for the Structural Reorganization of the Specified Textile Industries (the 1967 Law) aimed to foster excess capacity reduction, equipment modernization, and concentration of units of production to enhance efficiency (Ike 1980: 540). MITI, now under the influence of the "industrial policy bureaucrats," was more willing to step in to regulate textile competition, but still resisted the industry's demands for substantial financial assistance (Johnson 1982; Uriu 1996: 75). Although the LDP's Special Textile Committee attempted to triple the original MITI budget for textiles, in the end the allowances were very close to MITI's first proposal (Uriu 1996: 74–77).

After the textile wrangle, government assistance to the textile industry expanded significantly in 1971. For two years, the Japanese and US governments conducted tense trade negotiations that were also linked to the return of Okinawa. The Japanese textile industry (both the natural yarn and synthetics sectors) opposed export caps in their shipments to the United States. The Japanese government resorted once more to financial compensation in exchange for industry acquiescence on export limitations. Mirroring the intensity of domestic opposition to the trade agreement, the side payments made this time were extremely large: 183 billion yen earmarked through the Temporary Special Countermeasures for the Textile Industry (Hirai and Iwasaki 1985: 135).

The purpose of the Temporary Law for the Structural Reorganization of the Textile Industry (the 1974 Law) was to heighten the industry's technological sophistication, to continue promoting vertical integration, and to assist the apparel sector as well (Uryu 1990: 13). The 1974 Law paid particular attention to the needs of smaller companies through preferential government loans for structural improvement. Unfortunately, the 1974 Law was never very successful. Since the large firms were excluded from the structural improvement plans, no real improvements in technological sophistication and equipment modernization were feasible. In addition, the oil shock dragged the textile industry into a deeper recession than had been anticipated. Inflated prices of inputs derived from oil, plus a general contraction of domestic demand and export caps, resulted in lower rates of operation for synthetic textile machinery and a collapse in profits. Orderly competition through production cartels was the response of the private sector to these adverse developments (Ito 1993: 174, 175).

The Japanese textile industry was the target of special legislation to facilitate adjustment for most of the postwar period. Therefore it was no surprise that the first comprehensive law on structural adjustment—the 1978 Industry Stabilization Law—targeted several textile sectors. The primary goal of this law was to reduce excess capacity by scrapping existing facilities. To facilitate this adjustment, the government offered financing through a trust fund and sanctioned the creation of cartels to coordinate cuts. On the eve of the second oil shock, the Japanese synthetic industry had only considered limits on capacity expansion and output levels. Dispirited by the gloomier prospects for growth after the oil hike, the industry readily endorsed the scrapping goals set forth in the Industry Stabilization Law (Hirai and Iwasaki 1985: 144). Yet the trust fund initiative was poorly received by the targeted industries. Firms would have preferred public low-interest loans and found it difficult to obtain commercial credit once their industry had been designated as structurally depressed. Of the 100 billion yen in the trust fund, a mere 23.2 billion yen was utilized. Among the textile sectors, only discontinuous acrylic fiber (3 billion yen) and worsted yarn spinning (1.2 billion yen) relied on this form of public assistance (Sekiguchi 1994).

The government continued to regulate textile capacity with the 1983 Structural Improvement Law. However, three years later (in 1986), the manmade fiber industry did not seek to preserve its status as a depressed sector. Amelioration of the excess capacity problem, stabilization of profit rates, and improved prospects for growth encouraged fiber makers to manage competition on their own (Uriu 1996: 174). Although synthetics "graduated," the rest of the textile industry continued to participate in the government programs for structural adjustment, especially smaller companies, which continued to benefit from special legislation and financial support (Dore 1986; Uryu 1990). Even the synthetics sector favored some form of managed competition. The JCFA required notification of all capacity expansions to both the association and MITI, and this ministry continued to produce supply and demand outlooks aiming to influence private sector investment behavior (Uriu 1996: 174).

Evaluating Domestic Adjustment in Textiles

The Japanese textile industry's record on rationalization is mixed at best. Although the number of establishments in the textile industry fell dramatically—from 150,000 in 1977, to 66,257 in 1985 and 51,326 in 1994—the growth of the apparel sector in the second half of the 1990s reversed this trend. In 1999 the number of textile establishments was up to 94,530 (Nihon Kagaku Sen'i Kyōkai 2001: 4). The evolution of textile equipment stock further calls into question the merits of publicly subsidizing capacity scrapping. The number of spindles decreased little between 1960 and 1980 (from 16,000 to 12,000), despite the continuous government support for capacity curtailment. The same was true in the weaving industry, in which the number of looms hovered around 600,000 during this period. In spinning and weaving, major reductions in equipment capacity were carried out only after 1985, when the sharp appreciation of the yen rendered many Japanese textile operations uncompetitive. The number of spindles contracted to 4,000 in 1999, and the stock of looms declined to 150,000 in 1999 (ibid.: 14).[4]

The ambiguous record on textile adjustment has generated heated debate over government intervention in declining industries. Some believe the Japanese government hampered rather than expedited the process of industrial change by acting as a lender of last resort to minimize corporate bankruptcies and offering to buy excess equipment; such assistance gave firms negative incentives to remain in the industry (Ike 1980: 546). Others concur, pointing out that industrial politics slowed down the pace of adjustment (Uriu 1996), or that the registration system was used by small firms as a "property right" to avoid being wiped out by market competition (Dore 1986: 240). But Japanese industrial adjustment programs have received high marks elsewhere, especially when compared with more obtrusive forms of intervention (trade barriers) so prevalent in other industrialized nations facing economic maturity (see Patrick 1991). Moreover, Yamawaki (1992) finds the provision of low-interest government loans statistically significant in explaining the lingering comparative advantage of Japanese textiles in synthetic textiles, as well as their relatively smooth exit from the labor-intensive segments of the industry.

Despite their differences, analysts of Japanese textile policy all agree that the industrial hierarchy remained intact during the postwar period. "Orderly downsizing" emerged as the guiding principle of industrial policy for textiles owing to the intense lobbying campaigns of industry associations, the support of politicians with strong textile connections, and MITI's desire to avoid politicizing textile adjustment programs. Notwithstanding this consensus on taming excess competition, sharp differences separated the natural yarn and fiber sectors, and strong firms (Nisshinbo, Kanebō, Tōray, Teijin) on occasion spurned industrywide consensus in favor of open competition. Politicians supported by the JSA/JCFA acted as guardians of the textile industry, pushing forward palatable legislation and government subsidies and finance. However, they were not completely successful. Their attempts to increase the subsidization of the textile industry were at times checked by the bureaucracy, as was their budget in the 1967 Law.

MITI found itself in the uncomfortable position of helping stabilize, or perpetuate, an increasingly uncompetitive industry. At the request of industry, MITI stepped in to manage capacity curtailment. In 1964, when the ministry argued for deregulation in textile adjustment, industrialists galvanized the support of politicians to preserve the regulatory mantle. Moreover, although MITI emphasized over time preferential financing over direct subsidization, it had to "buy" textile industry understanding on export limitations on two different occasions.

Labor too aimed to influence the policy prescriptions for textile adjustment. Zensen Domei, the Japanese Federation of Textile Industry Workers' Unions, participated in the advisory committees in charge of textile legislation, resisted large-scale layoffs after capacity scrapping, and fought to compensate workers whenever management was incapable of maintaining the promise of permanent employment. The two priorities for Zensen Domei were to stabilize capacity curtailment and to protect the employment of its members (full-time, mostly male employees). Because the adjustment programs endorsed by management and government shared these goals, the union was sympathetic to the industry's restructuring efforts.[5]

The Japanese government disbursed a significant amount of public money in endorsing the "orderly scrapping formula." Hirai and Iwasaki (1985: 135) estimate that the cost of the textile adjustment programs amounted to 620 billion yen by 1984, of which 567 billion yen was channeled through preferential financing. Although public relief for textiles first came through direct subsidization, the totals were modest (1.6 billion yen between 1956 and 1963). With the New Textile law the government shifted the focus of its assistance to low-interest loans (which would not impose as large a burden on the budget). Only after 1967 did the size of the textile adjustment programs grow to significant amounts (191 billion yen between 1967 and 1973). Judged by the allocation of government assistance, political compensation seems to have overshadowed the economic goals of rationalization at critical junctures. Subsidies in the Old Textile Law were meant to placate cotton spinners' opposition to export quotas, and huge amounts (183 billion yen) were delivered to textile industrialists in 1971 and 1973, when domestic opposition threatened not only textile trade accords but also the smooth conclusion of the negotiations over Okinawa.

Industrial adjustment in textiles did not remain a purely domestic phenomenon by any means. In fact, international strategies were a crucial element of Japanese firms' efforts to ensure survival and profitability. Mirroring the domestic situation, Japanese companies were quite vocal in asking for government support to facilitate their international adjustment. The Japanese government responded by generously financing the offshore investment plans of textile firms. One institution alone, the Japan Eximbank, provided 266 billion yen in overseas investment loans to textile enterprises (roughly half the amount of credit earmarked for domestic rationalization). The following section tells what has been until now an untold story: how preferential financing facilitated the multinationalization of a contracting textile industry in Japan.

Relocating a Declining Industry Abroad

The importance of textiles for the development of Japanese multinationalism cannot be overstated. In both the prewar and postwar periods, textile firms pioneered the move to manufacture in foreign countries and became the undisputed leaders in early Japanese outward investment. The story of FDI in Japanese textiles is of interest not only because it is old, but also because it is continuously changing. The oldest transnational manufacturing corporations—the spinners—were displaced as the core investors abroad by synthetic fiber makers, and more recently by apparel companies.

To better grasp the shifting patterns of Japanese textile FDI, I have divided its fifty years of postwar history into four periods (see Table 5.2). Cotton spinners inaugurated Japanese textile FDI in the mid-1950s, and the industry's investments abroad represented close to one-fifth of all Japanese manufacturing FDI in the following ten years. In the mid-1960s, synthetic fiber companies also initiated foreign production. Both upstream sectors (natural and man-made fibers) actively invested overseas, producing the first textile FDI boom in 1973. Indeed, overseas investment in textiles constituted approximately 30 percent of all Japanese industrial FDI between 1965 and 1974. The brisk expansion of foreign activities proved short-lived, however. The two oil shocks dried up overseas investment capital and the textile recession spread to the synthetic sector. Between 1975 and 1984, offshore textile investment represented a mere 6 percent of manufacturing FDI. The contraction in textile FDI reflected not only the lack of new investment funds, but also the closure of several factories operating abroad. However, after the yen appreciation of 1985, the Japanese textile industry renewed its interest in overseas investment. Indeed, textile FDI between 1985 and 1999 reached $7.3 billion dollars (78 percent of the postwar total).[6] This time, however, upstream companies were left behind by apparel firms, wholesalers, and general traders who sought to produce low-cost clothing in neighboring Asian countries.

OVERSEAS INVESTMENTS

The Japanese cotton spinning industry had already established a significant manufacturing base in China during the prewar years.[7] Despite this long experience with foreign production, after World War II it was difficult for textile firms to quickly restore their international operations. The textile industry as a whole was seriously weakened by the war effort, since as a "peace industry" it had been deprived of capital and inputs, and its equipment had been confiscated for military supply purposes. Moreover, the industry lost all its overseas assets, foreign currency was scarce, and throughout Asia the environment was hostile to any investment initiative (Yoshioka 1979: 8–9). Not surprisingly, textile firms made domestic reconstruction and export-led growth their priorities.

TABLE 5.2
The Multinationalization of Japanese Textiles, 1955–1999

Stage	Amount (million US$)	Investment cases	Share of manufacturing FDI (percent)	Main traits
Inauguration (1955–64)	58	72	19.7	Cotton spinners pioneer overseas production
Expansion (1965–74)	861	469	29.2	First FDI boom; synthetic fiber makers invest overseas
Retreat (1975–84)	1,138	597	6.0	Stagnation in overseas investment drive
Boom (1985–99)	7,334	2,725	3.3	Second FDI boom; apparel firms, retailers
Total (1955–99)	9,391	3,863	3.9	A highly transnationalized textile industry

SOURCE: Prepared by the author with MOF statistics.

Inauguration, 1955–1964

Domestic recovery was speedy. Indeed, the outbreak of the Korean War led to the industry's first boom in 1950. And by the mid-1950s the cotton spinners had regained the will and the capacity to open spinning and weaving facilities abroad. No other Japanese textile firms followed the example of the spinners during the 1950s (see Table 5.3). In the first half of the 1960s the industry undertook some synthetic and downstream investment projects, but cotton spinning continued to dominate overseas investment during the first stage of Japanese textile FDI. Between 1955 and 1964, natural fiber spinners were responsible for 41 percent of all outward investment cases, and downstream processing and synthetics trailed behind with 27 percent and 17 percent, respectively.

The Japanese cotton spinners had powerful reasons to embark on foreign production. First, through FDI in resource-rich countries (those with cotton and wool) they could circumvent the foreign exchange quotas that had constrained their importation of raw materials (Take 1982: 17). Moreover, because many developing countries were beginning to develop their own textile industries and could benefit from cheaper local inputs, the spinners deemed it

TABLE 5.3

Pioneers of Japanese Textile FDI

Stage	Synthetic fibers	Synthetic spinning and weaving	Natural fiber spinning and weaving[a]	Knitting and dyeing	Downstream processing	Total
Inauguration (1955–64)						
Number of investment cases	2	5	17	5	11	41
Share of total (percent)	5	12	41	12	27	100
Expansion (1965–74)						
Number of investment cases	26	79	44	86	103	364
Share of total (percent)	7	22	12	24	28	100

[a]Includes cotton, wool, silk, and jute spinning and weaving.

SOURCE: Nihon Kagaku Sen'i Kyōkai, *Sen'i Handobukku*, 1978.

necessary to manufacture directly in those low-cost economies to maintain their market share. And finally, companies saw outward investment as a way to reduce excess productive capacity at home and to export idle equipment to new factories abroad (M. Fujii, 1979: 217). Indeed, numerous firms, such as Tōyōbō, sent their excess spindles to their new ventures in Brazil (Murakami 1977: 156).

The cotton spinners' FDI strategy is reflected in the geographic distribution of their investments. In the late 1950s, Tōyōbō, Kanebō, and Unitika invested actively in South America, producing what has been called the "Brazil boom" (Ueno 1977: 271).[8] The spinners' search for resource-rich economies also produced a significant number of investments in Africa. Indeed, these two regions, which had never figured prominently in the overseas expansion of Japanese capital, were the location of 20 percent (Africa) and 16 percent (Latin America) during this first state of FDI in textiles. Although not the original locus of expansion, Asia gradually reasserted its place as a main recipient of Japanese FDI. By 1964 more than half of all outward investment ventures were established in this region (M. Fujii 1979: 216). Japanese companies transferred small-scale, labor-intensive processes (mostly sewing operations) to Asia. Even though this trend became far more noticeable and influential in the late 1960s, wage disparities between Japan and its neighbors were already growing, and Hong Kong in particular emerged as an attractive site for manufacturing (Nishimura 1977: 302). The amount of money committed to the apparel ventures was very modest, though, and upstream projects (cotton spinning) accounted for most of the outward investment during this period.

Expansion, 1965–1974

In the second stage of textile FDI the cotton spinners were dethroned. Indeed, the composition of Japanese textile FDI changed significantly as synthetic spinning and weaving, midstream processing (knitting and dyeing), and apparel making overshadowed cotton spinning investment abroad (see Table 5.3). During this period, the number of overseas investments in synthetics manufacturing surpassed those in natural fiber spinning and weaving. Knitting and dyeing projects for the first time gained prominence among foreign investment projects, and small-scale investments in sewing continued to grow.

The synthetic fiber makers originally developed an FDI strategy to sustain their export drive. For this reason, most projects undertaken abroad during the 1960s were not in fiber manufacture, but in spinning, weaving, and dyeing (Kaigai Tōshi Kenkyūkai 1978: 48). By relocating the processing of synthetic fibers overseas, Japanese companies successfully locked in a constant demand for fiber produced in Japan (Okamoto 1988a: 73). Nevertheless, the expiration of synthetic fiber patents in the second half of the 1960s, and the resulting desire of the host nations to manufacture their own fibers, forced Japanese companies to transfer abroad some of the more technology- and capital-intensive manufacture of polyester, acrylic, and nylon filaments (Yoshioka 1979: 23–24).

Although overseas investment picked up markedly from 1967 onward with the transfer of costly synthetic fiber manufacturing, the real boom in textile FDI took place between 1972 and 1974. In these three years alone, the Japanese textile industry spent $664 million in FDI, 77 percent of all investment during the period 1965–74.

Both external and internal factors stimulated the investment by all textile subsectors during these years. First, the international business environment abruptly changed after the 1971 Nixon shocks led to exchange rate uncertainty, a revaluation of the yen, and US quotas on Japanese textiles. Japanese textile firms responded to this threat to their international competitiveness by redoubling their FDI efforts. The Japanese government's liberalization of capital outflows to stem revaluatory pressures on the yen further encouraged the transfer of the manufacturing base overseas. On the domestic front, too, it was difficult for Japanese textile companies to stay afloat. Labor shortages and wage increases were eroding the competitiveness of the more labor-intensive textile sectors. For instance, between 1968 and 1973 the yearly average wage increases in textiles (20.1 percent) was much higher than for the rest of manufacturing (17 percent) (Iwami 1977: 80). Moreover, in 1973 pollution regulations in Japan were significantly tightened, affecting especially chemical processes in textile manufacture.

Reacting to foreign exchange fluctuations, export market closure, and domestic excess capacity (in natural and synthetic fiber sectors), to an unrelenting wage spiral (in weaving and sewing), and to stricter pollution monitoring (in dyeing), Japanese firms at all stages of the textile production chain resorted to foreign manufacturing. The result was a very distinctive pattern of Japanese FDI: integrated production overseas from upstream to downstream activities. European and American fiber companies did not pursue integration abroad as aggressively as their Japanese counterparts did. Hirai and Iwasaki (1985) consider this "one set" pattern of overseas investment—from fiber manufacture to textile processing (including investment by *keiretsu* firms)—a distinctive trait of Japanese multinationalism.

Retreat, 1975–1984

The boom in textile FDI came to an end with equal speed. From a peak of 107 ventures in 1973, the number of investments dropped to 11 in 1975, 10 in 1976, and only 3 in 1977. New foreign investment funds dried up, and companies shut down existing overseas factories. After 1975 manufacturers withdrew from foreign markets more quickly, with 254 having done so by 1984 (Horaguchi 1992). Big spinners and fiber makers alike slashed the number of their overseas affiliates. Tōray and Kanebō were the most active, closing down fourteen and nine foreign ventures, respectively. Both Teijin and Asahi Kasei closed six foreign affiliates, and Tōyōbō did away with four (Okamoto 1988a: 82).

Abrupt international changes were once more responsible for the revision of Japanese textile firms' overseas investment plans. The oil shock severely damaged the financial condition of synthetic fiber makers, who for the first time recorded operating losses. As noted in Chapter 3, the Japanese government reversed its previous policy of capital outflow promotion and imposed strict controls on overseas projects. Host countries' divestment of foreign capital further discouraged Japanese textile firms (Yoshioka 1979: 15), but perhaps most disheartening was the low profitability of overseas ventures in a climate of worldwide stagflation. In 1972, for example, the average after-tax profit among Japanese textile ventures abroad was 7.8 percent; in 1974 it had dropped to 0.8 percent, and by 1977 it was 0.1 percent (Okamoto 1988a: 81).

Although the oil shocks were a setback to foreign investment, the multinationalization of the Japanese textile industry had reached unrivaled dimensions. Notably, investment in synthetics dwarfed the overseas investment in natural fiber textiles. As of 1977, FDI in synthetic fiber making, spinning, and weaving totaled $537.5 million, equivalent to 53 percent of all Japanese textile investment. FDI in natural fibers (especially cotton) was not minor by any means: it amounted to $311.8 million (31 percent of the total). The FDI amounts for knitting and dyeing were more modest: $77 million. Investment amounts in downstream processing such as clothing were particularly small ($26 million) (Nihon Kagaku Sen'i Kyōkai 1978).

Through these offshore investments, Japanese synthetic textile firms dominated Asian manufacturing by the late 1970s. Not surprisingly, Japanese firms held the largest shares of host country productive capacity in staple and filament manufacture (as much as 100 percent in Indonesia, and Malaysia). Indigenous firms in Southeast Asia lacked the capital and technology to engage in synthetic fiber making, and since European and American firms concentrated their investments elsewhere, Japanese companies dominated in these countries.

In spinning and weaving, Japan's share of Southeast Asia's textile equipment was especially significant in Malaysia and Singapore (44 percent and 33 percent, respectively) (Arpan, Barry, and Van Tho 1984: 148). Japanese textile manufacturers did not establish this dominant position in Asia completely on their own: they enlisted the general trading companies as offshore investment partners. More than half of all overseas affiliates of Japanese textile oligopolists in 1977 were in joint ventures with the traders: twenty-nine of forty-three subsidiaries for Tōray, thirteen of twenty-six affiliates for Teijin, twelve of twenty-three ventures for Tōyōbō, and twelve of fourteen subsidiaries for Kanebō (Nihon Kagaku Sen'i Kyōkai 1978). For fiber makers and spinners alike the alliance with general traders was crucial in sustaining their overseas expansion.

At the end of the 1970s, the most active Japanese overseas investors (the big fiber makers and their *sōgō shōsha* partners) had already developed a sizable manufacturing base in Southeast Asia, mostly to serve local and third-country markets. Japanese textile MNCs did not see the need for substantial additions to overseas productive capacity, so for the rest of this period FDI grew slowly (between 1979 and 1984 Japanese textile FDI averaged $85 million per year).

The Endaka Boom, 1985–1999

The 1985 Plaza Agreement marked the beginning of an eventful decade for Japanese textile overseas investment. For the first time since the boom of 1972–74, Japanese FDI in textiles broke new records. While FDI continued to grow sluggishly in 1985 and 1986 (registering $28 million and $65 million respectively), in 1987 FDI reached $206 million, $796 million in 1990, and peaked in 1995 at $1 billion. However, FDI in the second half of the 1990s tapered off to $341 million and $260 million in 1998 and 1999, respectively. Cumulative Japanese FDI during this fourth stage amounted to $7.3 billion, far more than the $861 million registered in the previous boom years of 1965–74 (see Table 5.2).

The sharp yen appreciation (*endaka*) and the consequent realignment of comparative advantage in the Asia-Pacific region were decisive in revitalizing overseas investment activities. Currency realignments not only put a brake on Japanese exports, but also opened the Japanese market to a flood of cheap textile imports. Moreover, domestic labor shortages widened the wage gap between Japan and neighboring Asian countries. In 1988 the hourly labor cost in the textile industry was fourteen dollars in Japan, three dollars in Korea, and less than one dollar in Malaysia, the Philippines, Thailand, China, and Indonesia (Dicken 1992: 248).

In its most recent phase, a new set of actors was responsible for the post-*endaka* boom: apparel makers, clothing wholesalers, and trading companies. Yen appreciation and labor shortages affected the most labor-intensive sectors of the industry, and the growing import penetration by foreign labels forced downstream companies to begin manufacturing overseas. In a MITI survey of FDI by textile firms, 78 percent of the 233 overseas investments recorded between 1988 and 1992 were in apparel. The share of investment by previously dominant sectors was minor: 6 percent for spinning, 6 percent for weaving, and 7 percent for dyeing.[9] Overseas investment in fiber making seems to have lost steam altogether: only one instance was reported in this survey (MITI 1994b: 176).

The motives for undertaking foreign production in apparel were distinct from those that encouraged up- and midstream Japanese textile firms to set up shop abroad. The same MITI survey reports that all textile firms, with the exception of apparel companies, aimed to capture local markets through FDI. In contrast, clothing firms sought to sell their offshore production back in the home market. Only 7 percent of clothing firms with overseas investments did not count on sales to Japan, and more than two-thirds of the firms planned to sell more than 75 percent of their production in their home country (MITI 1994b: 211). These "reverse imports" have further politicized the debate on textile trade protection in Japan.

Low-wage economies emerged as the new production hubs for the Japanese apparel industry. Concentration in Asia became more pronounced than ever (82 percent of all textile investment projects between 1989 and 2000). Industrialized nations hosted close to 15 percent of Japanese textile ventures abroad, while Latin America (with 1.1 percent of FDI projects) virtually disappeared from the overseas expansion plans of Japanese companies. Within Asia, China and ASEAN nations captured the lion's share of Japanese FDI. Between 1989 and 2000, 66 percent of Japanese textile investments in Asia took place in China and 24 percent in ASEAN nations (based on FDI statistics from the Ministry of Finance).

The role of China as the leading clothing supplier to Japan is in fact underestimated by the FDI statistics. The internationalization of the Japanese apparel industry proceeded not only through overseas investment, but also through outward processing (subcontracting with foreign firms), "compensatory trade" (local companies paying for textile machinery exports by providing sewing services), and specialized lines (commissioning the output from the production line of a factory abroad) (MITI 1994b). These production arrangements, together with Japanese-owned factories, redefined the composition of Japanese imports. In 1999, 70 percent of all Japanese apparel imports originated in China, and most of them were either produced or commissioned by a Japanese company (Nihon Kagaku Sen'i Kyōkai 2001: 122–23). Thus the fragile domestic consensus on avoiding overt trade protection was undermined by the import avalanche.

Textile MNCs: An Overview

The textile oligopolists established an integrated system of production abroad. Upstream firms ventured into mid- and downstream activities in their overseas factories (see Table 5.4). However, spinners and the fiber makers emphasized different areas in their offshore operations. The fiber makers supplemented their numerous investments in synthetic fibers (especially Tōray) with forward integration into spinning, weaving, knitting, and dyeing, but they rarely undertook downstream processing. The spinners were very active in the midstream segments of textile production and invested

TABLE 5.4

Textile MNCs: The Upstream Oligopolists, 1995

	Total number of overseas affiliates	Synthetic fibers	Spinning and weaving	Knitting and dyeing	Downstream activities	Nontextile manufacturing
Fiber companies						
Asahi Kasei Kōgyō	26	3	4	4	1	18
Kuraray	5	0	0	0	0	5
Mitsubishi Rayon	13	4	2	1	0	6
Tōray	42	9	10	12	0	22
Unitika	13	1	5	1	3	4
Teijin	12	3	1	1	0	7
Tōhō Rayon	2	2	0	0	0	0
Spinning firms						
Nittō Bōseki	10	0	0	0	0	10
Kanebō	29	1	6	2	4	16
Nisshin Bōseki	8	0	3	0	1	4
Tōyōbō	16	0	10	5	2	4
Kurabō	8	1	4	1	2	0
Omikenshi	2	0	2	0	0	0
Fuji Bōseki	2	0	1	0	0	1
Shikibō	4	0	2	2	1	0
Daiwa Bōseki	4	0	2	1	1	0
Total	196	24	52	30	15	97

SOURCE: Compiled by the author from Toyo Keizai, *Kaigai Shinshutsu Kigyō Sōran*, 1995.

somewhat more in downstream operations, but rarely did they establish synthetic fiber factories overseas. Even though domestically the spinners moved aggressively into synthetic manufacturing, they did not do so abroad. The large amounts of capital required for synthetic fiber projects, and the fact that they were not technological innovators in the field but late arrivals, may have deterred them from doing so.[10]

Although upstream textile firms invested actively abroad, midstream companies (weavers and dyers) exhibited little appetite for foreign production. In the early 1970s as few as five dyers owned overseas subsidiaries, and they were all joint ventures with upstream firms or trading companies (Iwami 1977: 99). In the mid-1990s, there were only three dying firms with investments abroad (a total of eight affiliates). Among weaving companies only three (Kawashima Orimono, Nippon Keori, and Miyuki Keori) owned a total of eight subsidiaries (Toyo Keizai 1995).

Apparel firms frequently co-invested with general trading companies in offshore manufacturing ventures. In 1995, nineteen firms had sixty-five apparel subsidiaries overseas; clothing wholesalers undertook twelve of these projects, and another nineteen were joint ventures with general trading companies or apparel wholesalers (ibid.). The saliency of *keiretsu* ties in apparel FDI reflects the central function of apparel wholesalers and general trading companies in organizing clothing production within Japan. General trading companies have supplied fabric both to the wholesalers and to smaller apparel concerns, and have taken part in the distribution of the more standardized clothing goods. Wholesale apparel makers, in contrast, have operated as manufacturer/trader hybrids, producing some of the apparel they sell and also commissioning garment production to affiliated subcontractors. The apparel wholesalers were able to finance and organize their overseas factories mostly on their own, while the smaller apparel firms used their domestic alliances with wholesalers or *sōgō shōsha* to implement their FDI projects.

One of the most salient traits in the multinationalization of the Japanese textile industry is the central role of "group investment," in particular, the liaison between textile manufacturers and general trading companies (see Table 5.5). Trading companies zealously assisted overseas production at all stages of textile manufacturing. The general traders accompanied the upstream textile firms as they initiated overseas production and also actively undertook garment manufacturing in the most recent wave of textile FDI. Textile manufacturers and trading companies closely coordinated their offshore manufacturing expansion so as to replicate abroad their domestic preferential transaction arrangements.[11]

Textile firms embarking on offshore production looked for business partners with whom they had previously tackled export markets who could also

TABLE 5.5

Foreign Direct Investment by General Trading Companies as of 1990

	Synthetic fibers	Spinning and weaving		Knitting and dyeing	Downstream activities	Total[a]
		Synthetics	Natural fiber			
Mitsui Bussan	3	10	1	7	9	30
Mitsubishi Shōji	2	7	2	3	10	24
Marubeni	2	7	7	4	13	33
C. Itoh	2	4	6	3	6	21
Sumitomo Shōji	1	1	1	—	3	6
Nisshō Iwai	—	2	2	—	2	6
Tomen	—	—	—	—	—	0
Nichimen	—	1	1	4	2	8
Kanematsu	—	1	3	2	7	13
Toyo Menka	3	5	4	5	8	25
Chori	—	2	1	1	3	7
Itoman	—	1	—	1	—	2
Total[b]	13	41	28	30	63	175

[a]Exceeds the actual number of investments because some factories produce more than one type of product.

[b]Exceeds the actual number of investments because some are joint ventures between two or more trading companies.

SOURCE: Compiled by the author from *Japan Textile News*, May 1990, pp. 55–63.

provide logistical support and contribute financially. The *sōgō shōsha* participated in FDI projects to protect their commercial rights (*shōken*). Joint ventures abroad provided a way for traders to lock in business opportunities as suppliers of inputs and machinery, and to market goods in local markets and third countries (Yoshihara 1978: 124).

Japan development of a highly multinationalized textile industry over fifty years of foreign investment was not emulated elsewhere. In other industrialized nations, the textile industry remained a highly protected and *domestic* industry, never leading the way in offshore manufacturing. In the United States in 1980, for instance, textile FDI represented only 1.7 percent of the manufacturing total; the figures were 1.4 percent in Germany, 2.6 percent in France, and 4.3 percent in England (UNCTC 1987: 26). Although the largest textile firms in Europe and the United States did engage in limited foreign direct investment, the vast majority did not (Arpan, Barry, and Van Tho 1984: 130–35). Moreover, textile FDI from industrialized nations was largely circumscribed to synthetic fiber making, rendering Japan the only advanced nation with numerous investments in cotton spinning (ibid.: 47).[12] Japanese textile FDI is remarkable not only for its magnitude, but also for its industrial composition.

Japan's accomplishment in setting up an overseas network of textile production challenges conventional understanding of the adjustment strategies available to structurally depressed industries. The textile industry in other countries has not invested heavily abroad because they do not have the firm-specific advantages that economic theories of FDI deem essential for outward investment: technological sophistication, high capital intensity, and an oligopolistic industrial structure.[13]

Lacking the ability to undertake foreign production, textile firms in industrialized nations have responded to structural decline *solely* through domestic means: rationalization, diversification, and protection. Japanese firms chose to internationalize production because the incentive structure in Japan was very different from that in advanced market economies: overt trade protection was not granted to textile industrialists given the strong international pressure to further liberalize market access, and the Japanese government enhanced the outward investment capabilities of Japanese textile firms through preferential FDI credit.

THE HAND OF THE STATE IN OFFSHORE MIGRATION

The Japanese government supported textile FDI for several reasons: to procure key raw materials, to promote textile machinery exports, to secure access to local markets abroad, to establish export footholds targeting third countries, and to alleviate the problem of redundant domestic capacity. The common aim in the government's sanctioning of outward investment projects was to enhance the competitiveness of an industry in gradual but unfaltering decline.

Government and industry hammered out "visions" of the proper management of industrial change in textiles. These reports from *shingikai*, or deliberation councils, included not only domestic policy recommendations on vertical integration, rationalization, or diversification, but also an FDI prescription (McNamara 1995: 12). For instance, in June 1973 the Japan Chemical Fiber Association issued a report calling for vertical integration and rationalization at home, and for active promotion of outward investment (M. Fujii 1979: 223). A few months later the textile advisory council, under the aegis of MITI, ratified the central role of offshore investment. Its report argued that the industry should upgrade technologically and undertake foreign production. Interestingly, the council noted that overseas expansion should proceed in an orderly fashion (Ito 1993: 166). Nevertheless, state endorsement was predicated on commitments by the Japanese textile MNCs to retain R&D and higher-value-added production activities in Japan, to provide for labor adjustments (no massive layoffs), and to limit imports back into the homeland.

State support for textile FDI was backed by substantial public credit. The pioneers of Japanese FDI in textiles, the cotton spinners, received generous support from government banks. The first beneficiaries of the Japan Eximbank's FDI loans were the spinners, who captured 96 percent of all overseas investment credit granted by the bank in the early 1950s. In those initial years they invested in four projects in Latin America (in Brazil, El Salvador, and Mexico). Because of the foreign currency limitations that Japan faced at that time, as well as the prevailing policy that FDI projects should generate exports, most of these projects were financed in kind (that is, with textile machinery). Government financing for cotton spinning also helped these firms procure cheap cotton, maintain market share through local production in foreign countries, and provide investment opportunities to firms that were beginning to feel the pinch of an overcrowded domestic market (Japan Eximbank 1983: 57–58).

Cotton spinners were not the only textile firms to enjoy public largesse. The Japanese state also assisted the chemical textile industry in its efforts to acquire inexpensive natural resources. The largest FDI project supported by the Japan Eximbank was for the extraction of lumber in Alaska. This project was conceived in 1951 as a joint enterprise of the Japanese pulp, chemical textile, and paper industries to develop and import pulp, lumber, and wood chips. But it had to be revised when the United States insisted that some form of processing take place locally. Only the Japanese chemical industry decided to go ahead with the production of pulp, a key ingredient in the manufacture of rayon.

In 1956 a Japanese cabinet resolution designated the Alaska Pulp venture a national project, and one year later the Japan Eximbank extended it a line of credit. Between 1957 and 1967 it provided financing of approximately $45.5 million (almost 50 percent of lumber and pulp FDI during those years). Moreover, in the Alaska Pulp project the bank for the first time guaranteed the bonds issued by a foreign joint venture. In total, the guarantees were worth $27 million. In this way, the Japan Eximbank demonstrated its commitment to the survival of the project and had to provide additional financing, extend repayment deadlines, and lower interest rates in periods of difficulty. Indeed, already in the 1960s the financial health of the project was compromised by the decline in chemical textiles, as synthetics came to dominate the market. It became increasingly difficult to find buyers for the pulp, and the venture required government assistance to stay afloat (Japan Eximbank 1983: 90–91, 120).

The synthetic fiber firms also sought and obtained sizable FDI credit from the Japan Eximbank. During the first decade of textile investment (1955–64), when only the cotton spinners ventured abroad, Japan Eximbank FDI loans represented around 20 percent of total textile FDI. In the second period (1965–74), dominated already by the synthetic fiber firms, the Japan Eximbank financed close to 34 percent of all outward investment in textiles. This support helped the synthetic fiber firms cope with the growing closure of export markets as developing countries upgraded their own textile industries into synthetics. Public credit was even more necessary given the more demanding capital requirements of the integrated production system (from spinning, weaving, and dyeing to fiber manufacture) that textile firms were implementing abroad in this period (Japan Eximbank 1983: 239).

In fact, the rapid surge in outward investment in the early 1970s made the government worry about a "disorderly investment rush," and MITI proposed to regulate the overseas expansion of Japanese textile MNCs. In particular, the bureaucrats were concerned about the brisk growth of reverse imports, and about the riots that erupted in Asian host nations over an "overpresence" of Japanese multinationals. MITI toyed with the idea of requiring textile firms to provide prior notification of their investment plans. An advisory council would be created to review and approve all investment projects abroad. Authorized projects would benefit from financing by public financial institutions, while those that seemed likely to disrupt local and domestic markets would be restrained. In other words, the deliberation council on overseas investment was conceived as a parallel body to the advisory council already in place to regulate internal capacity expansion (Osaka Chemical Research 1973: 4).

The public regulation of outward investment through a deliberation council was never implemented, mainly because the events of late 1973 made it unnecessary. The oil shock reversed overnight the Japanese balance of payments and led to the first serious recession in the synthetic textile industry. Consequently, offshore investment capital in textiles dried up. Big firms (whether spinners or fiber manufacturers) were the core textile clients of the Japan Eximbank, so when large manufacturers froze their overseas investment plans, public credit for outward investment also decreased markedly. After the first oil shock, most investment projects were carried out by downstream (small) enterprises that were outside the domain of Japan Eximbank credit. As a result, the industry's reliance on public financing during the third stage of textile FDI (1975–84) was very low: a mere 3 percent.

The importance of public financing in the overseas expansion of Japanese textiles did not wither away permanently, though. In the most recent post-*endaka* FDI boom, the textile industry once more enjoyed ample backing from public financial institutions. Between 1985 and 1994, the Japan Eximbank financed roughly 15 percent of all textile investment abroad. More important, government banks have been keener on financing the new agents of Japanese textile multinationalism: the apparel makers. For the first time, the Japan Eximbank dedicated a substantial amount of its FDI credit to small companies. Between 1989 and 1995, 52 percent of the bank's outward investment loans for textiles were allocated to large firms, and 48 percent to small enterprises.

As mentioned in Chapter 4, since 1987, when the government banks in charge of SME loans received a greater mandate to finance overseas ventures, they have catered to textile interests. In March 1995, only two other industries received more FDI credit from the JFS. Between 1992 and 1994, the JFS alone financed 30 percent of the SME textile projects abroad. Government SME banks therefore actively promoted small clothing companies undertaking foreign production. But these newly minted multinationals disregarded the tacit understanding that overseas factories should not target the home market. Besieged domestic producers in turn pressed more aggressively for trade protection.

The Political Battle over Textile Multinationalization

Free trade has not been common practice in textiles. Efforts in the postwar era to liberalize trade, which culminated in the creation of GATT in 1947, did not extend to textiles. On the contrary, cheap textile imports from Japan exacerbated pressures to isolate national industries from international competition. The European countries refused to eliminate restrictions on Japan even after it became a GATT member, and in the 1950s the United States began pressuring Japan to cap textile exports. Japan complied in 1957 with a "voluntary" restraint on its textile exports to the United States.

Protectionism in textile trade acquired new momentum with the adoption in GATT of the "market disruption" principle—that is, the imposition of restrictions on large import increases that are not attributable to foreign subsidies or dumping. The United States took the lead in 1961 to draft the international Short-Term Agreement on Textiles based on the disruption-of-markets principle (Cline 1987: 146–47).[14] A long-term agreement was signed in 1962 to perpetuate textile restrictions. The protectionist mantle was extended to man-made fibers with the signing of the Multi-Fiber Agreement (MFA) in 1974 and its successive renewals until 1994.

The first breakthrough in the liberalization of textile trade took place during the Uruguay Round of trade talks. The Agreement on Textiles and Clothing established a ten-year period (1995–2004) for the phasing out of MFA restrictions. Although quotas will be eliminated, textile trade is still subject to protectionist pressures. The elimination of quantitative restrictions is heavily backloaded: 50 percent of the textile quotas will not be eliminated until the end of 2004 (Hoekman and Kostecki 1995). Moreover, industrialized countries imposed stiff tariffs on textile products (higher than the manufacturing average) and increased their use of safeguard and antidumping measures to block market access to cheap textile imports (Spinanger 1999; Reinert 2000). National governments have jealously guarded their textile industries in international trade negotiations.

A BROKEN CONSENSUS ON ORDERLY IMPORTATION

In sharp contrast to the heavy trade protection granted by states to their textile industries, Japan maintained the lowest textile tariffs among industrialized nations and never invoked the MFA to impose quotas. Overt protection remained an elusive goal for the Japanese textile sector, despite its continuous efforts to obstruct imports. The protectionist lobby in Japan first emerged in 1973–74 in reaction to an unprecedented import surge. Through their industry associations, both spinners and weavers asked MITI to take prompt action to check the import flood. They wanted the ministry to create a surveillance committee on imports, to administratively guide importers into moderating their intake of foreign products, to carry out bilateral negotiations with foreign countries to sustain "orderly imports," to abolish a scheduled 20 percent reduction in tariffs, and to implement the MFA in order to keep imports at bay (Ito 1993: 180; Yamazawa 1988: 415). MITI rejected the industry's petitions, arguing that textile barriers in a trade-surplus country would prompt retaliation from trading partners.

As the synthetics industry, last bastion of Japan's textile export drive, felt the pinch of decreased foreign sales and growing import penetration, the protectionist lobby acquired new strength. In 1978–79, the Japan Textile Federation (this time with the support of the man-made subsector and the labor union

Zensen) continued to press for textile quotas and for the dismantling of the Generalized System of Preferences (GSP). MITI had become more sympathetic to the industry's plight and informally asked South Korea and Taiwan to restrain exports. Nevertheless, the ministry refused to implement the MFA or to abolish the GSP (Friman 1990: 126–31). MITI's resistance to modifying the preferential tariff system could be overcome only in 1981 when the Tariff Council of MOF recommended suspending the GSP for sensitive textile products (silk yarns, cotton yarns, and cotton fabrics).

The partial victory on GSP did not translate into success on the MFA front. Inconsistent demands by the textile subsectors were responsible for this outcome (Friman 1990: 133). The cotton weavers pressed for an import ceiling of 10 percent of domestic production to invoke the MFA; labor was willing to settle for a limit of 25–30 percent of domestic consumption. The producers of upstream fibers (cotton and synthetics) were willing to forgo explicit ceilings if MITI would act in the event of large import surges.

The lack of more tariff or quota protection continued to strain bureaucracy-industry relations. The spinners decided to switch tactics and in December 1982 announced they would file an antidumping suit against South Korea and a countervailing-duty suit against Pakistan. MITI did not immediately reject the suit petitions, and using this tacit acceptance as leverage the Japanese industry moved quickly to engage its foreign counterparts in negotiations. The intraindustry talks yielded results: Korea announced a VER in March 1983, and by the summer Pakistan had eliminated export subsidies (Friman 1990: 134–35). A new pattern of import protection had thereby been established: intraindustry accords to avoid legal action.[15]

The increasing vulnerability of the Japanese market in the *endaka* era once more rendered MFA implementation a bitter point of contention for policymakers and industrialists. Foreign-made textile products steadily replaced Japanese production. Import-penetration ratios for most textile categories grew, and by the early 1990s close to half of the Japanese textile demand was met by imported goods. Imports as a percentage of domestic consumption in Japan increased in cotton yarn from 26 percent in 1986 to 36 percent in 1992, and a similar increase occurred in cotton fabric (from 25 percent to 39 percent). The man-made fibers market remained relatively immune to imports, its import ratio being only 8.7 percent in 1992. Foreign-made apparel took over, however. In 1992 the import penetration ratio for knitted sweaters was as high as 76 percent, and for cotton outerwear 59 percent (MITI 1994b: 159).

Cornered by the import avalanche, Japanese textile industrialists redoubled their efforts to raise tariff and quota barriers. Only in November 1994 did they make substantial headway, when MITI finally announced domestic rules to petition for quota relief. However, the textile lobby soon became frustrated with MITI's ample discretionary power. Whereas in Europe numerical ceilings are set to determine the use of quotas, MITI announced that its decision to invoke the MFA provisions would be based on several policy considerations: the degree to which Japanese companies contributed to the import surge, whether Japanese firms would use the quota relief to pursue genuine industrial upgrading, and whether the quantitative restrictions would harm trade relations with exporting nations. Moreover, through the cumbersome process it envisioned, it could take a year from the time of application for quotas to their actual implementation ("Sen'i yunyū seigen no hatsudō kijun" [Criteria for invoking restrictions on textile imports], *Nihon Keizai Shimbun*, November 25, 1994).

The protectionist lobby sought to use the new international trading rules on textiles to check imports. Since 1995, spinners and weavers have repeatedly requested the implementation of the safeguard provisions contemplated in the World Trade Organization to reduce textile imports (especially from China). The sequence of events has invariably been the same: a Japanese industry petition for safeguards against imports from China, followed by a pledge of self-restraint from the Chinese and a bureaucratic decision to delay the implementation of quotas ("Chūgokusan menpu sefugadu miokuri" [Letting go of safeguards against Chinese cotton cloth], *Nihon Keizai Shimbun*, November 7, 1996). Only in December 2000 did MITI agree to simplify the safeguarding rules, deciding to no longer require an industry restructuring plan to be in effect during the life of the quota ("Sen'i sangyō, yunyū seigen o yōsei—shōhisha no rikai hitsuyō" [Textile industry demands import restrictions, understanding from consumers is necessary], *Nihon Keizai Shimbun*, December 21, 2000). But the Japanese state has remained adamant about imposing quantitative restrictions (either old-style MFA restrictions or new transitional safeguards), and has continued to prefer bilaterally negotiated export restraints.[16]

Concern over foreign retaliation is not the only reason the government avoided overt trade protectionism. Domestic divisions among textile subsectors and companies also weakened the protectionist lobby. Most of the companies responsible for the latest FDI boom (traders and apparel makers) strongly objected to trade restrictions. The new businesses responsible for an increase in imports (retailers and supermarket chains) understandably opposed any effort to block the sale of cheap, low-quality textile products to the Japanese consumer.[17] But even the old hands in textile trade (the *sōgō shōsha*) have shown few qualms about importing apparel back to Japan. Consequently, the general traders too oppose restrictive trade policies. In fact, the general trading company Marubeni took unprecedented action in June 1995 when it co-invested with a Korean spinner in Indonesia. Until then the *sōgō shōsha* had teamed up only with Japanese spinners, never with their foreign rivals ("Kokunai menbōseki, sonbō no kini tsukakachi takame kyōsōryoku" [Life or death opportunity for domestic cotton spinning, the competitive power to increase value added], *Nihon Keizai Shimbun*, August 10, 1995). The fissures in the domestic alliance were evident.

Enticed by the government, the pioneers of Japanese textile FDI (the upstream oligopolists) frowned on reverse imports.[18] With the deteriorating trade balance, Japanese weavers and spinners increasingly pressed the bureaucrats to restrain import growth. But the old tacit agreement among large textile manufacturers on shielding the domestic market from imports was swept away as some fiber firms scrambled to maintain profitability. The case of Tōray's reverse imports into Japan was much commented on in industrial circles. In justification, the company's president said: "We would rather fill the market with foreign-made Tōray products than sit back and see imports from foreign companies eating away the market share" ("Textile makers importing from offshore plants," *Nikkei Weekly*, March 20, 1995).

The previous consensus in the textile establishment restricting reverse imports collapsed. Moreover, the extensive import networks developed by Japanese firms helped foreign countries deflect Japanese pressure to adopt export caps. Chinese officials insinuated to a Japanese delegation in May 1994 that before they moved to restrain exports to Japan the Japanese should put their own house in order; that is, they should restrain the behavior of Japanese companies operating in China ("Sensan shinteigen 'yunyū kisei' ni yureru gyōkai" [Industry rocked by the proposal from the textile deliberation council to "regulate imports"], *Nihon Keizai Shimbun*, May 18, 1994).

Japanese manufacturers and traders are responsible for much of the current import flood into Japan. According to some estimates, Japanese companies participated in close to half of all apparel imports from Asia (MITI 1994b: 134). Of course, the involvement of Japanese companies varies by product: it is more substantial in apparel (29 percent of all cotton outwear imports and 15.4 percent of knit underwear imports) than in midstream (4 percent of all imported fabric) or upstream products (6 percent of all yarn and fiber). Reverse imports from Japanese-owned factories abroad were estimated to constitute 38 percent of all textile imports, whereas subcontracted imports are believed to amount to 39 percent (ibid.: 195, 194).

In the past, accusations that Japanese FDI had the perverse effect of increasing import penetration could be easily dismissed because most imports did not originate in countries where Japanese companies were actively investing (Yoshioka 1978). This is no longer true.[19] As Japanese factories abroad became increasingly oriented toward serving the home market, the domestic alliance that had sustained a relatively stress-free transnationalization strategy looked increasingly fragile. Conflicting interests now set apart spinners, fiber makers, and general traders.

DOGS THAT DON'T BARK: LABOR UNIONS AND OFFSHORE INVESTMENT

The split between traders and textile MNCs that import back to the homeland and the producers that wish to restrict these reverse imports was the main source of opposition to the multinationalization of the textile industry. Remarkably, labor did not lodge an active campaign to prevent management from investing abroad. The nature of textile unionism helps explain workers' quiet stance on FDI. The labor federation Zensen Domei has always been considered center-right, willing to cooperate with management. Its membership includes not only the large-enterprise unions but also local unions for smaller establishments, and it is reputed to exert more influence over its member unions than most industrial federations (Dore 1986: 217).

Zensen joined forces with the national union federation Domei, which in turn maintained close ties with the former DSP (Democratic Socialist Party).[20] Affiliation with Domei had important implications for the muted belligerence of Zensen, since Domei was among the first private sector union groups to accept the inevitability of rationalization policies and labor adjustment. Already in 1967, and pressed by pending trade and capital liberalization, Domei favored industrial restructuring to strengthen the international competitiveness of Japanese manufacturing. In exchange, however, Domei asked for the establishment of a prior consultation procedure between management and labor within each industry, and for representation at the economic deliberation advisory councils (Kume 1998: 165–66). Both of these petitions were eventually granted.

A decade later, Domei once more achieved a landmark success with the passage of the Law on Special Measures for the Laid-Off Workers in Targeted Structurally Depressed Industries. The post–oil shock recession forced many Japanese manufacturing sectors to cope with excess capacity and structural decline. Domei took the pragmatic stance that rationalization was inevitable but that workers' interests should not be disproportionately damaged. Zensen and the synthetic chemical union, both member unions of Domei, actively lobbied in support of the Special Measures Law. Union representatives met with officials of the Ministry of Labor and gained LDP support for the bill. With the new law, the Japanese labor union movement succeeded in extending the state's commitment: in addition to facilitating industrial restructuring, it would after workers' welfare in depressed industries (Kume 1998: 172–73).

Despite the practical posture of Zensen Domei in trading compliance with rationalization for some form of compensation, it is still remarkable that labor-management relations in textiles did not turn more confrontational given the major reductions in employment in the industry. In the late 1990s, textiles employed fewer than half the number it had thirty years earlier. Some textile subsectors fared worse than others: employment in yarn manufacturing dropped from 33,000 in 1965 to 655 in 1998); in synthetic fibers employment went from 48,000 in 1965 to 16,000 in 1998. In turn, apparel consolidated its position as the largest employer in the industry with 544,000 jobs (*Japan Statistical Yearbook*, several years; Nihon Kagaku Sen'i Kyōkai 2001: 4).

Two other factors helped mitigate labor activism despite the loss of job opportunities in textiles: nonconflictive labor adjustment practices and the selective targeting of the weaker groups in the workforce for job reduction. The nature of Japanese labor adjustment largely explains the relatively benign response of organized workers to both the domestic rationalization and overseas investment strategies of their employers. Though the industry lost jobs over the years, Japanese firms did not engage in massive layoffs. Instead, they pursued a variety of labor adjustment practices: overtime reduction, temporary layoffs, moderate recruitment, seconding personnel to a related *keiretsu* company, reduction of part-timers, and "voluntary early retirement" (Dore 1986: 209–13). Management and unions went to great lengths to uphold the principle of employment security and to provide some compensation when deviating from it.

But not all workers held on to their jobs. Nonunionized workers in small firms, female employees, and part-timers were not protected by the principle of employment security. These groups suffered most. Employment of women in the cotton spinning industry between 1965 and 1985 dropped by 63,000 jobs; employment of men dropped by only 6,000 (Uriu 1996: 91). Since most regular union members retained their employment, Zensen Domei regarded the rationalization and FDI strategies favorably.[21]

There is one more reason the unions did not contest FDI strategies in textiles. Quite simply, in a structurally depressed industry with a chronic problem of excess capacity, foreign direct investment was not seen as the main culprit. For this reason, Zensen did not campaign against offshore investment and limited its efforts to developing an international network of Asian textile workers—though without much success (McNamara 1995: 44). The combination of a pragmatic union stance on rationalization and FDI with compensation, of conciliatory labor adjustment practices, and of passing the costs of adjustment on to unorganized workers tamed the potential antagonism of the labor movement toward domestic and international adjustment in the textile industry.

The postwar shift in comparative advantage rocked the Japanese textile industry, but free-market adjustment was not the policy prescription sanctioned by the Japanese textile establishment. Quite to the contrary, industrialists, politicians, and bureaucrats endorsed "orderly transition" as the best approach to managing decline. The result was stability amid change in all dimensions of Japanese textile adjustment: negotiated capacity curtailments, preservation of firm hierarchy, orderly overseas expansion, and moderate import growth.

Textiles sets Japan apart in the management of mature industries. It was the only industrialized nation to adjust to decreasing competitiveness by investing overseas. The availability of public credit made the strategy possible.

Most of the early FDI financing by the Japan Eximbank was channeled to cotton spinning; later, substantial loans were directed toward national projects to facilitate natural resource procurement and toward capital-intensive synthetic projects abroad. But this assistance was not distributed evenly among all textile sectors; it reached only the upper echelons of the industry.

For most of the postwar period an alliance to multinationalize production was forged among big textile capital, government banks, and large trading companies. In other words, state FDI financing favored strong players (upstream oligopolists) operating in a weak industry. In the 1990s, however, the small-firm lobby had some success persuading the government to introduce special FDI loans with soft terms. Since then, SMEs have captured a larger share of preferential public FDI credit, contributing to a boom in offshore investment in textiles.

With the appearance of new textile multinationals (the small apparel makers) and growing import pressure on the domestic market, domestic alignments on textile transnationalization are in flux. The new division of labor between domestic and offshore factories has profoundly divided Japanese textile firms. Tensions have grown between multinational groups that resort to foreign production to serve local and third-country markets and those that established factories to sell output back in Japan. Interestingly, the challenge to multinational production has come not from trade unions but from disadvantaged textile industrialists. Trade and FDI policy, therefore, are intimately connected, and "reverse imports" have further politicized the protection debate.

Politics has been at the heart of domestic and international adjustment in Japanese textiles. Management, labor, politicians, and bureaucrats toiled mightily to prevail over purely market-driven adjustment. Although they agreed on the need to restore competitiveness through orderly transition, the political actors are increasingly at odds over the specifics of the adjustment prescription.

Textile management tried to circumvent labor antagonism by adopting nonconfrontational practices and favoring unionized workers. For most of the postwar period, upstream textile firms, politicians with textile connections, and government banks managed to aid the relocation of uncompetitive industry without generating significant domestic opposition. In the early twenty-first century, though, the successful lobbying by small firms for an FDI soft loan program, and the resulting offshore investment by apparel makers targeting the home market with the aid of retailers and *sōgō shōsha*, has politicized FDI and trade policy in Japanese textiles. This political battle is still being waged.

CHAPTER 6

The Offshore Rebirth of Japanese Aluminum Smelting

ALUMINUM SMELTING in Japan was a virtually extinct industry that nonetheless undertook huge refining (and some hydropower generation) projects abroad. How could firms operating in a structurally depressed industry with operating losses and burgeoning debt afford to establish costly smelters overseas? This chapter tells how public financing enabled Japanese smelting companies to use FDI as an international adjustment strategy.

Japanese smelters, politicians, and bureaucrats hammered out a two-pronged strategy in which the gradual closure of the most inefficient plants in Japan would be matched by the establishment overseas of Japanese-owned smelters to maintain a stable ingot supply. While parent companies and group banks covered most of the costs of domestic rationalization, the Japanese government absorbed the lion's share of FDI expenditures. Despite the shared objective among MITI bureaucrats and smelters to supply the domestic market with ingot from offshore Japanese smelters, and the substantial preferential financing made available for this purpose, the efforts of the government to keep private investors vested in unprofitable national projects, and the refusal of downstream sectors to be "guided" into buying Japanese regardless of price, generated ample political friction.

The Politics of Domestic Adjustment

The creation of the Japanese aluminum smelting industry was a difficult and protracted process. Although aluminum fabricators began operations in Japan at the beginning of the twentieth century, ingot smelting suffered a thirty-year delay. Among the difficulties that plagued early attempts at smelting were a lack of bauxite resources, competition from cheap imports, poor electrolysis technology (needed to reduce alumina into aluminum), and an undeveloped electric power network (Nakajima and Muratsu 1976: 51).[1] It was not until 1933 that Shōwa Denko overcame these drawbacks and opened the first Japanese aluminum smelter. Rival companies soon joined in the competition for the nascent aluminum ingot market: Sumitomo Chemicals in 1936 and Nippon Light Metals in 1940, among others.

Stimulated mostly by military procurement contracts, production grew rapidly in the ensuing years, reaching a peak of 114,057 tons in 1943. The emphasis on aluminum production for military purposes enabled Nippon Light Metals (NLM) to bypass the opposition of established firms to its entry in the industry, and by the end of the war NLM had become the largest producer of aluminum ingot in Japan, with a 35 percent market share.

THE CONSOLIDATION OF THE INDUSTRY

Defeat in World War II and economic dislocation in its aftermath endangered the survival of the Japanese aluminum industry. Overseas smelters were lost, bauxite supply channels were interrupted, and in the first years of the Occupation it appeared as if the smelters' equipment would be used as reparations to Asian countries (Anzai 1971: 230–36). Nevertheless, Shōwa Denko, Sumitomo Chemicals, and NLM succeeded in maintaining operations and divided the market among themselves. Nippon Light Metals controlled most of it, supplying 64 percent of all aluminum ingot consumed in 1950. Over time, these three prewar smelters were joined by two more companies: Mitsubishi Chemical in 1963 and Mitsui Aluminum in 1970. The subsequent erosion of NLM's market predominance has been described as the shift from a "Gulliverian monopoly to a balanced oligopoly" (Nakajima and Muratsu 1976: 76).

The small number of firms operating in the industry reflects the high cost of entry. Because aluminum smelting is highly capital-intensive, large investments are required to obtain economies of scale (a minimum annual production of 100,000 tons). In Japan, the high cost of electricity made access even more difficult. New smelters faced inflated electric bills from oil-fueled power plants.

Despite these barriers to entry, two more companies joined aluminum smelting during the 1960s and in 1970, as pointed out above. Two factors in particular created windows of opportunity through which these additional players could gain access to the industry. One was the brisk expansion of the Japanese aluminum market. Consumption of primary aluminum grew at almost 21 percent annually during the 1960s. The second was that supply was not keeping pace with demand. The high cost of electricity in Japan made domestic aluminum smelters very sensitive to import competition. A key concern, therefore, was to maintain high operating ratios in order to check production costs. Consequently, established companies invested conservatively, and aluminum production capacity lagged behind demand. A few companies attempted to fill this gap as suppliers of primary aluminum (A. Goto 1988: 94, 96).

Given the relatively high barriers to entry, aluminum smelting had an oligopolistic structure worldwide. The Japanese industry was no exception, with only five producers in its market. But one main difference made the Japanese aluminum industry unusual: its lack of vertical integration. The international "aluminum majors" are complex transnational corporations that engage in bauxite mining, alumina production, aluminum smelting, and the fabrication of aluminum products.[2] None of the Japanese smelting firms replicated this pattern of corporate organization. Japanese companies failed to integrate upstream (into bauxite mining) partly because they arrived late to the competition for the richer deposits, which were already controlled by one of the six international aluminum majors. For historical and strategic reasons they did not integrate downstream into fabrication either.

By the 1900s several Japanese companies were rolling, pressing, and fabricating aluminum goods using imported ingot. But a domestic aluminum smelting industry made its appearance only thirty years later, and while fabricators were established as subsidiaries of mining and metal firms, aluminum smelters were set up as divisions of chemical firms. This divide between smelting and fabrication persisted because aluminum smelters saw few merits in downstream integration. Aluminum smelting was the domain of a few producers who enjoyed high and stable profits. In contrast, the fabricating end was characterized by intense competition among numerous firms. Entry into fabrication entailed a rapid expansion of equipment investment and reduced operating rates, which increased the burden of fixed costs and lowered profit rates (Kimura 1983: 9).

The intense rivalry between Japanese smelters and fabricators is exemplified by the controversy surrounding the establishment of a new smelting firm in 1976. The aluminum rolling firm in the Sumitomo group—Sumitomo Light Metals—challenged established practice by proposing to create its own smelting subsidiary, Sumikei. Sumitomo Chemicals sharply opposed the move: "Until now coordination between firms in the Sumitomo group has proceeded smoothly. However, the entry of two firms in the smelting industry goes against the group policy of one industry–one firm. This is not desirable because it will lead to a duplication of investment" (Sumitomo Chemicals 1981: 670). The other smelters shared the concerns of Sumitomo Chemicals, and negotiations for admission to the industry stalled. Sumitomo Light Metals was able to break the deadlock, and earn its entry, by asking for the mediation of Kakuei Tanaka, then minister of industry and international trade.

The Japanese aluminum smelting industry flourished in the first half of the postwar period. During those years, bauxite resources were cheap and plentiful, primary aluminum prices were stable worldwide, and the fast pace of domestic economic growth in the machinery, transportation, and building sectors sustained a growing demand for aluminum. Fueled by a larger consumption of ingot, the Japanese aluminum industry expanded dramatically in the span of two decades: production grew from 36,000 tons in 1950 to over 1 million tons in 1972. By the early 1970s, Japan possessed the second largest aluminum smelting industry in the world (McKern 1976: 149).

THE COLLAPSE OF ALUMINUM SMELTING IN JAPAN

Despite the dynamic growth of ingot production in Japan, the turbulent 1970s uncovered the fragile base upon which the smelters' competitiveness rested. Because energy costs were so high, Japanese smelting companies had never enjoyed export competitiveness. Production costs alone were higher than the average export price per ton charged by the six international aluminum majors. Tariff protection (a 10.6 percent levy) had enabled domestic producers to compete with foreign smelters (Tashita 1976: 6), so trade liberalization dealt a serious blow to the Japanese aluminum smelting industry. As part of the Kennedy Round of international trade negotiations, tariffs for primary aluminum were lowered to 9 percent for industrialized countries and 4.5 percent for developing nations in 1971 (A. Goto 1988: 101). In that same year, 1971, the collapse of the fixed exchange rate system further undermined the competitiveness of the Japanese smelters. As a result of the yen appreciation, the price of imported aluminum fell 28 percent, and domestic fabricators were quick to switch to foreign ingot (Tashita 1976: 12–13).

In the 1970s, trade liberalization and currency realignments had already made the Japanese aluminum smelting industry vulnerable to import competition. Then, the two oil shocks proved deadly. The source of electricity generation (oil, coal, or hydropower) is the most important determinant of the competitiveness of an aluminum smelter.[3] The oil price hikes of 1973 and 1979 were important not merely because they raised the cost of aluminum production worldwide; more significantly, they affected the profitability of aluminum companies differently depending on the power mix of their electricity generation.

After the oil shocks, the Japanese smelters were the most disadvantaged given their extreme dependence on oil for electricity generation. Seventy-one percent of the Japanese smelters' electricity was supplied by oil-fueled power plants. Compare this with European companies, which relied on oil-based electricity for only 11 percent of their power needs (Tilton 1996: 53). Smelters located in regions with plentiful hydroelectric power were thus able to reassert their lead as low-cost producers. The OECD (as quoted in

Peck 1988: 23) estimated that by 1982 the price of electricity for Japanese smelters was twice that paid by companies in the United States and three to seven times higher than in low-cost power locations such as Australia, Brazil, and Canada.

The lack of vertical integration aggravated the situation for Japanese companies in the aftermath of the oil shocks because these enterprises derived their income exclusively from primary aluminum (ingot) production. Once they lost competitiveness in ingot production, Japanese smelters had no other sources of profit. The six international majors were more diversified: their revenue from fabricating activities was four to ten times larger than that from ingot production (Kimura 1983: 4, 9).

Given the electricity price differential and their lack of alternative sources of profit, the Japanese aluminum smelters were easily wiped out by international competition. The performance of the smelting industry quickly deteriorated: in 1976 it recorded 30 billion yen in losses and 50 billion yen in cumulative deficits (ibid.: 14). The chemical companies reacted by separating the highly unprofitable smelting divisions into independent aluminum smelting subsidiaries.[4] In a few years, foreign ingot producers captured the domestic market. By 1981, the volume of imports had surpassed national production, and domestic smelters continued to lose out to foreign ingot. Ten years after the first oil shock, the share of aluminum imports reached 84 percent of the Japanese market, and at present, 99.5 percent of primary aluminum consumed in Japan is imported (Japan Aluminum Federation 2000). Aluminum smelting in Japan did not survive the oil shocks.

The swift dismantling of the Japanese aluminum industry may seem to suggest a laissez-faire Japanese attitude toward declining industries. But Japanese smelters, bureaucrats, and politicians did not just resign themselves to the extinction of the industry. Through their domestic and international adjustment strategies they tried to check or even preempt (through overseas relocation) the negative effects of abrupt and irrevocable loss of competitiveness. On the domestic front, the core of the adjustment program rested on orderly capacity curtailment subsidized through tariff rebates (Tilton 1996).

Faced with this dramatic reversal of fortune in aluminum smelting, the Japanese government established the Aluminum Subcommittee as part of the Industrial Structural Deliberation Council in October 1974. Four years later, the government designated aluminum smelting a structurally depressed industry and drafted a five-year stabilization plan. This plan recommended gradually reducing aluminum smelting capacity to 1.1 million tons per year by 1983 (see Table 6.1). To encourage industry compliance with these plant-scrapping goals, MITI approved a six-month recession cartel.

Subsidies, however, were the most powerful lever over industry. The 1978

TABLE 6.1

The Domestic Death of Japanese Aluminum Smelting, 1978–1999 (thousand tons)

Company	Initial capacity, 1978	1.1 million tons plan, 1978–83	Actual capacity, 1980*	700,000 tons plan, 1981–83	Actual capacity, 1982*	350,000 tons plan, 1983–88	Actual capacity, 1988	Production, 1999
Nippon Light Metals	377	198		136		64	35	11
Shōwa Light Metals	242	162		76		32	Closed	Closed
Sumitomo Aluminum Refining	408	296		181		83	Closed	Closed
Mitsubishi Light Metals	352	236		76		51	Closed	Closed
Mitsui Aluminum	163	144		144		125	Closed	Closed
Sumikei Aluminum	99	99		99		0	Closed	Closed
Total	1,641	1,135	1,136	712	743	354	35	11

SOURCES: Kimura 1983: 11; JAF 2000: 149; additional data provided by Nippon Amazon Aluminum.

* Individual company production data not available for 1980 and 1982.

report of the Aluminum Subcommittee approved a tariff/quota program that was first implemented during 1978–79. Through this system, importers would pay a smaller tariff (reduced from 9.5 to 5.5 percent) for an import volume equal to the consumption in excess of the domestic capacity to be maintained under the stabilization plan.[5] Imports that exceeded this quota had to pay the normal tariff. Nevertheless, importers could not retain the earnings they made from paying lower duties; they had to pay back their tariff savings to the Association for the Promotion of the Structural Improvement of the Aluminum Industry. In turn, this association distributed payments to smelting companies based on the value of capacity scrapped multiplied by a 6.6 percent interest rate. The purpose of the measure was to help smelters cover the annual interest cost of idle capacity (A. Goto 1988: 111). The tariff/quota system was extended for one more year at a lower preferential tariff rate of 4.5 percent.

Despite these government incentives for orderly capacity reduction, market realities forced a much faster dismantling of refining equipment. In 1980 actual capacity in the aluminum smelting industry was already at 1.1 million tons, three years ahead of schedule (see Table 6.1). The situation of the smelters turned dire with the renewed upheaval of the world petroleum market. The second oil shock forced a revision of the basic stabilization plan in 1981: the revised goal for 1983 was to bring smelting capacity down to 700,000 tons per year. To facilitate the shutting down of the smelters, in 1982 the government initiated a new tariff exemption system that allowed domestic producers to import, duty-free, a volume of ingot equivalent to the capacity they had scrapped (Sheard 1991). But the stabilization policy had little effect because the Japanese smelting industry contracted at such a dizzying pace. In 1981 there were six companies and fourteen smelting plants operating in Japan; a year later only five firms and seven smelters remained open. In 1982 smelting capacity dropped to 743,000 tons. Once more, actual scrapping surpassed the official blueprints for orderly downsizing.

The 1983 Structural Improvement Law adopted a new five-year adjustment plan for aluminum smelting. It recommended the reduction of refining capacity to 350,000 tons per year by 1988. However, by 1986 capacity had already contracted to 320,000 tons, and low operating ratios continued to haunt the industry. Moreover, the aluminum industry lost its major source of subsidies in 1987. In response to foreign criticism, the Japanese government terminated the tariff rebate program. The US government and Alcoa had complained, with merit, that tariff rebates discriminated against American exports. Since spot market transactions did not benefit from the reduced duties, the Japanese government used the rebate program not to deter imports, but to favor ingot supplied by Japanese smelters abroad or through long-term contracts (Tilton 1996: 60).

The collapse of domestic aluminum smelting was complete by the late 1980s. In ten years, Japanese aluminum refining capacity had dropped from 1.6 million tons to 35,000 tons. Since 1988 only one smelting plant in Japan has continued to operate. The Kanbara smelter of Nippon Light Metals survived because it relied on cheap hydroelectric power, but its 1999 annual production was a mere 11,000 tons. To some observers, the extinction of Japanese smelting in Japan speaks not of industrial restructuring, but of "destructuring" (Samuels 1983: 498).

POLICYMAKING AND BURDEN-SHARING

Rescuing the ingot refining business required compromises between government bureaucrats and different branches of industry, with politicians acting as key mediators. Tilton has argued that the state played the predominant role in defining the adjustment prescription for the smelters: "The particular pace and manner in which the industry was shut down reflected state priorities" (1996: 52). MITI was in charge of overseeing capacity cuts and allocating tariff rebates. The ministry was also responsible for monitoring recession cartels and for creating a stockpile system, and it launched a campaign to persuade refiners to buy domestic ingot.[6]

Finally, MITI influenced the negotiations on the assistance package for aluminum smelters by hosting the deliberation councils, or *shingikai*—and most important, selecting their members. However, the downsizing policies for the smelting industry revealed the limits of MITI's power. Market realities defied bureaucratic planning, and the ministry's plans for an orderly reduction of smelting capacity had to be revised downward constantly (Samuels 1983). And despite its determined efforts, MITI was unable to compel users of aluminum to buy overpriced domestic ingot (Tilton 1996: 70).

Adjustment policies were not dictated solely by refining corporate interests either. The smelters relied on their business organization, the Japan Aluminum Federation (JAF), to make the case for maintaining a sizable domestic industry. The smelters pointed to their positive contribution to stabilizing the aluminum supply, providing high-quality ingot, organizing overseas investment projects, speeding technological innovation, and preventing total reliance on foreign ingot to supply the Japanese market. However, some of smelters' most sought-after demands were not met: tariff increases, publicly supported ingot prices, and cheaper electricity rates (Tilton 1996: 60, 74).[7]

Smelters and MITI bureaucrats were not the only parties attempting to mold the future of Japanese aluminum smelting. Another major bureaucratic player was the Ministry of Finance, which opposed subsidizing an uncompetitive industry. MOF was particularly critical of the tariff rebate program because it circumvented the normal process of legislative oversight over industry subsidies, and because it trespassed on its own turf of tariff revenue collection (ibid.: 73). Policymaking for aluminum smelting restructuring was also highly politicized. The LDP intervened at key junctures, supporting the tariff rebate program and drafting specific party demands for financial assistance to the industry (Samuels 1983: 500). JAF enlisted the support of individual LDP politicians from regions where smelters were located. Hiroshi Yamazaki (head of the Subcommittee on Aluminum), for example, was from Shizuoka prefecture, site of NLM'S Kanbara plant. LDP support of JAF's demands was crucial in extending the tariff rebate in 1981 (at a lower preferential tariff rate) and in expanding the stockpile program in 1982 (Tilton 1996: 74–75).

The Aluminum Subcommittee was the forum where the various interest groups in aluminum smelting met.[8] Despite some of the disagreements noted above, stakeholders in aluminum restructuring managed to reach consensus on the two pillars for the transformation of the refining industry: gradual dismantling of the production base at home, and its replacement with a network of offshore Japanese smelting plants (Tilton 1996). The reestablishment of the Japanese smelting plant in locations with low-cost energy was firmly supported by both the government and industry. The first report of the Aluminum Subcommittee in February 1975, for example, advocated an "orderly overseas expansion" to foreign countries with ample hydropower resources. Subsequent reports endorsing capacity curtailment in Japan also recommended that Japanese smelters operating abroad supply in the long term roughly 50 percent of the Japanese consumption of ingot (Imuta 1993: 96, 103).

And yet the costs of the domestic and international components of the aluminum adjustment strategy were divided very differently between the state and the private sector. Business groups (both parent companies and main banks) absorbed the vast majority of the domestic adjustment costs of aluminum smelting (see Sheard 1991: 20–24). Between 1978 and 1986, public aid for domestic adjustment totaled 175 billion yen (83 billion yen in subsidies and 92 billion yen in JDB loans and guarantees on banks' loans to the stockpiling program). Compare this with the 389 billion yen in losses endured by parent and shareholder firms between 1981 and 1986. In addition to writing off losses, *keiretsu* firms came to the aid of the ailing smelters by investing an extra 186 billion yen in paper companies buying idle smelting capacity, and main banks also reduced or eliminated interest payments on their loans (around 25 billion yen).

The most generous financial assistance from the state to the smelters came in the form of loans for overseas investment—276 billion yen in Japan Exim-bank credit (ibid.: 20). Indeed, the government absorbed a much larger proportion of the expenses for the industry's international adjustment strategy.

The multinationalization of the aluminum smelting industry has not been as thoroughly analyzed as the domestic restructuring program. Therefore, the remainder of this chapter discusses both the early attempts to secure bauxite resources with FDI projects and the politics behind the massive public financing of national aluminum smelting projects once the industry was irreparably hurt by the oil shocks.

Preferential FDI financing for aluminum smelting was a strategic governmental response to the loss of comparative advantage in the domestic manufacturing of a key industrial input. It is also a useful window into the politics of government-business relations in Japanese MNC expansion. The national projects analyzed in detail here underscore the perils to the state of an open commitment to keep the offshore smelters afloat, the tensions between the government and private investors as they become investment partners abroad, and the ultimate influence of consumer power on the success of the policy to reestablish the Japanese aluminum smelting industry overseas.

The Politics of International Adjustment

Competition for resource acquisition among the large aluminum firms was acute in the postwar period (Tamaki 1969). The international majors sought mining concessions on the richest ore deposits, and by the mid-1960s vertical channels for bauxite procurement were firmly in place. The incentives for the international majors to integrate upward (into bauxite and alumina production) were strong because of the high risks and huge capital requirements of bauxite mining (UNCTC 1981). In turn, the six majors' dominance over the bauxite/alumina industry was ensured by their financial resources, superior mining technology, and marketing advantages (access to captive outlets). Altogether, the bauxite production of the six majors represented 80 percent of the total output of the free-market economies (Fukuhara 1969: 59–60). Consequently, bauxite and alumina were traded mostly in intrafirm transactions and the market for arm's-length sales was little developed.

The bauxite procurement policies of Japanese smelters differed from the methods employed by the six majors. In 1965, Japan obtained most of its bauxite through short- and long-term contracts, with only one instance of equity participation in a foreign mine (Seaba in Malaysia). In 1960, Nippon Light Metals acquired 25 percent of Alcan's South East Asia Bauxite and was thereby entitled to an output quota from the Seaba mine of 250,000–300,000 tons of bauxite per year (ibid.: 70–72). Nippon Light Metals' singular move reflected its close relations with Alcan (after World War II the Canadian giant acquired 50 percent of NLM's equity). As partners in Seaba these two firms cooperated in the area of bauxite procurement.

THE SEARCH FOR BAUXITE

The Japanese smelters' reliance on market transactions for raw materials supply was unique. In addition, the Japanese companies distinguished themselves by getting most of their ore from Asian bauxite producers, primarily Malaysia, Indonesia, and Australia. However, Japanese firms attempted to hedge their risks in two ways. First, these enterprises created dominant-buyer relations. As Kojima (1978: 204–7) points out, Japan's (monopsony) bargaining power is enhanced if a supplier depends to a large extent on the Japanese market as an outlet for its ore. This was true for two of the main bauxite suppliers, Indonesia and Malaysia. In 1973, Indonesia sold 93 percent of its bauxite to Japan, and Malaysia 95 percent. Still, Japan got 58 percent of its bauxite from Australia. So, to prevent their main bauxite supplier from acquiring monopoly bargaining power, Japanese smelters carefully cultivated alternative sources of supply (Malaysia, Indonesia, and India).

The second risk-hedging strategy was to sign long-term contracts. Spot transactions failed to guarantee a stable supply of bauxite for an extended amount of time at a reasonable price. For this reason, long-term contracts were deemed a better procurement alternative. In fact, the Japanese smelters were the most active buyers in a market characterized by scarce market transactions. Only six of the twenty-nine bauxite producers sold on the open market. The main customers for three of these firms (Comalco, Gove Alumina, and Aneka Tambang Mining) were Japanese smelters (Nippon Light Metals, Shōwa Denko, and Sumitomo Chemicals).[9] The emergence of arm's-length bauxite transactions—although limited—was in fact sustained by the "exchange relationships between the Australian and Southeast Asian producers, and the Japanese aluminum firms" (Stuckey 1983: 117). The ties with Comalco were particularly strong because some Japanese alumina refineries had been modified to suit the special attributes of its ore.[10]

Nevertheless, long-term contracting for bauxite procurement was jeopardized by the more vocal demands for control by states in bauxite-producing countries.[11] These governments refused to simply contract away their ore and let clients know they expected a deeper financial commitment (loans and equity) to their mining and refining projects. Just when host governments acquired a larger say in shaping conditions for bauxite supply, Japan's consumption of bauxite ore grew substantially, from 1 million to 4 million tons during the first half of the 1960s. To meet the larger bauxite requirements of the Japanese aluminum industry, a more active procurement strategy was necessary, with direct equity participation in third-world mining projects in Asia and elsewhere.

Consequently, several investment plans for bauxite mining were drafted at the turn of the 1970s. The newfound willingness to mine abroad is best exemplified by the creation of the Aluminum Resources Development Corporation (ARDECO) in 1970. Through this investment consortium the five Japanese rival smelters proposed to coordinate their overseas investment plans for bauxite and alumina production. ARDECO's initial paid-in capital was 250 million yen, but the smelters hoped to obtain an additional 350 million yen equity contribution from the Metal Mining Agency of Japan (MMAJ) to support the industrywide effort (K. Fujii 1971: 237).

ARDECO was an ambitious bauxite mining initiative comprising survey work, prospecting, and the development and marketing of the ore. Despite the high hopes for smelter collaboration in overseas mining projects, almost all plans were either postponed or abandoned (see Table 6.2). The only two significant exceptions were Seaba and Alcan-Weipa, both ventures undertaken by Nippon Light Metals and Alcan. Although four additional bauxite and alumina projects had been conceived for Australia, they did not materialize. Australian government policies (resource protection and foreign exchange restrictions) discouraged Japanese smelters from carrying out these plans (Jūkagaku 1976: 195). The other projects were casualties of weak growth in the aluminum market, soaring inflation in some host countries, and a decline in the corporate performance of Japanese smelters in the early 1970s (Jūkagaku 1976: 195; Sumitomo Chemicals 1981: 671–72).

Japan's FDI in bauxite lagged behind overseas investment in mining projects for other nonferrous metals. By 1974 only 441 million yen had been invested in bauxite exploitation abroad, whereas FDI in copper totaled 245 billion yen by 1980, and 35 billion yen for both zinc and lead (Jūkagaku 1976: 195; N. Tanaka 1991: 350). Three powerful factors contributed to the passive attitude of Japanese smelters toward overseas bauxite mining: the lack of a bauxite mining tradition, weak official support, and the ore's price stability. As mentioned before, because Japanese aluminum smelters evolved as refining divisions of chemical companies, they had no previous expertise in mineral extraction; nor could they develop it domestically, since Japan lacks bauxite deposits (Uemura 1969: 74). Moreover, by the time Japanese smelters entered the competition for raw materials, the richest bauxite deposits were already under the control of the six majors, and the remaining mines were more costly to develop.

The institutional machinery in place to support Japanese overseas mining projects was not helpful to aluminum smelters. The MMAJ initiated a program for overseas prospecting and mining in 1968, just a few years before the post–oil shock recession in Japanese aluminum eroded the demand for bauxite imports.[12] In addition, bauxite was not assigned a high priority on MMAJ's agenda for the overseas mining of nonferrous metals. In 1968 the metals targeted by MMAJ's assistance were copper, lead, zinc, and manganese; only in 1971 was bauxite added (H. Tanaka 1993: 393). Similarly, bauxite was excluded

TABLE 6.2

The Unrealized Venture: Bauxite and Alumina Projects

Project name	Country	Type of operation	Japanese investors	Product	Status in 1976
Darling Ranges	Australia	Prospect survey	Nippon Light Metals, Shōwa Denko, Sumitomo Chemicals	Alumina	Unrealized
Kinbare	Australia	Prospect survey	Sumitomo Chemicals, Shōwa Denko, Sumitomo Shoji, Marubeni	Alumina	Unrealized
Terabari	Australia	n.a.	ARDECO	Bauxite, alumina	Canceled
Weipa	Australia	Prospect survey	Nippon Light Metals, Shōwa Denko, Sumitomo Chemicals	Bauxite	Pending
Fidji	Fiji	Prospect and develop	Nippon Light Metals, Shōwa Denko, Sumitomo Chemicals	Bauxite	Canceled
Bintan	Indonesia	Prospect and develop	Nippon Light Metals, Shōwa Denko, Sumitomo Chemicals	Alumina	Under examination
Seaba	Malaysia	Prospect and develop	Nippon Light Metals	Bauxite	In operation
Alcan-Weipa	Australia	Prospect and develop	Nippon Light Metals		Operation at reduced capacity
Ghana, Kibi	Ghana	Prospect and develop	ARDECO	Bauxite	Suspended
Anantenia	Madagascar	Prospect and develop	ARDECO	Bauxite	Suspended
Rennel	Solomon Islands	Prospect and develop	Mitsui Light Metals	Bauxite	Under examination

SOURCE: Jūgaku Kōgyō Tsūshinsha 1976.

from the overseas equity investment program—for MITI-approved projects—launched by MMAJ in 1974 (Jūkagaku 1976: 67). Therefore ARDECO had no chance of receiving a capital injection from MMAJ.

Several traits of the world's bauxite industry also explain Japan's reluctance to invest abroad. Worldwide bauxite reserves were (and are) plentiful. UNCTC (1981: 4) estimated reserves at 5 billion tons in 1978, enough to sustain consumption for 300 years at then current levels. Moreover, the price of this ore was stable, and even declined during the 1950s and 1960s. Thus there was no need for a strategic response from industry and government to participate directly in the extraction of bauxite. The first attempts to significantly raise the price of bauxite were not made until 1974 by the newly formed producers' cartel (the International Bauxite Association).[13] By this time, however, turmoil in energy markets had reduced the competitiveness of the aluminum refining industry in Japan, making overseas smelting projects the priority both for industry and government.

RECREATING COMPARATIVE ADVANTAGE OFFSHORE

Domestically, Japanese aluminum smelting did not survive the oil shocks. Offshore, ingot production was reborn through FDI in large-scale projects. In 2000, there were ten smelters operating abroad with Japanese capital participation (see Table 6.3).[14] The overseas expansion of the Japanese smelting industry can be divided into four broad phases. Early projects (Intalco and Eastalco) were located in the United States, required small equity participation, and involved a trading company and two fabricating firms. The main purpose of these two projects was to gain access to a share of the output through a moderate contribution of capital by traders and consumers of the ingot. The smelters themselves were not yet involved in foreign operations.

During the second phase of aluminum refining FDI, Japanese smelting companies ventured into overseas production by forging ties with foreign companies and by undertaking commercial smelting projects—that is, without Japanese government equity participation. The investment requirements for NZAS, Alpack, Venalum, and Boyne Smelters were relatively moderate because they did not need to pay for the construction of a hydroelectric power plant to feed the smelter. In the case of Boyne Smelters (Australia), electricity was provided by a coal-fueled plant, and for the other projects the host governments paid for the hydropower plant construction.

The partnership between Sumitomo Chemicals and Comalco opened the way for the first overseas venture by a Japanese smelter. The NZAS project originated with an invitation from Comalco to participate in the construction of a smelter in New Zealand (to be fed with Comalco's bauxite). The Australian firm had obtained the New Zealand government's commitment to undertake the construction of the hydroelectric power plant and to

TABLE 6.3

Offshore Rebirth: Japanese-Owned Aluminum Smelters Abroad (thousand tons)

Project (country)	Annual capacity	Japanese intake	Power	Year production started	Japanese equity (%)	Company shares
Intalco (United States)	254	64	Hydro	1966	25	Mitsui Bussan (11%); Toyo Sash (7%); YKK (7%); Alcoa (75%)
Eastalco (United States)	160	40	Hydro	1970	25	Mitsui Bussan (11%); Toyo Sash (7%); YKK (7%); Alcoa (75%)
NZAS (New Zealand)	313	65	Hydro	1971	22	Sumitomo Chemical (22%); Comalco Australia (78%)
Alpack (Canada)	90	45	Hydro	1977	50	Nippon Light Metals (50%); Alcan Canada (50%)
Venalum (Venezuela)	450	90	Hydro	1978	20	Shōwa Denko (7%); Sumitomo Chemical (4%); Mitsubishi Aluminum (1%); Kobe Seikō (4%); Mitsubishi Materials (3%); Marubeni (1%); Compania Venezolana Guyana (80%)
Boyne Smelters (Australia)	490	224	Coal	1982	50	Sumitomo Chemical (4.5%); Sumitomo Light Metals (17%); Kobe Seikō (9.5%); YKK (9.5%); Mitsubishi Shōji (9.5%); Comalco Australia (30%); Australia Metals (20%)
Asahan (Indonesia)	225	133	Hydro	1982	59	Nippon Asahan Aluminium (five smelters, seven *sōgō shōsha*, and OECF) (59%); Indonesian govt. (41%)
Albras (Brazil)	345	169	Hydro	1985	49	Nippon Amazon Aluminum (five smelters, twelve *sōgō shōsha* and banks, fourteen users, OECF) (49%); CVRD (51%)
Alouette (Canada)	230	46	Hydro	1992	20	Kobe Seikō (13.33%); Marubeni (6.67%); Austria Metal (20%); SGF (20%); VAW (20%); Hogobenz (20%)
Mozal (Mozambique)	250	63	Hydro	2000	25	Mitsubishi Shōji (25%); Billiton (47%); South Africa Development Corporation (24%); Mozambique govt. (4%)

SOURCE: Japan Aluminum Federation 2000.

charge preferential electricity rates to the smelter. Comalco needed the participation of Sumitomo to reduce its capital contribution (Sumitomo took a 22 percent equity share) and to ensure an outlet for the ingot smelted. For Sumitomo too, the project had several merits: it guaranteed a long-term supply of Comalco's alumina and secured access to low-cost electricity (Jūkagaku 1976: 196).

The Comalco-Sumitomo relationship bore fruit again in the Boyne Smelters project. This time Comalco took a 30 percent equity share, the Sumitomo group 21 percent, three more Japanese companies 28.5 percent, and a local subsidiary of Kaiser 20 percent. The Boyne Smelter relies completely on alumina refined from Comalco's bauxite (Stuckey 1983: 124). Boyne Smelters is the largest refining plant in the world with Japanese equity participation (with an annual capacity of 490,000 tons) and is the largest supplier to the Japanese market.

Nippon Light Metals' first investment in a foreign aluminum refining venture (just as in the case of bauxite mining abroad) was eased by its strong ties with Alcan. In 1974 these two companies jointly set up the Alpack smelter plant in Canada, which began operation three years later. Alpack's annual capacity production of 90,000 tons is divided evenly between the two partners. Nippon Light Metals imports the ingot back to Japan, while Alcan sends its share to its Kitimat fabrication factory (Nippon Light Metals 1991: 121).

Venalum also originated as a collaboration between a Japanese smelting firm and one of the six majors. This time Reynolds courted the participation of Sumitomo Chemicals and Mitsubishi Light Metals in the construction of a smelter in Venezuela's Guyana. At the same time, another group of Japanese companies (Shōwa Denko, Kobe Seikō, and Marubeni) was negotiating with Venezuela the construction of a second smelter. The Japanese side offered to provide 80 percent of the equity capital in exchange for an annual ingot supply of 150,000 tons (Sumitomo Chemicals 1981: 673–74). After the first oil shock, however, the Venezuelan government intensified its policy of national control over natural resources. Venezuela consolidated the two ventures planned with Japanese companies into one and provided 80 percent of the equity capital. Japanese investors financed the rest after Reynolds dropped out of Venalum. Japan's intake of ingot diminished to 90,000 tons per year, and Japanese investors did not acquire managerial rights. Because Japanese firms were kept out of daily business matters, observers have considered the Venalum operation closer to a long-term contract in exchange for equity financing than to a Japanese development project of ingot production abroad (Jūkagaku 1976: 198).

The third phase of Japanese investment in overseas aluminum smelting is epitomized by the national project formula.[15] The officially endorsed projects—Asahan and Albras—were distinct in two respects. First, for the first time the Japanese government, prompted by the collapse of the domestic refining base, joined in an overseas smelting venture to guarantee a stable ingot supply. The second novel element of the national project was that all firms in the industry were required to participate in the venture. Although plans for an industrywide undertaking of aluminum smelting abroad had been made before, they had not materialized. ARDECO had identified five different projects for the joint participation of the five smelters and had assigned each smelter organizational responsibility over one venture. Of the smelting projects identified by ARDECO, only two were actually carried out once the Japanese government and industry sped up their restructuring efforts in the post–oil shock period.[16] By prearrangement among the smelters, Sumitomo Chemicals was the project leader in Asahan and Mitsui Aluminum in Albras.

The Japanese public-private overseas smelting ventures came onstream in the early and mid-1980s. Interest in overseas investment later receded, reflecting investors' depleted coffers after having committed huge amounts of capital to the two national projects. Only in the early 1990s did Japanese investors participate again in the establishment of an overseas smelter, the Alouette smelting plant. It was constructed by Japanese, Canadian, and European firms to make use of Canada's abundant hydropower resources. The 20 percent output share allocated to the Japanese partners was divided between Kobe Seikō (13.37 percent) and Marubeni (6.63 percent) (Marques 1994: 255).

The most recent Japanese investment in aluminum smelting is the Mozal project. A general trading company—Mitsubishi Shōji—acquired minority ownership in order to import back to Japan 63,000 tons of ingot per year. Interestingly, the fourth phase in aluminum smelting FDI closely resembles the first one: projects have been undertaken by fabricators and traders in liaison with foreign companies, and Japanese investors have preferred modest equity shares.

The Asahan and Albras projects are explored in more detail here because they represent the most direct response to the abrupt loss of comparative advantage after the oil shocks, and because they figure prominently in the subsequent discussion of foreign direct investment and resource diplomacy.

ASAHAN: ELUSIVE SELF-SUSTAINABILITY AND PUBLIC BAILOUT

The high altitude of Lake Toba and the high annual rainfall in the region make the Asahan River an ideal place for hydropower generation. Over the years the six majors and Japanese aluminum smelting companies expressed interest in establishing a smelter in North Sumatra. But foreign investors balked at the Indonesian government's need to borrow to construct the infrastructure for electricity generation.

In August 1972 the Indonesian government sent a special envoy to Japan to request public financial assistance to construct a hydroelectric power plant and aluminum smelter. The Japanese government delayed answering, but its reluctance to fund such an expensive undertaking disappeared quickly after the first oil shock, and negotiations between Japan and Indonesia then proceeded swiftly. By January 1974 the five Japanese smelting companies had hammered out a basic agreement with Indonesia.

The Japanese cabinet designated the Asahan venture a national project entitled to public financial support. With the official agreement signed between the two countries in July 1975, Japan ratified its commitment to a project of unprecedented proportions: three water dams, two hydroelectric power plants (Sigura-gura Falls and Tangga Falls), a transmission line, an aluminum smelter, and related infrastructure (including a port, a town, and roads). The major items in the construction bill were the power plants and aluminum smelter, which constituted 30 percent and 55 percent of the total cost, respectively.[17]

The Japanese investment consortium set up the company Nippon Asahan Aluminum (NAA), capitalized at 68 billion yen. The OECF held a 50 percent share, the five smelters 7.5 percent each, and the trading companies for each business group divided among themselves the remaining 12.5 percent.[18] In this way, the Asahan aluminum plant became the first overseas smelting venture undertaken jointly by all Japanese smelters. Each smelting company was entitled to a seat on NAA's board of directors, and the Japanese share of the Asahan smelter output was divided equally in five parts. In other words, the distribution of ingot production fell along *keiretsu* lines, with each smelter working out the marketing strategy for its ingot quota with its trading company. These arrangements notwithstanding, Sumitomo Chemicals had a powerful say in the running of NAA. Officials from Sumitomo Chemicals filled the key positions of chairman of NAA's board of directors and president of Inalum, and NAA is staffed mostly with Sumitomo Chemicals employees.[19]

In early 1976 the joint venture between Indonesia and Japan (Indonesia Asahan Aluminum, known as Inalum) was founded. Both parties agreed that Inalum would manage the hydropower plant–aluminum smelter complex for thirty years after the initiation of operations and would then transfer control to the Indonesian government. When Inalum was first established, Japan owned 90 percent and Indonesia 10 percent. However, when inflation drove up the estimated construction costs from 250 billion to 411 billion yen, Indonesia increased its capital contribution to 25 percent. Once the issue of extra financing was solved, the construction of the dams, power plants, and smelter proceeded as scheduled. In 1982 a smelting plant with an annual capacity of 225,000 tons began operation.

Although the Asahan project was completed successfully and was considered to be quite competitive internationally, it was saddled with a large depreciation burden and debt in a strong currency. Capital costs amounted to as much as 30 percent of total costs, making the Asahan smelter very susceptible to exchange rate and international aluminum price fluctuations.[20] In 1987 a plunge in world prices for ingot and the sharp appreciation of the yen put a severe financial strain on the project. The Japanese government responded with an emergency assistance package to reduce interest rates, extend repayment periods, and increase the equity/debt ratio. According to NAA, these measures rescued the Asahan smelter: "By these reconstruction measures Inalum was saved from the serious crisis. It is not an exaggeration to say that without NAA's efforts of that time Inalum would not have been able to survive."[21]

In addition, the Indonesian government agreed to increase its capital contribution to Inalum, thereby raising its ownership share to 41 percent. Nevertheless, a year later relations between the two partners deteriorated over a disagreement about the redistribution of output related to the change in ownership shares. The aluminum joint venture reached its low point in June 1988 when the Indonesian government decided to suspend all exports of aluminum ingot to Japan. Although the 1975 master agreement had stipulated that 66 percent of the smelted ingot would be shipped to Japan, until 1987 exports had been in the range of 75 percent of total production. After the financial restructuring in 1987, the Indonesian government demanded that its share of output be raised to 40 percent, and that it be free to sell to third countries whatever ingot was not consumed domestically.[22] Negotiations dragged on for six months until both Indonesian conditions were met.

Financial problems continued to plague the Asahan project. Between 1987 and 1993, the special assistance measures had saved as much as 23.2 billion yen in interest payments. However, the sharp appreciation of the yen in the early 1990s once again necessitated emergency action to salvage the Asahan project. In 1994 the Japanese cabinet approved a larger equity participation from the OECF, as well as lower interest rates with extended repayment periods for the loans awarded by the Japan Eximbank. Commercial banks agreed to ease their loan terms, and the other partners in the project (the Indonesian government and Japanese private investors) agreed to increase their equity participation to match the OECF's additional contribution.

Yet a few years later Inalum was once more facing a critical situation. In 1997 and 1998 a drought in the Lake Toba region forced a reduction in the smelter's production level, and led to steep losses. And once more, the yen appreciation multiplied the dollar amount required to serve the yen-denominated debt. This time the government did not offer an additional rescue package because Inalum continued to meet its payment obligations. But the financial condition of the Asahan project remained fragile because the cash flow was generated by postponing repayment of the principal to the end of the loan term.[23]

For the Japanese government, the Asahan smelter was a very costly commitment. And given the leveraged financial situation of the Asahan venture, a future Japanese government bailout of the project cannot be ruled out.

ALBRAS AND ALUNORTE: SCALING BACK A NATIONAL PROJECT

During the days of ARDECO, Japanese smelters identified the Amazon as a site with potential for aluminum refining. As in Indonesia, the oil shock was a powerful stimulus to carry out the project. In January 1974, Japanese investors reached an agreement with Brazil to jointly build the largest alumina/aluminum complex in the world, with an annual capacity of 1.3 million tons of alumina and 640,000 tons of ingot. Brazil's dream of becoming the seventh sister seemed close at hand (Marques 1990: 192).

In the original proposal, the aluminum joint venture was expected to make a significant financial contribution to the construction of the Tucurui hydropower plant ($800 million or 60 percent of total cost). In fact, in 1973 the Brazilian Ministry of Mines and Energy had drafted the "law of participation" to permit foreign investment in electricity by major consumers (Bunker 1994: 289). However, the Japanese side balked at financing a power plant/aluminum complex worth $3 billion after a 1975 feasibility study, which revealed the unit cost of ingot to be $4,700 per ton when the market price was only $900 (Marques 1990: 182).

To recapture Japanese interest in the project, the Brazilian government made generous concessions. It agreed to construct the Tucurui power plant and other infrastructure, to guarantee all international loans for the project, and to provide electricity at discounted rates. Moreover, the Albras smelter was scaled back to 320,000 tons, and the alumina plant became an independent project named Alunorte (with an expected capacity of 800,000 tons).

Enticed by these incentives, Japanese investors agreed to participate in the Brazilian aluminum venture, though it was evident that Japanese companies were losing their enthusiasm after the substantial financial commitments they had acquired in Indonesia.

First, Albras was freed from contributing to the construction of the Tucurui power plant, and the Japanese government did not offer financing for electricity infrastructure either. The Brazilian government resorted to tied French loans to finance the hydropower plant (A. Hall 1989: 55). Second, the Japanese government and private firms were more reluctant to disburse large amounts of money, even after the venture was designated a national project in September 1976. The OECF contributed only 40 percent of the equity capital for the investment consortium Nippon Amazon Aluminum Company (NAAC), and thirty-one firms had to be enlisted to provide the remaining funds.[24] The five smelters contributed 28.5 percent of the paid-in capital, ten trading companies 18.31 percent, and fabricators, ingot consumers, and two financial institutions covered the rest (Marques 1994: 246).[25] NAAC's membership expanded because aluminum consumer firms (such as Nissan) were also asked to make a financial contribution to the project. Many companies were unwilling to commit themselves to the Amazon venture, so Keidanren's muscle together with MITI's guidance was necessary to persuade them.[26]

Once the financial obligations of Japanese public and private investors were sorted out, two joint ventures were established in September 1978. Japan acquired a 49 percent equity share in Albras and 39 percent in Alunorte. Although in both cases Japanese investors were satisfied with a minority ownership share, safeguards were introduced to protect their interests: NAAC controlled all technical and planning matters and had a right to exit the contract if a disagreement with the majority shareholder arose (Marques 1990: 185).

Construction of Albras and Alunorte began in 1981, but a depressed international alumina market compromised the future of Amazonian oxide production. In 1983, NAAC insisted on suspending the construction of the alumina factory for three years and on using cheap imports from Alcoa's plants in Australia and Surinam instead. Brazil accepted its partner's demands because it preferred the option of slowing down to cancellation of the project.[27] The smelter's construction made steady progress, but the prospects for the alumina plant were dim.

In October 1985 the first phase of Albras began operation (a year after the Tucurui hydropower plant had been completed). But the Japanese retired from the Alunorte project in 1986 by converting the balance of loans committed to nonvoting shares. Skeptical about the financial viability of Alunorte in a depressed world alumina market, Japanese investors took unprecedented action by withdrawing from a national project. The Japanese move was strongly criticized in Brazil because it thwarted the original goal of downstream integration from bauxite mining into refining and smelting, and it forced a bauxite-rich nation and alumina producer since 1945 to import the oxide to feed the Amazon smelter (Machado 1994: 306).

In 1987 the Albras smelter also ran into trouble related to the sharp yen appreciation and recession in the aluminum market. As part of a rescue program, the Japanese cabinet approved an additional injection of OECF equity capital, extended the loan repayment periods, and reduced interest rates on the loans (from 7.14 percent to 5.0 percent for Japan Eximbank financing, and from 7.86 percent to 5.2 percent for commercial bank credit). Again in the 1990s the yen appreciation hurt the Albras project, which collected its revenues in dollars but repaid its debt in yen. The Japanese government approved a second assistance package in October 1994, consisting of the same elements: additional financing (NAAC supplied another 3 billion yen) and lower interest rates (reduced from 5.0 percent to 4.5 percent for Japan Eximbank loans, and from 5.4 percent to 4.9 percent for commercial loans).[28]

At the end of the century, the financial condition of Albras finally began to improve. In 1996 it still registered losses (38 million yen), but a year later it generated 98 million yen in profits. This turnabout was the result of a recovery in the world price of ingot, cost efficiency (with the smelter operating at full capacity), and successful reduction of the yen-denominated debt (by almost half). Almost thirty years after the establishment of NAAC, the Albras smelter is expected to yield its first dividends by 2005.

A recovery in international alumina prices gave Japanese investors second thoughts about their decision to drop out of Alunorte. They expressed interest in rejoining the alumina refining project as early as 1988, but negotiations between NAAC and the Brazilian state mining company remained inconclusive.[29] In 1993 the Brazilian government decided to wait no longer and completed the plant in collaboration with domestic firms. Alunorte (with a capacity of 1.5 million tons) began operation in August 1995.

Only in March 1996 did the Japanese return to the venture by converting back their nonvoting shares. But they made no fresh injections of capital despite additions to Alunorte's capacity. Instead, they used the previously committed funds to obtain a 12.2 percent equity share in the project.[30] The status of Alunorte as a national project became increasingly ambiguous, given Japan's unprecedented withdrawal and subsequent negotiations for reentry. The term "seminational project" had to be coined to explain a venture in which OECF and Japan Eximbank financing remained in place but in which the private sector had reneged on its original commitment and refused to risk new money. Japan's participation in the development of Brazil's aluminum industry effectively illustrates the limitations of Japanese public/private cooperation in a fluctuating international market.

FDI and Security of Supply: Government Policy on "Development Imports"

Japan's dearth of natural resources makes vulnerability to overseas supply a key concern of its foreign economic policy. Japanese policymakers coined the term "comprehensive security" to stress the additional perils that economies deprived of raw materials face. MITI could hardly assign more importance to continuous mineral imports: "Mineral resources are the lifeblood which sustains the life of the people and their industrial activity. Japan depends almost entirely on imports for its mineral resource requirements. . . . The availability of mineral resources could pose a short term sporadic threat or a protracted industrial menace to the economic security of Japan" (quoted in Kolenda

1985: 257). For Japan, therefore, securing sufficient and stable flows of key natural resources at reasonable prices is a national imperative.

A central component of the strategy for resource supply was the develop-for-import policy (DI). The Japanese government endeavored to secure access to foreign minerals and metals through preferential loans and equity participation in extractive and processing ventures abroad. DI called for ores and metals to be developed overseas for the sole purpose of importing them to Japan. A set of institutions (most of them under the jurisdiction of MITI) was entrusted with project identification, information gathering, and fundraising for natural resource ventures overseas.

The Japan National Oil Corporation subsidized the exploration and development of oil and natural gas abroad. The MMAJ supported the exploitation of nonferrous metals overseas. The OECF loaned money to foreign mining operations and provided equity participation in extractive and processing projects abroad. The Japan Eximbank gave priority to natural resource projects, with these ventures constituting a sizable share of its lending portfolio. Thus did Japanese government and industry rely heavily on DI schemes for a wide range of natural resources: copper, aluminum ingot, iron ore, coking coal, liquefied gas, and crude oil, among others. The FDI-based importation (that is, DI) of these resources accounted for 15 percent to 70 percent of all imports (Takeuchi 1990: 310).

Japanese resource diplomacy (through DI) was particularly active in the aluminum smelting industry. Soft financing allowed Japanese companies that were losing the domestic market to foreign rivals, plagued by low operating ratios despite repeated plant closures, and burdened with increasing debt and operating losses to invest abroad. Japanese smelters could undertake overseas production because they relied little on their own funds to do so. Moreover, government FDI financing helped Japanese smelters to ameliorate the political risk of overseas investments.

The enhanced leverage of host governments in establishing the conditions of operation of MNCs was not lost on Japanese investors. Fresh examples included the nationalization of the Guyana bauxite mines and the Venezuelan government's decision to marginalize Japanese investors to a minority participation with no managerial rights. Likewise, in national projects, Japanese companies benefited from the Japanese government's help negotiating crucial terms of operation of the offshore smelters with their host governments.

The government's crucial financing role is nowhere clearer than in the case of Asahan.[31] Remarkably, it provided more than 80 percent of the total funding for the Asahan project (see Table 6.4), the largest Japanese financial contribution to a single overseas project ever (Yamashita 1986: 7).

In the Albras-Alunorte national project, the Japanese government did not

TABLE 6.4

Public Financing and the Exodus of Smelters: The Asahan Project

	Amount (billion yen)	Ratio (%)	Fund procurement	Amount (billion yen)
Equity capital	91.10	22.2	Indonesian government	22.78
			Nippon Asahan Aluminum	68.33
			(1) OECF equity	(34.16)
			(2) Private sector equity	(34.16)
Loans	319.90	77.8	Indonesian government	31.99
			OECF's yen loans	61.55
			Nippon Asahan Aluminum	226.36
			(1) Japan Eximbank–sponsored loans to the Indonesian government	(59.11)
			(2) Japan Eximbank–sponsored loans	(151.99)
			(3) Japan International Cooperation Agency loans	(15.26)
Total	411.00	100.0	Total	411.00
Share of Japanese government financing: 84.2 percent[a]				

[a]Assuming the Japan Eximbank covered 70 percent of the syndicated lending for the shareholders' equity contribution to NAA.

SOURCE: Yamashita 1986: 6.

pay for the construction of the hydropower plant or other infrastructure. Japanese public financial institutions provided 32 percent and 28 percent of the Albras and Alunorte's funding needs, respectively (see Table 6.5). OECF (equity) and Japan Eximbank (loans) were the only Japanese public financial institutions involved in Amazon aluminum, and once more, Japanese smelters relied on Japan Eximbank–sponsored loans to shore up their equity contribution to NAAC.[32]

The results of the government's endeavor to replace domestic ingot with development imports are best evaluated by looking at the impact of this policy on the Japanese import market (see Table 6.6). The importance of development imports to the total supply of primary aluminum peaked in 1985, representing close to 50 percent of all imports. At that time, two large overseas smelters (Boyne and Asahan) had recently begun operation, supplementing the ingot procured by two other sizable refiners (NZAS and Venalum). After that, however, the share of FDI imports contracted to 31 percent in 1990, and gradually recovered to 42 percent by 2000.

TABLE 6.5

Public Financing and the Exodus of Smelters: The Albras and Alunorte Projects

	Amount (billion yen)[a]	Ratio (%)	Fund procurement	Amount (billion yen)
			Albras	
Equity capital	102.26	29.3	Brazilian government	52.15
			Nippon Amazon Aluminum	68.33
			(1) OECF equity	(20.04)
			(2) Private sector equity	(30.07)
Loans	226.9	64.9	Brazilian government	123.69
			Nippon Amazon Aluminum	100.58
			(1) Japan Eximbank–sponsored loans	(70.41)
Own resources	20.22	5.8		20.22
Total	349.38	100.0	Total	349.38
Share of Japanese government financing: 31.9 percent[b]				
			Alunorte	
Equity capital	30.58	37.6	Brazilian government and firms	25.69
			NAAC	4.89
			(1) OECF	(1.49)
Loans	48.49	59.6	Brazil	26.27
			Japan	22.21
			(1) NAAC	(3.40)
			(2) Japan Eximbank–sponsored loans	(18.81)
Own resources	2.31	2.8		2.31
Total	81.38	100.0	Total	81.38
Share of Japanese government financing: 27.9 percent[b]				

[a] 1982 exchange rate used for converting dollars to yen.

[b] Assuming the Japan Eximbank covered 70 percent of the syndicated lending for the shareholders' equity contribution to NAAC.

SOURCE: Data provided by NAAC.

TABLE 6.6

FDI in the Name of Security Supply: Japanese Imports of Primary Aluminum, 1985–2000 (thousand tons)

	1985	1990	1995	2000
All imports	1,351	2,426	2,400	2,425
Development imports				
NZAS	100	50	55	65
Venalum	170	200	125	130
Alpac	45	45	41	45
Alumax	45	110	174	176
Asahan	175	116	137	84
Boyne	110	117	128	224
Amazon	0	106	169	169
Alouette	0	0	43	48
Portland	0	0	29	78
Subtotal	645	744	901	1,019
Share (percent)	48	31	38	42
Long-term contracts				
Comalco	90	155	150	180
Subtotal	330	618	948	1,028
Share (percent)	24	25	40	42
Spot purchases				
Brazil	20	207	191	0
United States	130	437	4	0
Subtotal	376	1,064	551	378
Share (percent)	28	44	23	16

SOURCE: Marubeni, several company reports.

Imports of the aluminum the Japanese government has paid most dearly for, the Asahan ingot, dropped from 6 percent in 1995 to a mere 3 percent of total imports in 2000. Despite massive financial support from the government, the two national projects supply only 10 percent of the ingot consumed in Japan. A more traditional procurement strategy, long-term contracting, made a comeback during the 1990s. In 2000, ingot supplied through these contracts represents 42 percent of all imports. And despite the much-heralded expansion of arm's length transactions in aluminum ingot, spot purchases constituted a mere 16 percent in 2000.

There are both benefits and disadvantages to the government and private sector of investing in offshore smelters. The obvious advantage is that a portion of the output is earmarked to the Japanese market as part of the production sharing arrangement. With direct ownership, Japanese investors acquire inside information (such as reliable production cost estimates) useful in negotiating separate supply contracts with other ingot providers. Japanese FDI projects in aluminum smelting also diminished the market power of the six international majors by increasing the number of alternative sources of ingot (Kolenda 1985).

Among the disadvantages are output volumes that cannot be adjusted to meet fluctuations in domestic demand for ingot. Moreover, these enterprises are costly, requiring large injections of capital to cover construction and operating expenses. Finally, soaring yen-denominated debt has hindered the cost competitiveness of Japanese smelters overseas. Without vertical integration into downstream processing, Japanese offshore refiners have not compelled domestic consumers to "buy Japanese" regardless of price.

The Japanese state has been deeply involved in downscaling the domestic aluminum refining industry and transferring smelting capacity overseas. Japan attempted to tamper with comparative advantage by creating a competitive Japanese smelting industry anew, this time in foreign countries where it would have access to cheap resources (bauxite and hydropower). The Japanese government's vocal support for an overseas refining base led many to argue that strategic concerns about security of supply displaced profitability considerations in the conformation of these investment projects. Some maintain that Japanese extractive investments abroad were not been motivated by "narrow microeconomic" concerns with profitability but by national imperatives to stabilize supplies of resources (see Ozawa 1978, 1993; Kolenda 1985; and Bunker and O'Hearn 1993, 94).

However, there are strong reasons to doubt these claims. Japanese smelting companies were as motivated by self-interest as their Western counterparts. They resorted to foreign production to gain access to cheaper resources, and ultimately to ensure their survival when domestic production became uncompetitive. Although eager to acquire more equity metal, Japanese investors were not so bold as to ignore profit considerations.

The Amazon negotiations show that the Japanese were very cost-conscious and refused to finance mammoth projects that seemed unfeasible. Japanese smelters drove a hard bargain with the Brazilian government to liberate the joint venture from financially contributing to the Tucurui hydropower plant and scaled down the Albras-Alunorte project to more feasible proportions. NAAC's withdrawal from Alunorte attests to the private sector's unwillingness to remain in projects lacking adequate prospects for profitability. To the dismay of public officials, and despite its designation as a national project, Japanese investors retired from an untenable venture.

Although smelting projects overseas constitute remarkable showcases of government financial involvement and industrywide participation in natural resource development, they are also characterized by public/private disagreement, business rivalry, and the need to balance competing goals. Domestic politics greatly influenced the definition of the FDI prescription for aluminum smelting and the ultimate results of the international adjustment strategy. The state's concern about industrial restructuring and raw material supply, together with the political clout of a highly concentrated industry, explain the strong consensus in Japan to publicly finance the internationalization of the smelters. MITI bureaucrats and public financial institutions (the Japan Eximbank and the OECF) aided a dying refining industry prodded by the need to secure a key industrial input, but also pressed by the need to rapidly scale down a huge industry that overnight had become utterly uncompetitive.

LDP politicians responded to the industry's plea for greater public assistance by brokering tariff rebates and FDI financing. Moreover, government support for the creation of a new offshore aluminum refining base was so sweeping because the relocation strategy was politically unopposed at home. Aluminum smelting was a capital-intensive sector with a workforce of only modest size (14,000 workers in 1970). Labor adjustment proceeded smoothly because parent companies could absorb workers displaced by plant closings (Uriu 1996: 179). Unions therefore did not challenge the overseas relocation of the dying smelters. All smelting firms went multinational after the fatal blow of the oil shocks, so there were no purely domestic smelters to resent the multinationalization strategy financed with public money.

Tampering with comparative advantage through FDI yielded mixed results for the Japanese government. First, FDI in aluminum smelting proved to be a very costly enterprise. The public financial packages for the construction of Asahan and Albras assumed that these projects would be self-sustaining. The largest amounts of financial assistance were not aid loans and equity injections, but FDI credit, which had a repayment obligation. Yet the national project formula turned out to be an expensive open-ended commitment. The government financed the construction of the smelter and had to step in later with emergency financial packages to keep the official projects afloat.

Second, the Japanese government was not always able to trade private sector compliance for preferential financing. The private sector's withdrawal from Alunorte generated strong resentment among bureaucrats who were forced to downgrade the project to "seminational" status.[33]

Industrial politics has had the most enduring impact on the success of the FDI policy for aluminum smelting. MITI bureaucrats and the smelters were in agreement about the single most important objective in the offshore revival of the refining industry: to supply "Japanese" ingot to the domestic market. Conflicting interests among the branches of the aluminum industry rendered this an elusive goal. Although downstream firms did not prevent the exodus of the smelters, through their "consumer power" they called into question the wisdom of the policy. Simply put, fabricators (unconstrained by *keiretsu* loyalties) refused to buy high regardless of the security concerns of the state or the political clout of the smelters.

CHAPTER 7

Consumer Electronics and the Limits of State FDI Financing

AT THE TURN OF THE twenty-first century, the Japanese consumer electronics industry is at a crossroads. Traditionally a pillar of Japanese electronics, the consumer segment of the industry suffered great losses during the period of steep yen appreciation (1985–2000). The domestic production of the more standardized goods turned increasingly uncompetitive, and the industry had difficulty developing new core goods capable of generating strong demand and conquering the emerging field of home information appliances. Foreign direct investment, in order to recoup cost competitiveness, emerged as the dominant adjustment strategy for consumer electronics firms.

This international adjustment strategy was largely self-financed. Indeed, the electronics industry is an important reminder that public FDI credit was not essential to all Japanese industries, and it corroborates this book's hypotheses about when the state will allocate subsidized FDI credit to industries that are losing competitiveness. Consumer electronics firms possessed abundant resources to autonomously undertake FDI and traditionally shunned close interactions with the bureaucracy. These enterprises did not lobby the state for special legislation to cope with decline or for subsidized FDI credit. Despite the challenges of multinational production (high import penetration ratios and displacement of lower-tier subcontractors), FDI strategies did not galvanize domestic opposition either. This chapter discusses the political economy of self-financed multinationalization and explores why labor and domestic enterprises did not object to the offshore relocation of consumer electronics firms.

The Evolution of the Industry

When World War II ended, the Japanese electrical/electronic machinery industry was seriously underdeveloped. This sector represented a small fraction of Japanese manufacturing value added (3.8 percent) and employment (4.0 percent) in 1950. Production of vacuum tube radios had resumed in the mid-1940s, but the first breakthrough occurred only ten years later. In 1955, Sony, using technology licensed from Texas Instruments, was the first company to produce and commercialize all-transistor radios. After this first hit, the industry continued to develop new consumer products and grew steadily. Refrigerators, washing machines, and black-and-white television sets were referred to as the "three gods" of the "electrification boom" (*kadenka*). The steady increase of disposable income allowed Japanese consumers to satisfy their demand for these modern home appliances.

A RISING STAR IN JAPANESE MANUFACTURING, 1950–1985

Mirroring Sony's experience with radio production, Japanese firms relied heavily on foreign technology to start up the television industry. In 1952, Hasegawa (Sharp), Matsushita, and Tōshiba signed licensing agreements with RCA for the transfer of basic circuit technology. Japanese electronics firms also sought foreign know-how for the manufacture of key television parts. Matsushita arranged licensing contracts for picture tube technology with Phillips in 1953, and Hitachi and Tōshiba did the same with RCA. The manufacture of black-and-white televisions grew swiftly, and by 1960 approximately 8 million sets had been produced (Hiramoto 1994: 36). The diffusion of this product reached almost 80 percent in the early 1960s. The saturation of domestic demand encouraged Japanese firms to search for an outlet overseas (mainly in the United States). Exports of black-and-white TVs increased quickly in the mid-1960s and peaked in 1967 when 2.6 million sets were shipped abroad (Okamoto 1989: 50).

Color television (CTV) manufacturing repeated the cycle: from the introduction of foreign technology to domestic mass production and export success. In 1960, RCA agreed to license color picture tube technology to several Japanese companies. CTV manufacturing in Japan picked up in the second half of the 1960s, and in 1971 approximately 6 million were assembled (Okamoto 1988b, no. 7: 31). Early on, a sizable amount of production was destined for the export market (once again, mainly to the United States). Japanese TV makers first gained access to the US market through general retailers and specialized in the production of smaller, cheaper sets that American companies had neglected. In 1964 the retailer Sears, Roebuck began importing CTVs from Tōshiba to be sold under the Sears brand name. The same year, Sanyō signed export contracts with Magnavox and Sears. Other American retailers soon established partnerships with Japanese firms: Montgomery with Hasegawa and J.C. Penney with Matsushita in 1966 (Hiramoto 1994: 104). Exports grew rapidly, and Japanese firms consolidated their own brand shares in the American market during the early 1970s.[1]

Japanese firms relied heavily on foreign technology for the initial production of main consumer electronics (radios, black-and-white and color TVs), but the keys to their success were product quality and process efficiency. Among the technological innovations of Japanese firms were Sony's Trinitron system and the all-transistor color TV that Sony and Hitachi first manufactured in 1968. Following the oil shock, Japanese consumer electronics firms pursued automation, miniaturization, and integrated-circuit technology.

A major breakthrough was the manufacture in the mid-1970s of the videotape recorder (VTR): Sony developed the Beta format and JVC the VHS standard. Production expanded rapidly from 1.5 million units in 1978 to 30 million in 1985. VTRs became a major export item, representing 45 percent of the value of consumer electronics exports in 1985. The rapid process of technological innovation coupled with skillful targeting of overseas markets produced the dramatic rise of the Japanese consumer electronics industry to world competitiveness.

EROSION OF COMPARATIVE ADVANTAGE IN THE 'ENDAKA' ERA

Originally the engine of growth for the industry, consumer electronics was superseded by industrial electronics products and electronic parts in the 1980s and 1990s. Traditionally, between 40 and 50 percent of all electric/electronics produced in Japan were consumer goods (see Table 7.1). By 1980, however, the manufacture of industrial electronics overtook consumer products, and five years later the value of electronic parts manufacturing also surpassed that of consumer electronics. The decline of consumer electronics was greatly accelerated by the yen appreciation after the Plaza Accord on exchange rates in 1985. The production share of consumer electronics decreased from 27 percent in 1985 to 9 percent in 1997.

Similarly, the contribution of consumer goods to electronics exports dwindled over time. Consumer goods were responsible for more than two-thirds of the electronics industry's exports in 1960 and 1970 and retained their leading position until 1985. But their share of electronics exports contracted dramatically during the *endaka* (strong yen) years, from 39 percent in the mid-1980s to 10 percent in 1997. Industrial electronics and electronic parts displaced consumer electronics as the main exporter in the industry.

TABLE 7.1

Consumer Electronics Overshadowed: Production and Trade Performance, 1960–1997 (billion yen)

	1960	1970	1980	1985	1990	1997
Consumer electronics						
Production	241	1,473	2,932	4,912	4,436	2,235
	(49%)	(43%)	(33%)	(27%)	(19%)	(9%)
Exports	57	587	2,047	3,806	2,618	1,393
	(78%)	(68%)	(45%)	(39%)	(24%)	(20%)
Industrial electronics						
Production	108	1,030	3,396	7,614	11,335	12,794
	(22%)	(30%)	(38%)	(41%)	(47%)	(51%)
Exports	3	137	1,049	2,919	3,443	3,803
	(4%)	(16%)	(23%)	(30%)	(32%)	(28%)
Electronic parts						
Production	143	894	2,677	6,027	8,150	9,968
	(29%)	(26%)	(30%)	(33%)	(34%)	(40%)
Exports	13	138	1,462	2,971	4,880	8,482
	(18%)	(16%)	(32%)	(31%)	(45%)	(62%)
Total production	491	3,397	9,005	18,553	23,920	24,997
Total exports	74	863	4,558	9,695	10,940	13,677

NOTE: Figures in parentheses represent the percentage share of total electronic production or export.

SOURCE: *Denshi Kōgyō Nenkan*, several years.

Electronic parts alone accounted for more than 60 percent of the industry's exports in the mid-1990s.

The adverse currency realignments after 1985 hit Japanese consumer electronics particularly hard. This was the only segment in the electronics industry to register a drop in the value of production in the late 1980s. Exports plummeted during the endaka era to close to one-third of their value a decade earlier. Falling export sales, sluggish domestic demand, protectionism in industrialized markets, and growing competition from other Asian economies put companies in the Japanese electronics industry in a difficult position. Firms in all three segments of the industry suffered from decreased profitability after the 1985 yen appreciation, but the drop was most severe for consumer electronics: from 9.58 percent in 1985 to 1.54 percent in 1998 (MITI 1998).

Although the consumer wing of the electronics industry suffered a severe recession, it was not comparable to what happened to textiles and aluminum smelting. Both of those industries were officially designated as structurally depressed; and the most pressing issue in their industrial adjustment was capacity curtailment (rationalization).

For all of the losing industries analyzed in this book, though, onshore production was no longer competitive and domestic and international adjustment strategies were intimately linked. In consumer electronics, domestic adjustment involved moving into higher-value-added segments of domestic production (diversification), whereas international adjustment meant expanding overseas manufacturing of the more standardized products (FDI). The state played only played a marginal role in both adjustment strategies.

Adjustment Strategies to Cope with Decline

Unlike Japanese textile firms, electronics firms vigorously pursued intraindustry diversification (that is, manufacturing higher-value-added goods within the same sector) (Onoda, Kohama, and Urata 1991: 41). They did so in two ways: first, by climbing the technological ladder in consumer electronics (from simpler products such as radios and home appliances to CTVs, VTRs, CD players, and high-definition television [HDTV]), and second, by attempting to merge traditional consumer and information products into new home multimedia offerings. Neither domestic diversification strategy was an unqualified success.

In fact, the difficulty in developing "core goods" capable of boosting demand—as radios, TVs, and VTRs had done in the past—further strained relations between the industry and the bureaucracy. All segments of the electronics industry (consumer, industrial, and components) articulate their interests through the umbrella industrial association: the Electronics Industry Association of Japan (EIAJ). This industry association traditionally stood out for its independence from bureaucratic guidance, a position that developed into distrust of bureaucratic authority after the government acquiesced in the 1970s and 1980s to US demands for export restraints on CTVs and VTRs (Yoshimatsu 2000: 86; Okimoto 1989: 167). And the rift between the bureaucracy and the private sector grew larger in recent times. Indeed, the 1990s stagnation in Japanese consumer electronics produced the most overt friction between consumer electronics firms and the Japanese government, this time with the Ministry of Posts and Telecommunications. In February 1994, the broadcasting director of the MOPT rocked industrial circles by announcing an end to the Japanese government's support for HDTV.[2] Taken by surprise, EIAJ responded promptly and energetically. In a press conference the following day, business executives sharply criticized the abrupt shift in government policy. EIAJ's protests quickly produced a retraction from the bureaucracy (EIAJ 1998: 41–42).

DOMESTIC ADJUSTMENT: CLIMBING THE TECHNOLOGICAL LADDER

These modest results in expanding the market for high-definition television prompted Japanese electronics firms to emphasize a second path of intraindustry diversification: the shift to industrial electronics and electronic parts. The production profile of the electronics giants became ever more diversified: Hitachi, Tōshiba, Mitsubishi, Matsushita, Sanyō, and Sharp now produce everything from home appliances to electronic devices (Fujita and Ishii 1995: 6). For these general and consumer electronics firms, information, industrial, and component electronics occupy the largest share of their business activities. In 1970, home appliances and audiovisual equipment generated 82 percent of Matsushita's sales, and the company had not begun manufacturing industrial electronics and parts. In 1980 the company's share of consumer goods had decreased to 61 percent, and industrial and component electronics had expanded to 28.1 percent (Hara 1989: 26). By 1996, information, industrial, and component electronics accounted for the largest share of Matsushita's sales (48 percent). The same was true for Tōshiba (59 percent), Hitachi (50 percent), Sanyō (52 percent), Sharp (53 percent), and Mitsubishi (81 percent) (*Kaisha Shikihō* 1996).

In particular, the development of home information appliances (that is, the merger of consumer and information equipment) is deemed key to the future of the Japanese consumer electronics industry. Japanese and US firms compete fiercely for "supremacy" in home multimedia (EIAJ 1998: 510). After an onslaught in the 1980s by the more competitive Japanese enterprises, US firms engineered a comeback in the area of high-value-added industrial electronics.

The "Wintelist" revolution (Windows + Intel) changed the terms of competition in the world electronics industry. In this new phase, large assemblers with vertically integrated product design and manufacturing (such as IBM) were displaced by firms that dominate horizontal markets through de facto market standards (Microsoft's operating systems, Adobe's applications, for example) (Borrus 2000: 59–65). Japanese firms did not transition easily to the new realities of horizontal market competition where standard-setting is all-important (EIAJ 1998: 15). US and Japanese firms compete vigorously to supply the new generation of home information appliances through their anchor products: the TV receiver for Japanese enterprises and the personal computer for US companies. Who will win this race is not yet known.

Spurred by the modest achievements in the development of new-generation consumer goods (HDTV and home information appliances), Japanese electronics firms also responded to the slump with a massive transfer overseas of the more standardized business lines. For the first time, overseas production began to replace domestic manufacturing and export, with the Japanese market increasingly dependent on intrafirm imports for the supply of consumer goods.

INTERNATIONAL ADJUSTMENT: THE CHALLENGES OF MULTINATIONAL PRODUCTION

Among Japanese manufacturing sectors, the electronics industry was a pioneer in international production. Although early foreign investments were small in scale, over time the industry consolidated its position as an outward investor. During the 1990s this sector held the largest share of Japanese manufacturing FDI (30 percent). The multinationalization of Japanese consumer electronics unfolded in three phases: the first experience with overseas manufacturing (1960–73), production in advanced markets in response to trade friction (1974–84), and relocation in Asia due to the erosion in comparative advantage (1985).

Early Multinationalization, 1960–1973

The first investments overseas date back to the early 1960s as firms in the consumer electronics industry ventured into foreign production. Several factors encouraged Japanese firms to abandon their exclusive reliance on exports as a means to promote their overseas expansion. Greater competition from American firms producing in East Asia, escalating trade friction due to the Japanese export drive, and revaluatory pressures on the yen after the collapse of the fixed exchange rate regime in 1971 made FDI a more attractive option for consumer electronics firms (Ikeda 1979: 187).

In the decade 1961–71, FDI by the electronics industry totaled $101 million. Following the shift to a floating exchange rate system (in 1971) and the liberalization of capital outflow (1972), the outward investment activities of Japanese electronics firms reached an unprecedented $225 million in 1973. Most of the outward investment projects in the pre–oil shock era took place in consumer electronics and parts manufacturing (see Table 7.2). Moreover, Asia was the preferred location for Japanese electronics companies venturing into international production for the first time.

Until 1965, most overseas investments targeted protected local markets, usually through a joint venture with a native partner. In 1961, Matsushita established its first overseas production subsidiary in Thailand (National Thai) together with a local investor. Sanyō too invested early overseas, in Hong Kong in 1961. Still, most FDI projects in those years were concentrated in Taiwan, in what was called the "first Taiwan rush." Again in Taiwan, Matsushita (1962) and Sanyō (1963) were among the first to establish production

TABLE 7.2

Foreign Subsidiaries of Japanese Electronics Firms, 1970–2000 (number of subsidiaries)

	Asia					United	
	NIEs	ASEAN	China	Subtotal	Europe	States	Total
Electronics industry							
~ 1970	33	13	0	46	7	8	72
1971–85	97	35	7	146	36	46	250
1986–2000	87	297	266	679	100	108	941
Total	217	345	273	871	143	162	1,263
Consumer electronics							
~ 1970	7	10	0	17	2	0	22
1971–85	15	8	2	27	14	9	60
1986–2000	15	67	61	155	24	22	216
Total	37	85	63	199	40	31	298
Industrial electronics							
~ 1970	7	1	0	8	2	4	18
1971–85	12	10	3	25	12	13	56
1986–2000	19	42	65	135	31	28	203
Total	38	53	68	168	45	45	277
Electronic parts							
~ 1970	22	5	0	27	4	5	41
1971–85	82	25	4	115	16	28	168
1986–2000	60	222	158	450	54	63	602
Total	164	252	162	592	74	96	811

SOURCE: Electronics Industry Association of Japan 2000: iii–vii.

ventures. Those first plants sought a small and protected market by offering numerous products (radio receivers, refrigerators, washing machines, black-and-white TVs). As one company official explained it: "The idea was to set up 'small Matsushitas' in these countries that would supply a broad range of the consumer goods available as well in the Japanese market.[3]

After the establishment of the Kaohsiung Export Processing Zone in 1966, though, export-oriented investment became predominant among Japanese firms investing in Taiwan and Korea (which became a major recipient country for Japanese FDI in the early 1970s). The investment activities of US firms as well as rising domestic wages were both reasons for Japanese companies to set up export production bases elsewhere in Asia (Yoshihara 1978: 156). In response to the Japanese penetration of the US black-and-white TV market, many American firms had moved their factories to low-wage economies in Asia, and Japanese firms had lost market share in the United States (from 77.8 percent in 1971 to 50.9 percent in 1973) (Kawahara and Ishii 1980: 26). In 1969, Hitachi established a factory in Taiwan to produce TVs for export to the United States. And Sanyō (1969) and Matsushita (1973) did the same in Korea. This strategy paid off, and by 1975 Japanese brand products accounted for 60 percent of US TV receiver imports. Early Japanese FDI (offshore production targeting third-country markets) was heavily influenced by the export strategies of Japanese consumer electronics firms.

Protectionism and FDI, 1974–1984

During the 1970s, concern over the future of export markets continued to spur the internationalization of the Japanese electronics industry. This time, however, growing protectionist sentiment among labor and management in the primary destination market, the United States, threatened Japanese exports. In 1971 the three main American labor unions in the TV industry petitioned for import relief under the 301 clause of the Trade Expansion Act. The following year, Sylvania, Magnavox, and Zenith demanded that the Treasury Department impose a countervailing duty on Japanese TV exports, arguing that the Japanese government was effectively subsidizing Japanese exports. Finally, in 1976 labor and management joined in the creation of COMPACT (the Committee to Preserve American Color Television) to demand import relief under the new Trade Reform Act of 1974. In the end, the administration of President Jimmy Carter negotiated an Orderly Market Agreement with Japan. That 1977 agreement limited Japanese exports of color TVs to 1.75 million units per year for the next three years (Millstein 1983: 123, 125, 128, 134).

Sony had been the first Japanese company to react to the uncertain future of the US market by establishing a color TV assembly plant in San Diego in 1972. Two years later it began producing picture tubes as well. Other Japanese companies soon followed in Sony's steps: in 1974 Matsushita acquired the TV division of Motorola, and in 1976 Sanyō bought the TV maker Warwick. The other Japanese TV manufacturers arrived in the United States shortly after the signing of the OMA: Mitsubishi in 1977, Tōshiba in 1978, Sharp in 1979, Hitachi in 1979, and Japan Victor in 1982 (Sasaki and Edokoro 1987: 55–59). The share of Japanese CTV transplants in the American market increased from 17 percent in 1979 to 28 percent in 1985 (Hiramoto 1994: 197).[4]

During the 1970s, Japanese consumer electronics firms also consolidated their export platform bases in Asia, especially in Singapore, which had a highly qualified and relatively low-cost workforce, a tariff-free port with a well-developed industrial infrastructure, and favorable government policies toward foreign capital.[5] Nevertheless, during the decade 1975–84, half of all FDI projects in electronics took were in Europe and North America. Hence, avoidance of tariff or quota barriers was a powerful force behind the unfolding of Japanese electronics FDI in this decade.

The Erosion of Comparative Advantage, 1985

Despite the early inroads of Japanese electronics companies in offshore manufacturing, the multinationalization of the industry did not reach its height until the mid-1980s. The steep appreciation of the yen after 1985 eroded the competitiveness of domestic production for the Japanese and export markets, and forced Japanese enterprises to embrace overseas manufacturing more energetically. Japanese consumer electronics firms were responding both to adverse currency realignments and to competition from other Asian producers at the lower end of the industry (radios and televisions); they were also adjusting to import restrictions and local content requirements in industrialized markets. These were powerful incentives to expand foreign production (Urata and Kohama 1991: 71).

The outward investment flows during these years were unprecedented in both their size and their number. Overseas investment grew from $3.1 billion between 1971 and 1984 to $65.2 billion between 1985 and 1999. Every subsector in the electronics industry responded to the yen appreciation and the other competitive challenges with ambitious plans for overseas manufacturing. More than 70 percent of overseas investment projects in consumer, industrial, and component electronics were initiated after 1985 (see Table 7.2).

The evolution of the foreign production ratio—that is, the share of overseas production in total manufacturing—is profound evidence of the industry's restructuring. In 1985 several electronics products already exhibited sizable foreign production ratios: 56 percent for radios, 48 percent for stereos, and 40 percent for CTVs. A few years later the multinationalization of the industry had made great strides. By 1993, VTRs, record players, and CD players (whose foreign production ratio in 1985 was less than 6 percent) reported that foreign manufacturing accounted for 30–40 percent of total production. Likewise, color television, stereo, and radio manufacturing had the highest foreign production ratios (60–70 percent) in 1993 (Solís 1998: 415).

Rapid growth in outward investment since the 1980s also reoriented Japanese electronics geographically. Asia has reemerged as a major manufacturing base for Japanese electronics firms. Between 1981 and 1985, 13 percent of Japanese electronics industry investment took place in Asia, but the region's share increased to 20 percent between 1986 and 1990. Within Asia too, the location of consumer electronics factories shifted toward ASEAN nations in the second half of the 1980s, and toward China in the early 1990s.

In particular, Japanese firms moved the production of low-value-added consumer goods (such as radio cassettes, headphones, small TVs, refrigerators, fans, and vacuum cleaners) to Asia because technology is standardized for these products and therefore cost competition is acute (see Table 7.3). Within Asia, TV production is concentrated in Thailand, China, Malaysia, and Indonesia. Japanese stereo production took place primarily in China and Malaysia, and China was the country of choice for air conditioner production. The overseas production of more advanced consumer goods picked up more recently; in Malaysia several plants producing VTRs were established after 1988.

The internationalization of the Japanese consumer electronics industry during the *endaka* era is remarkable in two other dimensions. First, foreign direct investment emerged as a key strategy for combating the erosion of comparative advantage. In previous episodes of domestic recession the industry's main response had been to intensify the export drive (Hiramoto 1994). In the mid-1960s, when the diffusion of black-and-white television was high and growth in the domestic market stagnated, Japanese firms found an outlet for their goods in the United States. And in the late 1960s the same thing happened with color TVs.

During the post–oil shock recession, Japanese electronics firms aggressively pursued automation and product development to expand their export markets. In other words, exports were seen as the engine of growth for the electronics industry, and firms turned to foreign production when markets could not be served through the export route. In the 1990s recession, though, the export drive faltered and more firms turned to FDI.

Second, the strategy of setting up export platforms in Asian countries was superseded by a more complex scheme of cross-border production networks. The regionalization of manufacturing was particularly acute during the *endaka* era, as Japanese firms tried to reduce their dependence on expensive components shipped from Japan. Their Asian subsidiaries decreased their Japanese procurement from 45 percent in 1986 to 38 percent in 1990, and increased local sales from 42 percent to 49 percent (Aoki 1994: 66). And some Japanese firms, such as Hitachi, set up international procurement offices to find the most competitive electronic parts worldwide.[6]

Although Japanese firms' willingness to buy from low-cost component makers is a sign that the supply structure is broadening (Ernst 2000), the overseas relocation of Japanese parts suppliers seems to be a more dominant strategy. Offshore manufacturing of electronic components has been going on since the 1960s but accelerated rapidly during the *endaka* years. Between 1986 and 2000, 602 new investments were recorded, equivalent to 74 percent of all electronic component investments carried out in the postwar period (see Table 7.2).

That expansion spurred a wave of research on the influence of *keiretsu* ties

TABLE 7.3

The Internationalization of Japanese Consumer Electronics Firms, 2000 (number of foreign subsidiaries)

	Manufacturers of audiovisual equipment		Manufacturers of audio equipment				Manufacturers of home appliances			
Location	TVs	VTRs	Radios	Tape recorders	Stereos	CD players	Air conditioners	Refrigerators	Microwaves	Total
Korea	0	0	0	1	2	0	1	0	0	3
China	8	1	1	2	12	6	22	10	4	63
Taiwan	4	4	0	1	0	1	5	3	1	14
Hong Kong	1	1	0	2	2	1	1	0	0	7
Thailand	9	1	0	0	2	0	11	8	3	27
Singapore	1	0	0	0	3	1	4	0	1	13
Malaysia	6	8	0	3	14	7	7	2	0	32
Philippines	3	0	0	0	2	0	3	3	0	8
Indonesia	6	1	1	0	7	1	6	4	1	18
Asia	45	19	2	9	48	17	64	35	11	199
Europe	12	8	0	0	7	4	6	1	3	40
North America	14	0	0	0	3	1	9	2	2	49
Total	80	32	4	9	64	23	82	39	19	298

SOURCE: EIAJ 2000: ii.

on FDI flows (Kimura and Pugel 1995; Belderbos and Sleuwaegen 1993; Banerji and Sambharya 1996). In the electronics industry, though, subcontracting networks are weaker given the importance of independent suppliers for the manufacture of general components (Nishiguchi 1994). Not surprisingly, large and independent suppliers dominated FDI activities in Japanese electronic parts (Ishii 1996). For instance, in a study of the subcontracting practices of Japanese electronics firms in the United States and Mexico during the mid-1990s, Solís (1997) found that the vast majority of Japanese component makers in the region were independent suppliers, while subcontractors had a rather marginal participation in the transplanted supply structure.[7]

Moreover, electronics parent companies played a limited role in promoting subcontractors' FDI. Only a minority of affiliated suppliers (8.5 percent in the sample of machinery subcontractors) received parent-company requests to invest overseas (Kikai Shinkō Kyōkai 1987: 63). The assistance provided by parent companies to subcontractors stressed soft aid (such as information and human resource development), and downplayed direct subsidization.[8] Subcontractors with overseas investments list the following primary forms of assistance provided by parent firms: information (73 percent); guaranteed orders (54 percent); personnel (35 percent); capital participation (29 percent); financial support (8 percent); and land and equipment leases (2.7 percent) (multiple answers were allowed) (Kikai Shinkō Kyōkai 1987). Electronics parent firms in particular emphasized that the difficulty of guaranteeing stable demand for components and the pressure to increase local procurement ratios were the main deterrents to the overseas relocation of their subcontractors (Research Association on Subcontracting Firms 1986: 102).

Consequently, only a fraction of subcontractors—those at the top of the supply pyramid—pursued FDI strategies. A MITI survey revealed that 23 percent of first-tier subcontractors had overseas investments, whereas only 1.5 percent and 0.7 percent of second- and third-tier subcontractors did so (MITI, Small Business Agency 1994: 181). The overseas investment activities of affiliated suppliers of Hitachi and Matsushita corroborate this trend. In a sample of subcontractors to these two Japanese consumer electronics giants, only a minority of subcontractors undertook foreign direct investments (21 percent for Hitachi and 16 percent for Matsushita). Most of the affiliated suppliers remained domestically oriented.[9]

Lower on the subcontracting pyramid the negative effects of assemblers' overseas relocation were strong. Second- and third-tier affiliated suppliers were more susceptible to the competition from host-nation manufacturers of simple parts or labor-intensive assembly processes. A MITI Small Business Agency survey (1994: 201) depicted the precarious situation of many second- and third-tier subcontractors. Many of these firms were reducing their number of employees, and a third of the smallest subcontractors expected to move into other businesses or to shut down. The restructuring efforts of assemblers (through FDI) therefore created a serious adjustment problem for many subcontractors.

The increasing displacement of domestic production by foreign manufacturing, inexorable import penetration, and the financial straits of many domestic subcontractors profoundly altered the political economy of FDI in Japanese consumer electronics. Yet the adjustment of consumer electronics—with FDI as a core strategy—was not heavily politicized. The government played a small role in financing electronics FDI, and social groups disadvantaged by overseas relocation of consumer electronics did not contest the FDI strategies of the large assemblers and part makers.

Meager Public Support for the Overseas Expansion of Electronics

The meteoric rise of the Japanese electronics industry fueled a heated debate over the contribution of the Japanese government to this dynamic process of growth. To many observers, public support largely explains the superior export performance (and prowess as a foreign investor) of the Japanese electronics industry (Baranson 1981; Millstein 1983). Others doubt that the Japanese bureaucracy had much influence on the dynamic expansion of the Japanese electronics industry (Callon 1995; Okimoto 1989: 65). My own analysis of Japanese government assistance to the export and FDI drive of the electronics industry supports the latter view: that the Japanese bureaucracy played a marginal role in promoting consumer electronics at home and had a minor influence on the internationalization of these highly independent electronics firms.

PUBLIC POLICY AND THE INFANT INDUSTRY

MITI's role in the development of the machinery industry has been discussed primarily in relation to the temporary promotion laws passed in 1956 and 1957. However, bureaucratic efforts at industrial promotion began earlier and were more ambitious; and their failure led to the adoption instead of provisional legislation. In 1953, MITI put forward the idea of creating a public corporation to help the machinery industry modernize its manufacturing equipment and improve its export performance. To this end, 30 billion yen in subsidies for 530 firms, 39 billion yen in Japan Development Bank financing, and 292 billion yen in loans from foreign banks were anticipated. But difficulties putting the financing in place forced MITI to reduce the planned assistance to 1,600 million yen to seven companies. When it was finally implemented in February 1955, only four companies received loans of 810 million yen (T. Hashimoto 1990: 559–61).

In November 1955, MITI's Heavy Industry Division proposed the establishment of an Association for the Promotion of the Machinery Industry, whose main tasks would be the rationalization and modernization of equipment. The paid-up capital for the association was expected to be 34 billion yen, all from public coffers. In the end, the idea of an association was discarded after the Machinery Division of the Industrial Rationalization Council argued that the new body would duplicate the functions of the JDB, result in soft credit for private firms, and strain public finances. MITI had strongly favored the association because it considered that novel formulas (such as the leasing of machinery) would promote equipment modernization more effectively than JDB loans heavily guided by financial considerations: "From the point of view of policy goals, the concept of the association was considered superior, and JDB financing was judged to be a second-best policy" (ibid.: 566).

MITI therefore had to settle for a legislative framework that did not embrace its preferred method to support an infant machinery industry. In 1956 the Temporary Measures Law for the Promotion of the Machinery Industry was passed for an initial five-year period and was renewed twice before 1971. Its main elements were bureaucratic planning and public financing: MITI would draft a rationalization plan and JDB would offer credit to entice firms to participate. The law also contemplated cartelization. "Concerted action" would be permitted to attain the production, technology development, and parts procurement goals (Friedman 1988: 78–79).

In the first term of the law (1956–61), JDB loans in this program amounted to 112 billion yen, or 84 percent of MITI's expected financing. The top recipients of these JDB credit included makers of machine tools (with 22.5 percent of the total), cutting tool dies (15 percent), gears (13.5 percent), and automotive parts (11.3 percent) (T. Hashimoto 1990: 575).

These loans notwithstanding, the impact of MITI's modernization policy on the machinery industry was limited. None of MITI's planning goals in the machine tool industry were actually met (Friedman 1988: 82). Production costs were expected to drop, but instead they increased by 121 percent in 1960 and by 9.4 percent in 1965. Exports reached only 40 percent in 1960 and 66 percent in 1965 of the planned amount; and output far exceeded the 1960 goal by 221 percent, but was 52 percent below the 1965 target. And in all of the machinery sectors selected, investments in equipment were much higher than anticipated in MITI's plan (T. Hashimoto 1990: 578).

The government singled out electronics as the object of public support with the passage in 1957 of the Temporary Measures Law for the Promotion of the Electronics Industry.[10] The special focus on the electronics industry responded to the fear that the technological gap between Japan and other countries would expand in the absence of public assistance. The goals of the law were to assist in the development of production technologies not yet available in Japan, to help consolidate production levels for several products, and to foster improvements in quality and precision. The law contemplated financial assistance (through JDB and JFS loans) and cartelization. In addition, the bill granted depreciation allowances based on export performance, and tax exemptions for international marketing expenditures. However, just as with the Machinery Law, the limits on MITI's planning abilities became evident early on. In 1959 the production volumes of several electronics sectors far exceeded the planned amounts (by 78 percent for receiver and broadcasting equipment, for example) (T. Hashimoto 1990: 597–98, 604).

In fact, the unexpected performance of many sectors forced MITI to revise the entire five-year plan; and its subsequent efforts also had little influence on consumer electronics. The Provisional Measures Law for the Promotion of the Electronic Industry (1971–78) selected only a few items related to consumer electronics (such as high-capacity picture tubes and color TVs); the main target of the promotion was industrial electronics. This effort was reinforced with the passage of the 1978 Law on Provisional Measures for the Promotion of the Specific Machinery and Information Industry, whose main goal was the development of the computer industry (Baranson 1981: 58–59).

Baranson (1981) regards public support for technological innovation as an important factor in the growth of the Japanese electronics industry, in particular its support for public research at the Japan Broadcasting Corporation (NHK) and for private R&D in color television manufacturing. But both the small size of the public research program and the fate of some joint research plans raise doubts about the effectiveness of government policy in this area.[11]

The Committee for the Trial Manufacture of Color TV Picture Tubes, established in 1957, is a case in point. This committee (consisting of officials from MITI and MOPT, NHK personnel, picture tube manufacturers, and scientists) was entrusted with the task of joint research for the national manufacture (*kokusanka*) of picture tubes. MITI allocated experimental subsidies for the next four years.

The collaborative research effort yielded some results: by 1959 all participating companies were producing picture tubes for seventeen-inch color TVs; in 1961 Hitachi and Tōshiba started the production of picture tubes for fourteen-inch TVs, and so did Matsushita a year later. However, the life span of these newly developed picture tubes was not very long: by 1961 Matsushita had already discontinued the manufacture of the tube for seventeen-inch TVs. Moreover, efforts to develop an indigenous technology did not eliminate the dependence on foreign know-how. Hitachi and Tōshiba in 1960 and Mitsubishi in 1962 entered into an agreement for technology transfer with RCA.[12] MITI considered this a serious setback: "If [foreign] know-how is still necessary, that will mean that the manufacture of picture tubes with nationally developed technology was not achieved, and that this research ended in failure" (quoted in Hiramoto 1994: 95).

MITI's influence over the evolution of the consumer electronics industry was felt primarily in the area of trade policy. In the early 1950s, foreign goods flowed rapidly into the Japanese market. More than half of all broadcasting equipment was imported, as were large quantities of TV receivers. In MITI's view, some form of sheltering was necessary for a national electronics industry to develop. Therefore in 1953 the ministry announced it would limit imports of TV receivers to 5,800 units during that fiscal year. Only those products that did not compete with the local industry (sets with large picture tubes) or that were necessary for research and trial production would be allowed into the Japanese market.[13]

Soon after CTV manufacturing got under way in Japan, domestic enterprises demanded some form of protection. In 1961 the department store Mitsukoshi asked for authorization to import 5,000 CTVs, manufactured by RCA, to be sold at 21,000 yen each. Given that Japan's production at the time was only 4,736 units, and that domestic prices set were much higher (35,000–44,000 yen per set), Japanese television manufacturers strongly opposed Mitsukoshi's proposal. Initially, MITI tried to reach a compromise to reduce the number of sets imported and increase their retail price. Opposition from the manufacturers was relentless, however, and the import authorization was postponed (Hiramoto 1994: 103).

Under pressure to ease its trade controls, the Japanese government included color TVs in the list of items subject to commercial liberalization beginning in 1964. During the second half of the 1960s tariffs for color TVs remained at 30 percent. In 1971 customs charges were reduced to 7.4 percent, and in 1973 to 4 percent (less than the US tariff of 5 percent).

At this writing in 2003, no tariffs are applied to the import of color TVs. Much more difficult to assess is the impact of nontariff barriers (NTBs) on protecting the Japanese electronics industry. Conceivably, the role of NTBs has decreased because capital controls that prohibited black-and-white and color TV production, together with foreign exchange quotas for imports, were eliminated (Baranson 1981: 65).[14] A quantitative study of NTBs in Japan supports this idea. Sazanami, Urata, and Kawai (1995) found a large discrepancy between the imported and domestic producers' unit values for radio and television sets (607 percent). However, these authors doubt this price differential is due to NTBs. In the *endaka* era, Japanese electronics companies have continued to export high-value-added goods from Japan and have begun to import back less sophisticated items produced by their subsidiaries overseas. Therefore, "large unit value differentials in the case of radio and television sets mainly reflect differences in quality between Japanese and foreign products" (ibid.: 28).

Protection at the infant stage of the electronics industry cannot sufficiently explain the speed at which this sector achieved international competitiveness. The Japanese electronics industry got started in the postwar period with a delay of ten years, and in 1960 it was still a backward sector in terms of labor productivity and product design. However, in the span of a decade Japanese consumer electronics firms managed to outperform their American competitors in production and export. This was a decade of rapid technological innovation through *private* efforts. Some of the major accomplishments of Japanese firms include Sony's development of the Trinitron system, the rapid substitution of vacuum tubes for integrated circuits, and the successful commercialization of the all-transistorized CTV. Corporate strategies, with their emphasis on product and process innovation, their concern with filling niches in export markets, and their preoccupation with quality improvement and cost reduction, largely paved the way for the rise of the Japanese consumer electronics industry.

PUBLIC POLICY AND THE MATURE INDUSTRY: THE INDEPENDENT PATH TO INTERNATIONALIZATION

The relative unimportance of the electronics industry in Japanese industrial policy is borne out by the data. Throughout the postwar period (1955–90), the electronics industry showed dynamic growth, but was not a major recipient of government aid (Beason and Weinstein 1993). Among thirteen manufacturing sectors, the electronics industry ranked seventh in government financing, ninth in subsidies awarded, eighth in trade protection received, and eighth in corporate tax breaks (Bearon and Weinstein 1993).

Even as the consumer electronics industry entered a major restructuring phase, the government's role remained marginal. In 1988 MITI's Machinery Information Division, private manufacturers, and the Electric and Electronic Industries Associations formed the Roundtable on the Long-Term Prospects of the Home Appliances Industry. The creation of this government-business group was triggered by the structural changes that Japanese firms faced in the second half of the 1980s: yen appreciation and shifts in international competitiveness, acute rivalry with other Asian producers, rapid expansion of Japanese FDI, and greater import penetration.

In its 1991 report the Roundtable concluded that a more harmonious international division of labor should be created, and that in order to meet price competition from Asian countries Japan should specialize in high-value-added goods. The Roundtable emphasized avoiding the American experience with deindustrialization by fortifying the domestic technological base as Japanese firms pursued their globalization strategies. Interestingly, the Roundtable circumscribed the sphere of government action to the diplomatic realm—that is, to government officials in multilateral institutions that deal with issues of importance to the electronics industry: dumping, countervailing duties, local content requirements, and intellectual property rights. Domestically, public policy should focus on avoiding excessive competition among Japanese firms through administrative guidance (Roundtable, 1991: 70). It did not envision a much more sustained effort to develop consumer electronics through special legislation authorizing subsidies and public loans.

This brief examination of Japanese industrial policy in electronics shows that the Japanese consumer electronics industry was not the main object of industrial targeting during the expansionary period; nor did it receive major government aid during the phase of structural restructuring. In fact, the Japanese electronics industry was one of the most self-reliant industrial sectors in financing its domestic investment. For example, the share of outstanding credit from public financial institutions for manufacturing was 6.5 percent in 1960, 12.8 percent in 1970, 11.9 percent in 1980, and 11.9 percent in 1990. For the electronics industry the figures were 3.7 percent, 7.5 percent, 9.5 percent, and 11.5 percent (Bank of Japan).

Still, the reliance of the electronics industry on public credit to finance overseas investment projects fluctuated widely over the past fifty years. When electronics firms first embarked on multinational production they tapped public resources (Japan Eximbank FDI loans represented 14 percent of FDI in electronics between 1953 and 1970). But during the second wave of overseas investment (1971–84), firms self-financed their FDI strategies to circumvent industrial market protectionism: public credit represented only 3 percent of total FDI flows. It was only when export competitiveness eroded in response to the sharp yen appreciation that public financing again played a larger role (14 percent of total FDI).

Despite their greater reliance on public loans in recent years, electronics firms never depended on public FDI credit to the same degree that structurally depressed industries have. Moreover, because electronics firms resorted more frequently to Japan Eximbank credit when commercial interest rates were low, the public subsidization of FDI (the difference between public and private interest rates) was more modest for the electronics industry.

Overcoming Domestic Resistance to the Emigration of Industry

Unlike US labor unions, the Japanese union movement did not strongly resist the FDI strategies of Japanese multinationals. Despite the very high foreign production ratios for key electronic consumer goods (CTVs, VTRs) no widespread opposition from labor unions emerged in this industry. The stance on FDI from the umbrella labor organization (Denki Rengō, the

Japanese Electrical, Electronic, and Information Union) remained unchanged during the *endaka* era. Denki Rengō supported FDI because it helped maintain the international competitiveness of Japanese goods, alleviated trade friction, and fostered the economic development of recipient countries (Denki Rengō 1986; 1994).

However, it considered the protection of domestic employment to be of the utmost priority and urged some restraint to avoid a large negative impact on Japanese jobs. In particular, Denki Rengō advanced the principle of "prior consultation" with labor on overseas expansion. By Denki Rengō's own definition, consultation in advance mostly means that management should provide the union with information about the effects of foreign production on domestic employment and anticipated corporate countermeasures. Denki Rengō stopped short of establishing industrial guidelines on this issue by leaving the specific form and content of prior consultations to be decided at the enterprise level. In fact, there was wide variation in the degree to which these prior consultations took place.[15]

LABOR AND THE EXPORT-OF-JOBS DEBATE

The absence of a union movement against FDI did not reflect a lack of concern about the erosion of the employment base. Reflecting popular concern about *kūdōka* (deindustrialization), a number of studies over the years have tried to estimate the employment effect of accelerated FDI flows in the electronics industry. The Japan Institute of Labor (1984: 281) estimated that cumulative FDI until 1979 produced a net loss of between 30,000 and 58,000 jobs in the electronics industry (the range depending on whether the replacement ratio of exports by FDI is 33 percent or 100 percent). Considering that in the early 1990s the electronics industry employed close to 1.7 million people, the estimated job losses even in the worst-case scenarios were not considered very damaging to the industry.[16]

Contrasting labor adjustment practices in the United States and Japan were also responsible for the marked differences in union attitudes toward foreign direct investment in the two countries. For the Japanese electronics industry, the need to cope with the problem of excess workforce due to structural changes in demand was not new. The post–oil shock recession of 1973–75 had posed the first labor adjustment challenge. During those years, the electronics industry experienced the largest reduction in employment up to that point: 185,000. Significantly, these employee cuts were not achieved through large-scale dismissals of regular workers (as often happens in the United States). Part-time employees, especially women, shouldered most of the labor adjustment. A survey of fifty-one companies showed that these enterprises reduced their employment of part-timers by 57.5 percent between 1973 and 1975. Since women fill most part-time positions, and automation particularly affected the production processes entrusted to female workers, the proportion of female employees in the electronic industry's workforce decreased markedly in this period.

The other means of adjustment pursued by electronics companies were temporary layoffs and early voluntary retirement. Companies used temporary layoffs only until the worst of the recession was over (27,000 people were let go temporarily in 1974–75). Early voluntary retirement plans were in place for a longer period. Between 1971 and 1981, 10,671 persons participated in these programs (Takeo Kinoshita 1984). Survey evidence on employment practices during this period also suggests differences by size of establishment. Large firms often transferred employees to subsidiaries, limited new recruitment, left vacancies unfilled, and restricted overtime hours. Medium-sized firms encouraged early retirement more strongly and used selective dismissal (Shimada 1980: 26).

The structural transformation of the electronics industry during the *endaka* era once more exacerbated the need for labor adjustment. Overall employment levels in electronics did not change much after 1985 (see Table 7.4). But the composition of employment in the industry was transformed by large reductions in the number of employees (especially in audio equipment, home appliances, and TV and radio receivers). The pains of adjustment were felt most strongly by smaller establishments, where, for example, the share of employment in the TV and radio receiver industry for firms with fewer than 300 employees decreased from roughly 30 to 15 percent between 1985 and 1992 (estimated from data in *Kōgyō Tokeihyō*, several years).

Labor adjustment practices in electronics firms in Japan proved resilient. In the 1990s (just as they had twenty years earlier), large firms relied mostly on the internal reallocation of the workforce and on temporary transfers or secondment to related firms; medium-sized firms engaged more actively in temporary dismissals and early retirement. Large-scale layoffs were not a major means of adjustment for large or medium-sized firms, and these companies requested employment subsidies to sustain their existing policies (Denki Rengō 1993: 6).

Labor adjustment practices in the Japanese electronics industry stand in sharp contrast to the massive dismissal of excess workforce undertaken by American consumer electronics firms in the 1970s and 1980s (see Abraham and Houseman 1989). In the United States, firms reduce their payroll more quickly in response to changes in demand, and production workers are hit hardest. In Japan, there is greater employment stability, but some adjustment has taken place. The fact that in Japan the less unionized workforce (small-firm employees and female part-timers) shouldered most of the adjustment burden, and that management avoided the dismissal of regular employees,

TABLE 7.4

Labor Adjustment in the Endaka *Era, 1970–1998 (number of employees)*

	1970	1980	1985	1988	1998	Change, 1985–98
Electronics industry	1,341,072	1,357,669	1,825,314	1,891,477	1,665,857	–159,457
Home appliances	99,568	113,151	138,224	129,715	109,409	–28,815
TV and radio receivers	85,547	48,989	26,943	19,957	10,768	–16,175
Audio equipment	152,026	200,450	210,966	162,008	71,712	–139,254
All manufacturing	11,679,680	10,932,041	10,889,949	10,911,123	10,399,378	–490,571

SOURCE: *Kōgyō Tōkeihyō*, several years.

largely explains organized labor's benevolent attitude toward outward direct investment.

FOREIGN DIRECT INVESTMENT AND REVERSE IMPORTS

Import penetration, of either foreign brand products or goods assembled abroad with national components, acted in the United States as a powerful incentive for trade protection and lobbying for constraints on multinational activity. The creation of COMPACT (Committee to Preserve American Color Television) in 1976 provides one of the clearest examples of a labor-management coalition to obtain relief from import competition. This group argued for quantitative restrictions on imports of finished CTV receivers and openly expressed its desire "not to see their plants and jobs relocated to foreign shores" (Millstein 1983: 128). COMPACT signified a large rift among American consumer electronics firms, in which companies with underdeveloped offshore networks (Zenith, Sylvania, and Magnavox) joined labor in their demand for trade protection.[17]

In Japan, dependence on electronics imports for the first time became a potentially disruptive issue during the *endaka* era (see Table 7.5). Before 1985 imports played a marginal role in the Japanese consumer electronics industry. However, following the yen appreciation the weight of imports in total domestic demand grew for all products, especially rapidly for VTRs (56 percent in 1997), tape recorders (46 percent), and TV receivers (24 percent). Despite the retreat of onshore production, import penetration generated little domestic opposition, and no voice was raised in favor of trade protection (unlike in the textile industry). Two main factors were responsible for this outcome: (1) foreign producers did not capture a larger share of the Japanese market, and (2) all Japanese consumer electronics firms engaged in reverse importing, thereby avoiding the potential clash between internationally and domestically oriented firms.

In order to understand why rapidly increasing import-penetration ratios did not generate a political response from Japanese management or labor, it is important to note first that foreign brand goods were not responsible for the expanded import volumes in the 1980s and 1990s. Japanese firms remained well entrenched in Japan, where in 1991 seven Japanese brands held 94 percent of the CTV market (see Hiramoto 1994). It was the spectacular rise in "reverse importing"—mostly from Japanese subsidiaries in Asia—that produced the changes in the trade structure of Japanese electronics.

A quick overview of Japanese trade and investment relations with Southeast Asia reinforces this point. Southeast Asia is the most important source of Japanese consumer electronics imports; its share increased rapidly, from 47 percent in 1985 to 69 percent in the early 1990s. Most imports from ASEAN nations were goods manufactured by Japanese-affiliated companies in the re-

TABLE 7.5
Retreating Domestic Production: Evolution of the Import Penetration Ratio, 1970–1997 (percent)

Product/Industry	1970	1980	1985	1988	1992	1997
TV receivers	0.0	0.3	0.5	2.5	7.7	24.2
Videotape recorders	0.0	0.0	0.0	1.9	6.4	55.9
Tape recorders	0.9	10.8	4.4	15.9	31.7	45.8
Consumer electronics	0.5	4.1	2.1	4.5	9.0	32.4
Industrial electronics	12.0	11.3	7.8	5.9	8.1	18.9
Electronic parts	8.4	23.2	16.7	18.5	26.4	68.5
Electronics industry	7.2	13.7	10.5	9.4	13.9	33.6

NOTE: The import penetration ratio is estimated as follows: imports / (production – exports + imports). If the import penetration ratio had been estimated using monetary values, the figures would probably had been lower given that Japan usually exports higher-value-added goods and imports low-value-added goods.

SOURCE: *Denshi Kōgyō Nenkan*, several years; EIAJ 1998.

gion (H. Tanaka 1993: 32). Countries where Japanese investment was concentrated in the recent past emerged as leading exporters of electronic consumer goods to Japan. In 1993, Malaysia led in exports of tape recorders to Japan (4,007,000 units), and was second in exports of VTRs (244,000 units) and color TVs (1,033,000 units). Thailand was third in color TV exports to Japan, having increased its shipments from 39,000 units in 1991 to 541,000 units in 1993 (EIAJ 1995).

MITI's surveys further corroborate the fact that reverse importing emerged as an important strategy for Japanese electronics multinationals. Whereas in 1980 only 2 percent of the exports of Japanese electronics subsidiaries in Asia were shipped to Japan, in 1992, 27 percent were directed to the home market. Not surprisingly, almost all reverse imports (90 percent) were intragroup transactions (MITI 1993b: 190).

There is another equally important reason for the calm response of both the Japanese electronics industry and the government to the rapid rise in import penetration ratios: reverse imports never became a source of political controversy. All major Japanese firms in this industry became full-fledged multinationals; none remained purely domestic in location of production or destiny of sales. Manufacturers therefore had no reason to oppose growing import volumes from overseas.

Finally, unlike in the textile industry, where upstream and midstream firms opposed the importing behavior of apparel companies, consumer electronics firms continued to rely mostly on Japanese components (through in-house manufacturing, quasi-vertical integration, or long-term trading with independent suppliers), and FDI only negatively affected the weakest link in the production chain: small, labor-intensive, lower-tier subcontractors. Rifts among segments of the Japanese electronics industry, therefore, did not emerge as a threat to the multinational strategy.

From the mid-1980s through the turn of the twenty-first century, the Japanese consumer electronics industry confronted the challenge of restructuring; it avoided losing comparative advantage by using foreign direct investment, largely self-financed, as an international adjustment strategy. During the *endaka* era, foreign direct investment boomed and domestic production was increasingly replaced by overseas manufacturing. For the first time, reverse imports became a major factor in the industrial adjustment of Japanese electronics.

But contrary to the American experience, the emigration of industry generated little opposition from Japanese labor and capital. Foreign producers did not capture a large share of the domestic market, the Japanese business community was not divided over FDI strategies, and organized labor did not suffer.

Self-reliance characterized the multinationalization of the consumer electronics industry. Japanese electronics MNCs used state FDI financing only in moderation. In keeping with this book's hypothesis, the industry's abundant resources and its lack of close ties to bureaucrats and politicians made it an unlikely recipient of public FDI assistance. The Japanese government never targeted consumer electronics as a key industry for growth, but concentrated its efforts on industrial electronics (semiconductors) and computers.

Although domestic consumer electronics production is increasingly cost-inefficient, the industry did not fall into a structural recession requiring state-orchestrated capacity curtailment. And a traditionally independent industry association shunned state tutelage in its the international adjustment strategy. Firms used their own investment resources rather than political solutions to meet their competitive challenges.

Conclusion: Crafting Comparative Advantage Through FDI

The Politics of Migrating Industries and State FDI Financing

To a degree unparalleled elsewhere in the industrialized world, Japanese public financial institutions helped industries facing decline to adjust through FDI. The resources channeled through Japanese public financial institutions overshadowed the more modest commitment of American, European, and other Asian states to bank on multinationals. Especially in the early postwar period, but to a significant extent even at the outset of the twenty-first century, FDI loans from public institutions financed a substantial share of Japanese firms' overseas investment. And some sectors (iron, steel, and nonferrous metals) were extremely dependent on public money to afford investing overseas.

The Japanese state showed its activism in MNC policy not only by selecting some industries over others to receive FDI credit, but also by zealously monitoring capital outflows for more than thirty years. Despite the process of financial liberalization, MITI and MOF maintained broad powers to stop any FDI project they deemed undesirable for financial or industrial policy reasons. The state made enormous financial effort to sustain those FDI projects that had cleared bureaucratic review and was a vibrant force behind the unfurling of Japanese multinationalism.

Japan's large role in financing foreign investment is one of the greatest puzzles in the debate over the developmental state. Why would a government so keen on building a home-based industrial juggernaut support the relocation of production abroad? Why didn't the loss of jobs and export opportunities restrict state banking on multinationals, as it did elsewhere?

FDI POLICYMAKING IN JAPAN

The Japanese government generously financed overseas investment by Japanese firms in order to overcome market failure in natural resource procurement and industrial adjustment. Much of the government's generosity also responded to political demands to subsidize economically inefficient but politically powerful interest groups.

The creation of the institutional machinery to finance overseas investment was initially inspired by the need to secure strategic natural resources abroad. Soon afterward, the Japan Eximbank began extending outward investment loans to manufacturing sectors whose international competitiveness had deteriorated. Many of these large-scale industries experiencing structural decline after World War II were well connected with the political world. The role of politicians was often crucial in meeting the industrial federations' demands for greater public relief from assistance programs with an FDI component.

Big business was not the only one to cash in on close relations with the LDP; small enterprises also lobbied successfully for public financing of outward investment. In 1976, LDP legislators endorsed their claim that the Japan Eximbank should increasingly cater to small-firm needs, and a decade later, amid the recessionary years of the strong yen, the Diet agreed to subsidize the lending programs of financial institutions serving small and medium-sized enterprises.

Politics was never far removed from public loan programs. Public FDI loans were not priced equally for all producer groups. And Japanese bureaucrats and politicians clashed repeatedly over the budgetary design of public FDI credit institutions, because funding rules hold the key to soft finance. Indeed, the institutional design of public FDI financing in Japan allowed some compensation to take place, but prevented rampant subsidization. Most FDI loans were channeled through the Japan Eximbank, which faced institutional constraints on providing extensive soft financing. To operate, the bank had to generate its own funds or borrow from the Treasury-run budget.[1] In contrast, other financial institutions (those in charge of small-business financing and economic assistance programs) received large appropriations from the general account budget to subsidize their lending and were not constrained by the principle of self-sustainability.

Politicians were able to use these different rules to open the window of soft FDI financing: they created new public agencies to appease private sector demands, the OECF, and the JFS; they eased the loan approval conditions in these institutions; and more important, they relaxed the fund procurement constraints on soft financing by allocating substantial subsidies to the politically useful public credit agencies.

However, the struggle between bureaucratic rationality and political expediency was far from over. Economic contraction and the realignment of party politics exerted a powerful influence on the institutional framework of FDI financing. In pursuit of administrative reform, the coalition governments of the mid-1990s forced a merger between the OECF and the Japan Eximbank, the premier agencies responsible for FDI financing. For decades they had been locked in a struggle to separate, not integrate, their operations. And with its economic stewardship severely questioned in the wake of a serious banking crisis and charges of a bloated FILP system, the Ministry of Finance lost to the LDP in devising new budgetary principles for Japanese public corporations.

Interbureaucratic rivalry also shaped FDI policymaking in Japan. MITI and MOF vigorously competed over the definition of FDI policy in its two key components: capital controls and preferential financing. The desire of each agency to expand its own jurisdiction and to protect important clients led to protracted negotiations during the postwar period over capital outflow liberalization. Moreover, turf battles among Treasury and industry bureaucrats produced a notorious duplication of functions among FDI credit-disbursing agencies (most notably between the OECF and the Japan Eximbank before 1975).

Of great relevance to the developmental state debate, MITI did not manage the core of the financing program for multinational investment. This ministry shared in the supervision of OECF and JFS, and had jurisdiction over the JODC and the Association for Small and Medium-Sized Businesses. Interestingly, all of these public institutions enjoyed more budgetary leeway to offer attractive FDI credit terms to the industries and firms encouraged by the government to invest overseas. Yet the volume of financing provided by the institutions under joint or exclusive MITI jurisdiction was very modest in comparison with that provided by the Japan Eximbank. The largest FDI creditor (Japan Eximbank, and then the international financial activities account of the JBIC) remained in the exclusive domain of MOF. MITI failed to gain control over the allocation of Japan Eximbank FDI credit after the oil shocks. Critics of the developmental state model are therefore right on mark when they point out that MITI did not control the allocation of industrial credit (in this case for multinational investment).[2]

THE UNEVEN REACH OF STATE FDI FINANCING

The experiences of the textiles and aluminum industries reflect the Japanese government's attempts to craft comparative advantage through foreign direct investment. Textiles, an industry with a faltering export drive, was able to protect its market share by turning to offshore production financed to a large degree with public credit. Government agencies and textile business partners (*sōgō shōsha*) endorsed an FDI strategy to sustain the industry's competitiveness, increasingly through multinational production.

But perhaps the most spectacular example of tampering with comparative advantage is the case of aluminum smelting. To facilitate the industry's restructuring at home and stabilize the supply of ingot to Japan, the government financed two mammoth projects in Indonesia and Brazil. Yet those national projects also generated tensions between the state and business in their overseas partnerships. In the Alunorte plant, Japanese private investors were indifferent to the state's predicament of sustaining (regardless of cost) a key bilateral economic cooperation initiative. Japanese investors withdrew from the project and did not renew their participation until the alumina market rebounded, but without offering new capital. The vagaries of the Alunorte plant forced the Japanese government to coin the term "seminational project" to explain the status of a project in which public financing persisted despite private sector withdrawal (and subsequent reentry).

In consumer electronics, firms drafted their FDI plans mostly unassisted by public banks. Traditionally loose ties with bureaucrats and politicians, a relative abundance of investment resources, and long experience in international production allowed Japanese firms to self-finance their mutinationalization. The experience of this industry is a healthy reminder that the Japanese state affected foreign investment flows by assisting some, but not all, Japanese industrial sectors.

POLITICAL OPPOSITION TO STATE FDI FINANCING

The neutralization of political opposition to offshore production was an important precondition to the full-fledged development of state FDI financing. Often Japan's record at industrial restructuring is praised because of the lack of strife among labor. In fact, this book's case studies revealed that economic restructuring was not painless. The nonunionized workforce (small-firm employees and part-timers—mostly women) suffered the most from the domestic recession and the shift to offshore production. Because hiring freezes and dismissals affected these unprotected groups most, Japanese unions did not challenge the foreign investment plans of management.

The most serious threat to FDI arose not from labor but from other segments of the business community. In all of the three industries discussed here the ratio of multinational production to domestic manufacturing was very high, and domestic markets were heavily penetrated by imports. Despite these shared characteristics, business opposition to FDI strategies varied by sector.

Electronics was remarkable for the smoothness with which international production strategies unfolded; no disgruntled industrialists challenged the targeting of the home market by offshore Japanese factories. But aluminum fabricators did not adhere to the state's scheme of favoring ingot from Japanese smelters; their purchases were guided exclusively by price considerations. In textiles, reverse imports polarized the industry. The flood of cheap imports moved spinners and weavers to call for trade protection that would jeopardize the overseas investments of apparel makers who had moved their manufacturing to less expensive foreign locations.

One general lesson is evident from these otherwise varied alignments of domestic interests: industrial fragmentation was a key factor in generating entrepreneurial hostility toward foreign direct investment. In both aluminum and textiles the downstream sector was uncommitted to the success of the FDI strategies of upstream firms because they were not constrained by *keiretsu* loyalties (fabricators and smelters were the children of mining and chemical firms, respectively, and forward integration in textiles was very limited).

AN EVALUATION OF PUBLIC FDI FINANCING IN JAPAN

The Japanese strategy of financing the offshore relocation of sunset industries had a mixed record. Three criteria are important indicators of a successful state FDI financing program: the accomplishment of stated goals, the eventual weaning of targeted industries from public loans, and the impact of FDI subsidies on Japanese public finances.

Some of the goals of public FDI financing were met (such as maintaining the international market share of Japanese textiles). But political intervention could not prevail over all market forces: for example, imports from other sources were able to displace ingot produced by offshore Japanese smelters. And public financing engendered some private sector dependence: many favored sectors were unable or unwilling to eventually undertake offshore investment plans autonomously.

The financial health of the public system of FDI financing held up for most of the postwar period, though. The Japan Eximbank relied little on public subsidies and dutifully repaid its FILP loans and private sector bonds. Still, bureaucratic control over soft financing rules may be hard to preserve with the prolonged economic contraction, as politically powerful constituencies lobby harder for FDI subsidization.

In Japan, the hand of the state visibly prodded the multinationalization of declining industries. Japan's financing of overseas investment was guided by the economic goals of raw materials procurement and industrial transformation, but also by the political motivations of protecting bureaucratic clients and cementing relationships with constituencies that could provide funds or votes. The sustainability of publicly supported FDI hinged on carefully circumventing the opposition to offshore relocation by disadvantaged sectors (labor and domestic capital). This is, in short, the political dynamic that characterized the emigration of declining industries in Japan.

Broader Implications of a Political Economy Model of FDI

The political economy of Japanese foreign direct investment also sheds light on some broader issues pertinent both to international and comparative political economy scholars and to Japan specialists. The broader implications of this book extend to three different areas: the IPE understanding of the adjustment options and political responses of sunset industries; the relationship between home governments and multinationals; and the complicated balance between strategic planning and pork-barrel politics in Japanese industrial policy.

This study of domestic support mechanisms for FDI strategies may also inform scholars concerned with national responses to changes in the world economy, and with the domestic political dynamics of international economic policy. The incentive structure for firms facing adjustment not only is guided by the protection and free-trade options, but also is affected by the costs of setting up a factory abroad. Thus the presence or absence of domestic institutions that support overseas investment may explain why firms in different countries react differently to the loss of comparative advantage.

This book underscores the shortcomings of political models of industrial adjustment and economic FDI theories that rule out the international mobility of sunset industries. Domestic institutions (government banks) can be catalysts in the multinationalization of declining industries and weak firms. Specifically, declining industries can travel across borders with the assistance of low-cost public financing.

This analysis also broadens existing views of the relationship between home states and multinational corporations. Conventionally, home government policy is limited to the use of diplomatic tools to prevent nationalization or unfair treatment of foreign companies abroad; the adoption of ad hoc measures (taxes, insurance, balance-of-payments safeguards) that influence the climate for overseas expansion; and the imposition of capital controls to monitor FDI projects.

Here I expand the possible scope of government action to include the offering of public credit to private corporations for offshore investment. Some states, but not all, have been eager to promote the international expansion of corporations to meet industrial policy goals for resource security and industrial adjustment, or to placate powerful constituencies. This view of home governments casts them in the role of bankers to MNCs; it also challenges the mainstream view that home government policies tend to converge. In fact, my finding that public financing of multinationalism differs from state to state opens up a new line of research in IPE: namely, why governments have been very concerned with negotiating sophisticated international rules to curb the national subsidization of exports (such as the OECD regime on export credit), but have not been equally concerned with restricting FDI subsidies.

At least two factors may have tamed the demand for an international regime governing FDI credit: (1) because the Japanese government financed sunset industries, there was no strong international concern that Japan used public credit to unfairly advantage vanguard industries with important spillover effects and high-value-added products;[3] (2) because the Japanese government did not massively subsidize FDI, there was no strong international incentive to negotiate international rules in this area. Future comparative work on state FDI financing should refine our understanding of why this area of national credit remains internationally unregulated.

Finally, this book addresses the domestic sources of foreign economic policy and the debate over the quality of public industrial financing. First, I caution against using Japan's lead in FDI financing as proof of Japanese mercantilism. My analysis debunks the myth of the cohesive and strategic state orchestrating the overseas expansion of Japanese multinational corporations; and it documents the high-profile conflicts between the private sector and the Japanese government in their partnership in large-scale investment projects abroad.

Second, I tackle a core debate over the quality of Japanese industrial policy. There is strong consensus in the field that in some areas of the Japanese political economy pork-barrel practices are prevalent (agriculture and construction, for example), but that in others bureaucracies and public agencies have remained insulated from interest group influence. However, this only begs the question of what kind of institutional checks prevent rent-seeking (subsidization of inefficient economic sectors) from growing to unbearable proportions, thereby thwarting the Japanese state's agenda of industrial upgrading.

This book's insight is that budgetary design influences whether pork-barrel practices emerge in public financing. In other words, budgetary rules act as focal points for the struggle among interest groups, politicians, and bureaucrats over the strings of soft financing in Japanese industrial policy. And because these battles are fought in each public financial agency, compensation and efficiency coexist closely, even within a single issue area.

In the early postwar period the Japanese bureaucracy was able to discipline its public lending program to carry out its developmental goals, but over time politicians became more influential in the FILP approval process and pressed for the establishment of soft financing agencies. This implication of my research, that budget structure affects the politicization of Japanese public financial institutions, should be of interest both to Japan specialists and to students of interest group pressure on the allocation of government industrial financing.

The political economy of state FDI financing thus illuminates the contours of government-business relations in Japan and, more generally, the role of domestic institutions in shaping the expansion of national industry across borders. This book aims to contribute to the fields of international and political economy by explaining how declining industries, if politically assisted, can be internationally mobile; how states bank on multinationals; and how institutional budgetary design in Japan served to check subsidization while leaving some room for political compensation.

Toward a Portable Model of State FDI Financing

Japan has far surpassed other industrial nations in its commitment to promoting multinational corporations. Does this mean that a political-economy model of FDI is applicable to only one country? Quite to the contrary, the benefit of the political-economy model developed here is that it helps explain the wider range of experience in other countries with public financing of overseas investment. Although some governments have been quite prepared to solve market failure in raw materials procurement and industrial adjustment through FDI loans, others have shied away from providing such subsidized credit. In order to explain this variation in state commitment to FDI financing, I offer a mini case study of South Korea's FDI policy, and conclude with a comparative discussion of Japan, the United States, and South Korea (henceforth Korea) that identifies the factors responsible for encouraging or hindering public banking on multinationals.

STATE BANKING ON MULTINATIONALS IN SOUTH KOREA

Korea's overseas investment dates back to 1968 with a timber project in Indonesia. But not until the late 1980s and 1990s did FDI flows become significant. Between 1968 and 1980, for example, overseas investments totaled a mere $145 million. During the 1980s, outward FDI increased to $1.8 billion, and in the 1990s a veritable boom in overseas investment took place: FDI reached $23.8 billion, equivalent to 92 percent of all Korean FDI in the postwar period (Seong-Bong Lee 2000: 3).

FDI Patterns

There are striking similarities between Japan and Korea in the industrial composition of their FDI flows. Natural resource procurement was the first motivation for Korean FDI, with forestry and mining dominating FDI flows until the 1980s. In 1984 investments in natural resources accounted for 51 percent of all cumulative Korean FDI (Chung Lee 1994: 283). Since the mid-1980s, however, manufacturing has played a much larger role, representing close to half of all outstanding Korean FDI in 1999 (Seong-Bong Lee 2000: 4).

In manufacturing, labor- and energy-intensive sectors operating with mature technologies accounted for a large share of Korean FDI. Basic and nonferrous metals, petroleum and chemicals, textiles and apparel, footwear, parts assembly, and miscellaneous products were heavily represented. These are the sectors in which Korea lost comparative advantage because of rising wages, spiraling energy costs, and currency appreciation (Keun Lee 1995: 218).[4]

A strong consensus exists among students of Korean FDI that these multinationals did not excel in the traditional firm-specific advantages associated with foreign direct investment (such as capital intensity, marketing outlays, technological superiority) (Kumar and Kim 1984; Keun Lee 1994; Sachwald 2001; Nicolas 2001). Rather, loss of comparative advantage and protectionism were the main drivers of Korea's business globalization.

Korean MNCs invested heavily elsewhere in Asia in order to regain cost competitiveness in labor- and resource-intensive manufacturing, and increasingly invested in industrialized nations in order to avoid tariffs or escape other trade retaliation measures (Keun Lee 1994; Nicolas 2001: 62). During the 1990s, the electronics industry emerged as one of the leading overseas investors. Most of its investments were in assembly operations in China and in more capital-intensive manufacturing in developed countries that raised protectionist barriers against Korean exports.

Capital Controls on FDI

The Korean government played a crucial role in the unfolding of Korean multinationalism, through its policies both of control and of promotion. The Korean state was worried not only that foreign multinationals could decrease the clout of its industrial policy, but also that overseas investments by Korean firms could result in the export of precious foreign exchange at a time of severe balance-of-payments shortages.[5] Therefore the government instituted one of the most rigorous systems of capital control, one that surpassed even Japan in its restrictions.

Draconian capital controls in the 1960s penalized illegal financial outflows of more than a million dollars with a minimum of ten years in jail or a maximum death sentence (Amsden 1989: 17). The government outlined the criteria for the authorization of FDI projects when it introduced outward FDI guidelines into the Foreign Exchange Control Law in 1968. It would authorize only FDI projects that promoted exports, that secured essential raw materials, or that were "*in industries in which competitiveness in the world market has been weakened under the nation's industrial structure*" (quoted in Kumar and Kim 1984: 52; emphasis mine). The government screened each potential FDI project and was adamant about monitoring the operation as well the performance of offshore subsidiaries—something that the Japanese state failed to achieve. Monitoring of FDI projects was so strict that "in the case of Korea, it is the government decision which ultimately counts in overseas investments" (Kumar and Kim 1984: 53).

A relaxation of balance-of-payments constraints in the 1980s as Korea's export-led industrialization took off, and international commitments to liberalize capital flows when Korea joined the OECD in 1996, forced the government to dismantle its tight regulatory regime. But until that point, the process of FDI liberalization was protracted and piecemeal.

In the late 1980s the government inaugurated a prior notification system for small FDI projects and gradually increased the amount a company could invest without prior approval from the government. In 1988 public officials for the first time allowed Korean investors to obtain funding for their offshore projects from foreign financial institutions (Park 2000: 593). The Korean state also progressively reduced the number of restricted sectors whose overseas investment activities were in principle prohibited: from fourteen business categories in the early 1990s to three areas in real estate in 1995. It eliminated them altogether when Korea joined the OECD.

Despite the progress made in easing FDI restrictions, the Korean government was prepared to reimpose controls if it deemed them necessary. In 1995, concerned about the deteriorating performance of offshore subsidiaries and the greater incidence of large Korean conglomerates (*chaebol*) financing their FDI ventures with foreign capital, it introduced ceilings for self-financing (equivalent to 20 percent of the project's value) and parent-firm payment guarantees. The goal of these measures was to slow down what it feared could be excessive expansion abroad in low-profit ventures (Park 2000: 596). Belated liberalization and the discretionary reintroduction of restrictions characterized the Korean policy on FDI controls.

Industrial Policy and the Promotion of FDI

The other side of Korean public policy toward multinationals—as in Japan—was the promotion through FDI financing of projects the government deemed compatible with its industrial policy objectives. The use of preferential financing to promote international business activity in fact fits neatly with Korea's industrial policy patterns. The Korean state's control over the entire financial system and its undisputed allocation powers over subsidized credit dwarfed those of the Japanese state.

The importance of preferential financing to the Korean developmental state cannot be exaggerated. Amsden (1989: 8) finds the key to the successful Korean industrialization drive in the ability of the state to exchange subsidies (most notably discounted loans) for high export performance among Korean firms. Woo-Cummings concurs, asserting that "at the core of [Korean] state power is its channeling of the flow of money. As such, money is not merely a medium of exchange but also a political tool" (1991: 2).

The Korean government, under the Chung-hee Park regime in the

1960s, adopted a far more interventionist approach than the Japanese state to achieve its industrial policy goals. In 1961 the government nationalized all commercial banks, taking complete control of the loan allocation decisions of these institutions. In addition, it instituted a program of policy loans that offered preferential interest rates, loan maturity, and collateral requirements. In 1981 these loans constituted more than 66 percent of all bank credit (Chung 1990: 117). Even in 1991—after a process of financial liberalization—policy credit as a share of total domestic loans was a hefty 30.9 percent (Cho and Kim 1995: 42). The Korean industrialization drive hinged on a credit-based system in which firms meet most of their corporate investment needs through bank financing (see Zysman 1983).

The other side of the coin in this intermediated financial system was of course highly leveraged private firms. By international standards, Korean enterprises were extremely dependent on bank credit. In the 1970s the debt/equity ratio for firms in Brazil and Mexico ranged between 100 and 120 percent, in Taiwan from 160 to 200 percent, and in Korea between 300 and 400 percent (Woo-Cummings, 1991: 12). The threat of bankruptcy was constant for highly leveraged firms that had to weather economic adversity despite high fixed costs (loan interest payments and redundant workforces that are hard to reduce). Because the government controlled the loan approval process and set interest rates, it held great sway over the private sector.

Differences between Japan and Korea were not limited to the degree of direct bureaucratic intervention in the financial system. In Korea, policy loans were not administered exclusively by public financial institutions as they were in Japan; they were also widely disbursed through banks even after banks were privatized in the 1980s. The two countries' preferential credit systems were also funded differently. The Korean government relied extensively on foreign loans, whereas the Japanese state avoided foreign financing and relied instead on the mobilization of domestic savings.[6] Finally, whereas in Japan fiscal funds (collected through the postal savings system) were essential in supplying the resources for policy loans, in Korea central bank credits and bank deposits played a much larger role. For instance, between 1973 and 1991, government funds accounted for only 7.6 percent of policy loans, whereas central bank credits were responsible for 35.1 percent (Cho and Kim 1995: 42–43).

The Korean government relied on preferential financing to promote export-led industrialization. Before the creation of the Korea Eximbank in 1976 the government was already promoting exports through special credit programs. Most notably, starting in the 1960s, firms with export letters of credit received automatic approval of their loan applications, and after the establishment of general trading companies in the mid-1970s these enterprises also qualified for special lines of credit.

Export credit was highly subsidized as Korea embarked on its heavy chemical industrialization drive in the 1970s. The interest rate on export loans (9.7 percent) was roughly half that of general loans (17.3 percent) (Cho and Kim 1995: 32). Credit support for exporters became much more systematized with the establishment of the Korea Eximbank in order to provide longer-term financing for capital-intensive goods purchased over time.

From the outset, however, the Korea Eximbank also endorsed the financing of Korean multinationals whose projects were deemed compatible with development guidelines. The Korea Eximbank consistently refused to finance projects it considered nonessential for industrial upgrading or resource security, including real estate, entertainment, banking, and insurance. For all other sectors, long-term FDI loans were available to Korean firms in an amount equivalent to up to 90 percent of the FDI project's costs (Korea Eximbank 1996: 25).

The Korea Eximbank's goals are clearly reflected in the industrial allocation of overseas investment loans. The main reason for launching the FDI financing program was to facilitate the procurement and processing of raw materials, and between 1976 and 1984 natural resource projects accounted for 61.8 percent of Korea Eximbank's FDI credit (mining alone represented 47.6 percent). After 1985 the Korea Eximbank dramatically reoriented its priorities. Manufacturing, which had received a mere 4 percent of all FDI loans before the mid-1980s, received 89.8 percent of all FDI credit between 1985 and 1997. Natural resource development receded in importance (with a 4.5 percent share), and trade never received more than 2.2 percent.[7]

FDI financing fluctuated in importance in the operations of the Korean Eximbank. In its early years, export financing was clearly the bank's raison d'être: it represented 92 percent of all loan operations between 1976 and 1983. Later, FDI gained prominence in the bank's activities, reaching 8 percent of all loan commitments between 1984 and 1996. Then, with the onset of the Asian financial crisis in 1997, the Korea Eximbank—pressed to generate precious foreign exchange—reverted to its original mandate as an export promotion agency. The share of export credit soared to 94 percent, and FDI financing declined to 4 percent of all loans approved between 1997 and 2002 (Koo and Lee 1985; Japan Eximbank 1999, several years; Korea Eximbank, *Annual Report*, several years).

Despite these fluctuations in the share of FDI credit in total loan operations, the Korea Eximbank continues to be the premier public agency for the promotion of Korean multinationals. As in Japan, other specialized agencies to promote FDI in mining and petroleum exploration were created; and reflecting a similar understanding of the interrelationship between economic assistance and private investment, in 1986 the Korean government inaugurated the Economic Development Cooperation Fund to administer the ODA program *and* to finance investment projects of Korean enterprises in the developing world. The legendary disputes in Japan between the Japan Eximbank and OECF were not replicated in Korea, however, because the Economic Development Cooperation Fund is administered entirely by the Korea Eximbank; it is made available only to projects that did not qualify for bank financing, small enterprises, and nonmanufacturing ventures (Korea Eximbank 1996: 26–27).

The lion's share of the FDI loans continued to be administered by the Korea Eximbank. This public financial institution had a powerful influence on Korean multinationalism through its credit program. In the early 1980s the Bank of Korea released information showing that the share of Korean Eximbank's loans for equity investments in offshore projects was 26.9 percent in forestry, 35.3 percent in fishery, 59.6 percent in mining, and 17.9 percent in manufacturing. On the basis of these statistics, Koo and Lee concluded: "There are few domestic banks in Korea which can finance Korean firms' foreign investment since domestic banks are in a perennial shortage of funds. Thus, the Korea Eximbank remains the only bank in Korea which provides financing for such investments" (1985: 84).

Firms' dependence on the state to fund overseas ventures was not eliminated with the passage of time either. In 1997, the Korea Eximbank's overseas investment loans represented 13.8 percent of cumulative FDI in mining, 23.9 percent in manufacturing, and an extraordinary 61.6 percent in forestry, fisheries, and agriculture combined.[8]

Capital Liberalization and the Erosion of State Autonomy

The clout of the Korean developmental state, however, decreased over time in response to two fundamental changes: capital liberalization and the loss of state autonomy in relation to organized groups in society. In the 1980s, faced with substantial pressure from the United States, the Korean government eased its controls on financing. However, mirroring the case of capital controls, public authorities dragged their feet on the liberalization of the financial system. Although all banks were privatized in the early 1980s, the liberalization envisioned by this act was slow to arrive. The Korean state retained substantial control over these commercial banks: it introduced strict restrictions so that they could not be taken over by the *chaebol* (the maximum ownership share for single shareholders was fixed at 10 percent); and it continued to oversee the management of the banks, appointing the directors and issuing guidelines for loan approval (Woo-Cummings 1991: 196).

The government gradually liberalized interest rates, and since the early 1980s the gap in interest rates between policy loans and general loans has almost disappeared. However, in an economy where credit was still scarce, the allocation of policy loans continued to provide the government with powerful leverage over industry.

Other reforms in the late 1990s included liberalizing the influx of foreign capital, establishing nonbanking financial institutions without limitations on *chaebol* ownership, and lifting restrictions on the stock market. With these changes in place, *chaebol* could decrease their dependence on state financing, and in the mid-1990s massively increase their short-term foreign debt (Zhang 2003).

Just as the barriers on international financial transactions were gradually lifted, important changes in the relationship between the Korean state and organized society were in store. Some scholars attribute the rapid industrialization of Korea to its being a developmental state insulated from growth-retarding lobbying groups. According to Minns (2001), the high degree of state autonomy was the result of a unique historical legacy: the Japanese occupation of Korea, which eliminated the power of the landed aristocracy and hindered the development of a local entrepreneurial class; in addition, the US occupation authorities demobilized the radical peasant and workers' unions that proliferated briefly in the 1940s. And the emerging business groups—*chaebol*—were extremely dependent on public assistance to expand rapidly. Others claim, however, that the state never had such autonomy, even at the height of bureaucratic control during the 1960s and 1970s (Kang 2002: 178). In this view, bureaucrats were not impervious to private sector lobbying; and bribes (political contributions) were a prerequisite to gaining access to preferential state financing.

Despite their different interpretations of Korean state insularity in the early postwar period, both Minns and Kang agree that over time the explosive expansion of the *chaebol* brought about a major shift in the correlation of forces between big business and the Korean state. Quite simply, the government could not threaten to withdraw its support for a *chaebol* during an economic downturn because the fall of even one corporate giant would be so harmful to the economy. The erosion of state autonomy was also the result of a more militant labor movement during the democratic transition of Korea in 1987 (Kong 1995). Ultimately, independent unions, competitive elections, and civilian governments helped shelve the authoritarian developmental past.

The Rise of Union Power and the Hollowing-Out Debate

Labor-management relations in Korea and Japan resembled each other in their common practices of seniority promotion, enterprise unionism, and lifetime employment for white-collar workers in large enterprises (Lee, Kim, and Bae 2000). The similarities end there, however.

The Korean government established a highly repressive system of labor control that left little room for Korean workers to organize to improve their workplace conditions. In 1961 the Korean government eliminated all trade unions and established the officially sanctioned Federation of Korean Trade Unions as the sole representative of the worker class. In 1971 the government banned all strikes and severely restricted collective bargaining rights; and for the following decades it was prepared to use force to repress any sign of labor discontent with the exacting working conditions (nonimplementation of labor standards, long hours, and low salaries among them) (Vogel and Lindauer 1997). The authoritarian elite considered a docile and inexpensive labor force essential for advancing Korea's position in the international division of labor.

This system of tight labor control ended abruptly in 1987 after an unprecedented wave of massive worker strikes and student demonstrations forced the government to promise both improved labor representation and competitive elections. A much more vocal labor union movement emerged in South Korea, and two issues dominated the agenda of this empowered social actor: the consolidation of a genuinely independent labor union movement, and job security. These two objectives became increasingly intertwined.

To combat the economic crisis that the country experienced in the late 1990s, the government offered concessions on union representation in exchange for more employment flexibility. Although labor resisted and in January 1997 once again launched a spectacular strike campaign, in the end it had to accept the tradeoff. By the spring of 1998 the government had agreed to recognize the independent Korean Confederation of Trade Unions, to grant collective bargaining rights to public servants, and to lift the restraints on union political activities. In exchange, labor laws were revised to allow layoffs to eliminate redundancy and the hiring of substitute workers during strikes (Koo 2000: 246). The *chaebol*, much more so than their Japanese counterparts, jumped at this opportunity to downsize their workforces through layoffs. Consequently, the unemployment rate in Korea soared from 2.1 percent in 1997 to 9 percent in 1999 (Lee, Kim, and Bae 2000).

Intensive corporate restructuring and large-scale job dismissals led to friction with the union movement. The Korean labor movement laid the blame for the recent economic debacle on excessive foreign borrowing by the *chaebol* and rejected the IMF's prescriptions for employment flexibility to facilitate restructuring. However, Korean unions did not single out the internationalization of production as a contributor to the problem. Massive capital inflows—not outflows—were at the center of the labor critique of corporate behavior and state management of the economy.

The lack of union opposition to offshore production through subsidized public credit is not surprising considering the moderate, and in general positive, influence of outward direct investment on the Korean economy. Domestic investment and overseas investment expanded simultaneously between 1986 and 1990, suggesting that the growth of investment abroad did not detract from investment projects at home. The work of Kim (1998) determined that overseas investment stimulates the export of machinery and parts from the home country to the host nation and did not harm domestic employment opportunities either. When outward investment intensified in the late 1980s and mid-1990s, the unemployment rate in Korea actually fell and reached an all-time low of 2 percent in 1995. Quite simply, Korean overseas investment was too small to substantially affect the performance of the domestic economy. Cumulative foreign direct investment as a share of GDP in Korea was very modest by international standards: 2.2 percent in 1995. In contrast, it was 6 percent in Japan, 9.8 percent in the United States, and 31.2 percent in Sweden (Kim 1998: 17, 25).

Overseas investment did not foster deindustrialization in Korea, and yet the Korean government was quite prepared to intervene if it judged the offshore investments of a particular industry to be "excessive." The best-documented case is that of the footwear industry in the late 1980s. As many Korean footwear firms sought to relocate in lower-cost locations in Asia (notably Indonesia), the government moved to restrict FDI in footwear in an effort to prevent deindustrialization and loss of export opportunities. This measure backfired, though; the Korean footwear industry continued to lose competitiveness and several firms went bankrupt in 1992. A year later, the government eliminated the special restriction on FDI in footwear (Keun Lee 1994: 190–91).

Union opposition and concerns about hollowing-out were not responsible for more recent restrictions on state FDI financing. In 1997 the cause was the Asian financial crisis. Scrambling for funds in the stormy years following the currency crisis, the Korean Eximbank very abruptly reoriented its financing priorities. Overseas investment loans contracted by 96 percent in 1998–99 (that year amounting to only 5 billion won), as the bank required large capital subscriptions from the government in order to fund its operations; it more than tripled its paid-in-capital from 870.9 billion won at the end of 1997 to 2,675.8 billion won at the end of 2002. Only in the years 2001 and 2002 did the bank return to international capital markets—traditionally a major funding source—through syndicated loans and bond issues. Demonstrating Korea's strong desire to promote MNCs—and perhaps more fundamentally the bank's improved financial condition—overseas investment credit quickly recovered in 2001 and 2002 to 153 billion and 398 billion won, respectively (Korea Eximbank, *Annual Report*, several years). This sharp fluctuation in public FDI finance underscores once more the key importance of robust fund procurement structures for a state to perform the role of banker to MNCs.

WHEN SHOULD WE EXPECT THE GOVERNMENT TO BANK ON ITS MULTINATIONALS? SOME REFLECTIONS

The contrasting experiences of the United States, South Korea, and Japan with state FDI financing shed light on the factors conducive to an active public loan program for multinational corporations. Three issues in particular seem to directly influence whether a state will assume the role of banker to MNCs: (1) the existence of market failure in raw materials supply and industrial adjustment, *and* the relative attractiveness of public FDI financing over other state solutions; (2) the legitimacy of an active industrial policy that gives the state leverage over the private sector in order to interdict or subsidize multinationalization strategies; and (3) national labor adjustment institutions that neutralize the potential opposition of unions to FDI subsidies that favor internationally mobile capital.

Solving Market Failure Through Subsidized FDI

State intervention in the economy is usually justified in cases where the market, left to its own devices, would generate inferior outcomes. Market failure can occur for a variety of reasons: high risk and uncertainty, insufficient investment capital, and others. Raw materials supply and industrial adjustment in particular can be plagued by market failure, prompting state intervention. For instance, the capital intensity and high sunk costs of large raw materials processing projects may deter private firms from investing in the developing world. And the market itself may be very thin if, instead of arm's-length transactions, host governments or a handful of MNCs already control the production and commercialization of these commodities. In the case of industrial adjustment, the reallocation of factors of production from industries that have lost comparative advantage to new growth sectors may also fail to occur. The difficulty of retraining labor and redirecting industry specific capital to new sectors may spur labor and management campaigns to keep a dying industry alive.

States have different options for dealing with market failure in resource supply and industrial restructuring. To secure access to raw materials, they may promote domestic production, acquire colonies, or protect the ownership rights of their multinationals; or through public FDI financing they can both lower the financial costs of these huge investments and reduce political risk by making the home state a shareholder in an offshore investment project. To facilitate industrial adjustment, states can rely on cartel policy and offer rationalization subsidies; they can insulate an industry from international competition through trade protection; or they can subsidize the relocation of production to lower-cost locations abroad with FDI credit.

All three countries discussed here have faced the challenge of resource security and industrial change. Japan and Korea, however, chose different solutions from the United States. The United States is well endowed with natural resources, and after World War II it emerged as one of the most powerful countries in the international system. It therefore emphasized domestic production and a foreign policy protecting US multinationals against the risk of forced disinvestment or nationalization.

Japan and Korea faced other constraints and consequently responded differently to similar challenges. Raw materials are scarce in both countries, and in the postwar period neither one had the political clout to actively protect the ownership rights of its multinationals. Japan lost all of its colonies and was diplomatically isolated from its neighboring Asian countries. Korea regained its independence from Japan, but was quickly partitioned and suffered great destruction in the Korean War. In order to regain access to essential supply lines of raw materials, both Japan and South Korea emphasized economic cooperation projects with resource-rich nations, relying heavily on home state financing through both ODA loans and FDI credit.

In all three countries, industries that had lost competitiveness in international markets sought some form of public relief. Again, the options entertained by each state for dealing with industrial restructuring were very different. The US government, lacking both an interventionist industrial policy and the budgetary means to downsize industries, dealt with industrial adjustment issues mostly through trade policy. Japan and South Korea, increasingly pressured by the international community to liberalize their markets, used a combination of covert protectionism (nontariff barriers), rationalization subsidies, and FDI loans to relocate mature segments of the industry abroad.

FDI Industrial Policy and National Credit Programs

Reflecting their broader industrial policy traditions, these three nations articulated very different FDI policies. The United States adopted a laissez-faire attitude: it neither monitored the investment plans of its firms nor provided them with any significant public funds to undertake overseas investment. In contrast, Japan and South Korea attempted both strict oversight of FDI projects and subsidization of desirable offshore ventures. But the policies of Japan and Korea also differed in fundamental ways. There is no doubt that South Korea imposed much harsher capital controls: the penalties for unauthorized overseas transfers were much stiffer than in Japan, and the South Korean government was able to do what its Japanese counterpart could not: monitor the offshore subsidiaries of Korean enterprises.

The more encompassing Korean financial industrial policy was likely responsible for the success of the state in exerting tighter control over its multinationals. Although both Japan and Korea had credit-based systems in which the state for most of the postwar period controlled the allocation of scarce investment capital, the Korean government pursued a far more interventionist policy: it nationalized all banks in 1961, and despite the privatization process of the 1980s it retained substantial control over the operation of the commercial banks. Japan, rather than displacing the private sector, followed a market-conforming credit policy, offering discounted interest rates and longer-term loans.

In addition, Japan funded its large national credit program mostly with citizens' private savings in the postal system. Korea relied more on foreign funds and central bank credit. Thus the Korean (FDI) public credit program was always more at risk of generating inflation and was exposed to sharp fluctuations in the availability of foreign capital. This vulnerability became evident during the 1997 financial crisis, when FDI loans from the Korea Eximbank contracted sharply.

These differences in national credit programs had important political implications. In Japan, the bureaucracy and the ruling party competed to control the allocation of the vast FILP resources; but in Korea the political contest over soft public financing was played differently given the moderate importance of fiscal funds to the state's indicative credit policies.

It is undeniable that both the Japanese and Korean governments lost leverage over their multinational corporations owing to the process of capital outflow liberalization and the internationalization of corporate finance. They abandoned their very strict monitoring mechanisms and replaced them with ex post facto reporting requirements. The result was much less discretion on the part of national authorities to block FDI projects. Moreover, many MNCs diversified their sources of financing by tapping bond and stock markets at home and abroad.

However, the shift toward internationalization and securitization of corporate financing was much more pronounced among large and profitable firms. Smaller enterprises and firms in contracting industries remained much more dependent on public loans to meet their offshore investment needs.

Domestic Unions and Multinational Capital

Despite the headline appeal of hollowing-out stories, none of the studies in these three nations confirmed a link between foreign direct investment and deindustrialization. Instead, these analyses consistently found FDI to be positively correlated with export performance and to be unrelated to the unemployment rate in the United States, Korea, or Japan.

Once more, however, the Korean and Japanese governments stood out for their willingness to intervene and slow down FDI plans that might disrupt individual industries. The Japanese government worried about textile reverse imports, and the Korean authorities were concerned about the FDI rush by footwear producers. And yet the experiences of these two industries are a sober reminder of the limits of state intervention.

The Korean restraints on footwear FDI backfired; the industry continued to lose export competitiveness and many enterprises went bankrupt. A year later the government had to lift its special controls and allow footwear companies to try to recoup competitiveness in lower-cost locations. The Japanese government effectively restrained reverse imports in the upstream segment of the textile industry, but when it had to graduate textiles from the list of restricted sectors subject to more stringent FDI controls, it was increasingly unable to moderate the apparel makers' aggressive targeting of the home market. Government officials found themselves trying to mediate between different textile subsectors with conflicting trade preferences.

National unions played a very different role in the politics of FDI support in these three nations. Only in the United States did unions consistently challenge the FDI plans of management and circumscribe the range of action of OPIC by forcing public agencies to consider whether an FDI proposal would affect domestic employment. A combination of high job insecurity, worker strikes, and national mobilization of industrial federations was responsible for this outcome.

The history of the South Korean labor movement could not be more at odds with the US tradition of active unions and conflictive labor-management relations. For most of the postwar period, the Korean state effectively repressed the labor movement, preventing the formation of any independent union and condoning low wages and inferior labor standards. The Korean labor movement successfully challenged state power, playing a key role in the democratic transition of 1987. But the independent union movement did not question the government's use of public credit to promote MNCs. The labor movement was willing to exchange concessions on job security for the expansion of its political representation rights; and it attributed the recent economic contraction and rising unemployment rate to the vagaries of massive inflows of short-term portfolio capital, not to the outflow of financial resources in the form of direct investment.

In Japan, national labor adjustment institutions were also central in explaining the absence of union opposition to state FDI financing. Despite the prolonged recession, Japanese large enterprises were much more reluctant than their *chaebol* counterparts to engage in massive layoffs; instead they used well-proven labor adjustment practices (hiring freezes, reduction in overtime, and the like) to minimize clashes with unions over employment security. The nonunionized sector of the Japanese economy absorbed most of the adjustment burden: female employees, part-timers, workers in small enterprises, and lower-tier contractors lost jobs when industries contracted domestically and shifted production overseas.

This brief comparison of the United States, South Korea, and Japan reveals some of the conditions necessary for the emergence of state financing of overseas investment. Among them are market failure in raw materials procurement and industrial restructuring, robust public loan programs, and the neutralization of labor opposition. When these conditions exist, states do bank on multinational expansion and can exert a powerful influence in the internationalization of industry.

Reference Matter

Notes

Introduction

1. I adhere to Komiya's (1988: 242) definition of FDI as "a form of long-term international capital movement made for the purpose of productive activity and accompanied by the intention of managerial control or participation in the management of a foreign firm." Throughout the book I use the terms *FDI* to refer to outward direct investment flows, and *multinationalism* to denote the expansion of firms undertaking foreign production.

Chapter 1: Preferential FDI Financing and International Industrial Adjustment

1. One notable exception is the work of Ozawa (1986), who was the first to point to the crucial role that the Japan Eximbank played in promoting Japanese multinational corporations. This book seeks to build on that insight by providing a political economy model of state FDI financing that can explain why Japan leads internationally in the public funding of overseas investment, what the domestic politics are behind the allocation of FDI subsidies, and what the experience of Japanese sunset industries has been with publicly funded international adjustment strategies.

2. Owing to balance of payments concerns, the United States did impose capital controls on overseas investment between 1963 and 1974 in the form of interest equalization taxes and voluntary capital restraints (Safarian 1993; Berhman and Grosse 1990: 76–78).

3. The United States did stand out in the past for its active diplomacy of sanctions and overt/covert intervention to protect ownership rights of American MNCs against the risks of expropriation and nationalization (Lipson 1985). But Krasner (1978) argues that Cold War security considerations better explain the pattern of US reprisals. Regardless of the economic or strategic motivations of US actions against expropriation, with the codification of investment protection rules both bilaterally and multilaterally, unilateral punitive practices have subsided (Rodman 1993).

4. Doremus et al. (1998) make a separate, but related, critique of convergence theory. These authors find significant differences in the behavior of Japanese, German, and US MNCs (in terms of R&D patterns, FDI strategies, and technology trade preferences) that can be traced back to distinct national systems of innovation,

finance, and investment. Although Doremus et al. do not specifically discuss home government FDI policy, my analysis of public FDI financing concurs with theirs on the divergent and significant influence of states on MNC expansion. In fact, both these arguments on distinctive MNC behavior *and* divergent home government FDI policy fit well with one of the most influential paradigms in comparative political economy—the varieties-of-capitalism model—with its emphasis on persistent differences across political economies in their basic institutional structures (such as corporate governance and labor markets) (Hall and Soskice 2001: 4).

5. Table 1.2 does not include the UK because the Commonwealth Development Corporation (CDC) was partially privatized in 1999. France is not included either due to the stiff requirements for FDI loan approval imposed by the French government. For example, Michalet (1997: 318) reports that until the late 1970s the French government required additional exports (seven times the value of the overseas investment amount) to release public FDI loans. Other countries that do not appear in Table 1.2 but also have public FDI programs include Denmark, Holland, and Canada. The FDI programs of these countries were even smaller, and therefore they were not included in Table 1.2 (Japan Eximbank *Gyōmu Binran* 1999: 287–90.)

6. JBIC was only created in October 1999 through the merger of the two most important government agencies financing FDI (the Japanese Eximbank and the Overseas Economic Cooperation Fund). For purposes of this cross-national comparison I use the consolidated JBIC, but Chapter 4 analyzes in depth the separate evolution of these institutions and the politics behind their integration.

7. I could not ascertain the precise amount of OPIC's direct FDI loans for the years 1993–2000 because the annual report for those years discloses only total FDI financing amounts (loan guarantees plus direct loans). Loan guarantees have always superseded direct loans (for example they totaled $2,429.5 million for the 1971–92 period), so I left out these years to avoid overrepresenting the actual direct financing of US FDI through OPIC. In any case, it is safe to conclude that the US government has provided very limited financial assistance for specific investment projects abroad, even for the more strategic raw material investments (Krasner 1978). Perhaps the most direct promotional measure for the internationalization of production in the United States has been the offshore assembly provisions of the US Tariff Code (formerly known as sections 806/807). It should nevertheless be noted that offshore provisions do not favor FDI over other forms of outward processing, such as subcontracting or licensing. It is, therefore, not surprising that large electronics and automobile manufacturing firms have self-financed their own factories overseas, while smaller and traditionally domestically oriented firms (textiles and apparel) have used offshore assembly provisions to commission production to foreign firms (Clark, Sawyer, and Sprinkle 1989).

8. Again, this finding on the importance of the state in financing Asian multinationalism fits well with Hall and Soskice's (2001: 18) observation that in coordinated market economies firms traditionally resorted to bank loans (from public and private institutions) given the underdevelopment of the stock market. The new insight offered here is that in some of these Asian countries public industrial financing not only targeted domestic investment but also supported FDI strategies.

9. As part of this effort to discipline its activities, OPIC was not allowed to make

equity investments abroad. In 1987, OPIC inaugurated the investment funds program to support private equity funds in emerging markets. OPIC, however, does not directly contribute capital to these funds and limits its participation to loan guarantees in case of default (GAO 2000).

10. For a strong critique of OPIC's portfolio performance and an argument for privatizing the institution, see Shields 1999.

11. Aid is tied when the recipient nation must use some of the economic assistance to buy products from donor country companies. The evolution of the OECD regime on government export credit is ably analyzed by Ray (1995), Moravcsik (1989), and Evans and Oye (2001).

12. The unrestricted application of export credit models to public FDI financing is compromised by the complexities behind the government's decision to finance overseas investment: Should location (domestic manufacture) or nationality (national firms producing across borders) be the preferred industrial policy goal? And how can the state neutralize social opposition (labor) to a preferential credit program that favors only internationally mobile factors of production (capital)? On the question of location versus nationality in Japanese foreign economic policy, see Samuels and Heginbotham 1998: 184, 200.

13. Bergsten, Horst, and Moran (1978: 125) point out that consumer states seek to secure the supply of raw materials through three different strategies: "developing self-sufficiency, acquiring colonies, and promoting foreign direct investment in order to have their 'own' companies as suppliers." US and European promotional measures have been limited to the protection of their firms' ownership rights abroad. The Japanese innovation in the area of FDI promotion is precisely the subject of this book: preferential FDI financing.

14. Economic considerations are of course not the only or the overriding objective of imperialism. Security, geopolitics, and prestige have also been decisive factors behind empire-building. For a good discussion of the varied motives behind colonial expansion, see Gann 1984.

15. One of the best discussions of the link between the reparations program and official programs of economic assistance continues to be Yanaga 1968.

16. The OECD supports "positive adjustment policies" that are transparent, temporary, and efficiency- and market-oriented. Critics of state involvement in industrial adjustment believe it perpetuates the existence of uncompetitive industry, eliminates market incentives for adjustment, and wastes public resources on industries without a future.

17. For a good overview of the history of US-Japanese trade frictions, see Cohen 1998.

18. Kojima 1978; Ozawa 1978; Wakasugi 1989.

19. Nelson (1988: 830) provides a good critique of endogenous tariff theory by noting the serious underdevelopment of the institutional structure through which protection is demanded and supplied.

20. The other key variable of importance to Uriu is industrial concentration: large firms possess the economic resources necessary to avoid political solutions.

21. Labor's opposition to FDI has been widely documented in the United States, but little studied in the case of Japan. One exception is J. Goto 1990.

22. Hymer in 1960 was the first to pose the idea that proprietary advantages are a precondition for foreign direct investment, and his insight has guided all microeconomic models of FDI. See Yamin (1991) for a good review of Hymer's contribution to international production theory. Kindleberger (1969) and Caves (1971) are other well-known exponents of the industrial structure approach to FDI, in that they both emphasize that overseas investment is concentrated in oligopolistic industries well endowed with the tangible and intangible assets necessary to outcompete local rivals.

23. Buckley and Casson (1976), Rugman (1982), and Buckley (1989) pioneered the application to FDI of Penrose's model on the growth of the firm, giving birth to what is known as the internalization approach. This approach presupposes another kind of market failure, this time transactional, causing firms to prefer internal trading to arm's-length contracts.

24. Clegg (1987) determined that Japanese transnational corporations in the first half of the postwar period (until 1975) did not have the same strong ownership advantages enjoyed by their counterparts in other industrialized nations. He concluded that Japanese FDI represents a different pattern of international production, since its direct investments had the lowest research and capital intensities (Japan was the only country in the sample with a negative coefficient for capital intensity).

25. Other scholars who have contributed to building a macroeconomic theory of FDI include Ozawa (1978; 1993), Wakasugi (1989), and C.H. Lee (1990). Case studies of firms' adjustment through industrial diversification and FDI can be found in Yoshihara 1978; Hara 1992; and Van Tho 1992.

26. Dunning (1992) points out that because of its neoclassical stance Kojima's theory cannot explain investment flows that are not guided by the distribution of factor endowments, but that are triggered by the need to overcome market failure through the exploitation of economies of scale, product differentiation, and other methods. Dunning argues that Kojima disregards the essence of multinational enterprise activity—the internalization of intermediate product markets—and that his endorsement of a perfect competition paradigm leads him to conclude that intrafirm resource allocation will always be inferior to market-dictated outcomes. Buckley (1983) also notes that Kojima's theory excludes direct investment flows between advanced countries and cannot account for cross-investment between two countries within an industry.

27. Government organizations (financial agencies and their responsible ministries) are not the only institutions that influence Japanese FDI industrial patterns. Economic institutions—that is, business groups, or *keiretsu*—also figured prominently in the multinationalization of Japanese industry. Ozawa (1978) and Kojima and Ozawa (1984) pioneered this line of analysis by demonstrating the pivotal role of general trading companies (*sōgō shōsha*) as organizers of offshore projects.

Later on, Hatch and Yamamura (1996) discussed the central importance of vertically integrated production networks (parent-subcontractor groups) to Japanese investment in Asia. I have argued elsewhere (Solís 1998; 1997) that this degree of interfirm coordination of FDI strategies is indeed remarkable, but is in fact limited to those industries where relational transacting is predominant.

General trading companies—key members of the intermarket *keiretsu*—organized structured patterns of interfirm exchange to replace spot contracting with recurrent, long-term transactions. To sustain their trade intermediation business, the general trading companies (*sōgō shōsha*) offered their clients a variety of services: raw material supply, marketing of finished products, trade credit, and investment capital for offshore projects. Nevertheless, the *sōgō shōsha* constructed a system of governance for economic exchange that affected only a fraction of Japanese industry: mostly light and heavy sectors highly dependent on raw material supply and producers of standardized goods.

The exacting demands of product differentiation, sophisticated technology, and after-sales service prevented the general trading companies from accessing the distribution of consumer goods and high-tech products. Consequently, the *sōgō shōsha* played no role in the multinationalization of these industries.

The other major type of Japanese business grouping, the vertical *keiretsu*, emerged as assemblers attempted to solve the problem of customized manufacturing. The production of highly specific parts entails a serious risk for part makers who will not be able to sell to alternative customers, and to assemblers who must share sensitive product specification information (Williamson 1985). Therefore, substantial parental investments in subcontractors are essential to overcome the risks of custom-tailored part manufacturing. In the case of Japanese companies, this assistance included loan and equity links, joint R&D, production information exchange, and parental help with offshore relocation. Since customized manufacturing is pervasive in automobile production, but not in consumer electronics, the offshore relocation of Japanese subcontracting networks is prominent only in the former sector, but not in the latter industry.

28. Groups that are geographically concentrated or over-represented in electoral districts (farmers) are also likely to wield influence over politicians eager to capture their votes.

29. For a few firms the Japanese government substantially financed FDI from industries competitive in the international market, such as electronics and automobiles. Nevertheless, electronics did not receive public FDI credit for most of the postwar period, and only when its export drive faltered owing to yen appreciation did this industry figure prominently in the list of public FDI credit recipients. The Japanese government targeted the automobile early on for promotion as an infant industry, and support for automobile FDI met the need to achieve scale economies and maintain access to markets pursuing import substitution strategies. For a good analysis of the strategies of Japanese automobile companies in Southeast Asian markets, see Doner 1991.

30. Utmost care should be exercised in aggregating from assertions at the level of the firm to the level of the industry. Obviously, there will be weak firms in robust sectors and strong firms in declining ones. The case studies here identify which firms in an industry were responsible for most of the outward investment flows. Even in those cases where strong firms in contracting sectors were the main foreign investors, I have unearthed a political phenomenon of significance bypassed by economic theories: profitable and large firms making use of public soft financing instead of relying solely on their own resources to undertake international production.

31. Graham, for instance, finds no link between FDI by US firms and the do-

mestic unemployment rate; instead, he establishes a positive statistical relationship between outward investment and US exports (2000: 115, 119).

32. For a good review of this literature, see Piazza 2002.

33. One exception is Katz (1998), who does make the case for the current hollowing-out of the Japanese economy. Rather than blaming FDI for the deindustrialization of Japan, though, Katz believes that Japanese exporters are being chased away from the homeland because of two related factors: the protection of Japanese inefficient industries, which inflates the cost of inputs; and the artificial trade surplus, which translates into a soaring yen. Katz does not provide evidence, however, that in the aggregate, the Japanese economy is deindustrializing.

34. Shimada (1980) and Koike (1987) discuss the significant impact of Japanese enterprise unions on several employment practices: the elimination of preferential treatment of white-collar workers, the extension of the bonus system to production workers, the establishment of the periodical wage increase system, and the oversight of employee transfers.

Chapter 2: The Rise of Japan as an FDI Power

1. Wilkins (1988: 14) notes that in addition to the standard multinational corporation (a firm headquartered in the home country that opens subsidiaries and branches in foreign nations), Britain innovated with the creation of "free-standing companies." These companies were registered in England with the purpose of operating a single line of business in one foreign country and aimed to tap into the abundant financial resources of British individual investors.

2. Nevertheless, the share of world FDI stock attributed to Japan in this table is underestimated, because Japanese FDI statistics do not take into account reinvested earnings, whereas those of the United States, the UK, Germany, and most OECD countries do. Indeed, it is important to keep in mind that Japanese official FDI statistics have some serious flaws. Outbound direct investment statistics compiled by Ministry of Finance (MOF) do not take into account reinvestments or divestments, and report only nominal amounts. Changes in the FDI regulatory regime have also affected the coverage in these official statistics. Prior to 1980, MOF's FDI statistics covered approvals, but since then it has reported prior notifications, and currently it registers ex post facto notifications. The Bank of Japan's FDI statistics do report actual outflows (not notifications) but do not provide an industrial breakdown (Farrel 2000: 2, 56). Despite the shortcomings of MOF's statistics, they still remain the best database covering the entire postwar period having a detailed description of geographical and industrial trends, and therefore, will be used throughout this book.

3. The government restricted outward FDI both to preserve precious foreign exchange and to ensure that the incipient industrial base would not be burdened by reverse imports (Mason 1999: 29).

4. In 1971 the US president effectively terminated the Bretton Woods fixed-exchange-rate regime by ending the convertibility of dollars into gold, and also imposed a surcharge on US imports.

5. Encarnation and Mason (1994: 444–45) also conclude that Japanese multinationals in Europe conduct their operations differently from other MNCs. These au-

thors stress that some important remaining differences in the overseas operations of Japanese multinationals (such as the prevalence of *keiretsu* networks and the importance of intrafirm trade), cannot be explained away as "vintage effects—that is, as a reflection of the fact that Japan is at an earlier stage in multinational evolution.

6. The figures for Europe represent FDI flows from the UK, Germany, France, and Italy.

7. In manufacturing, SMEs are officially defined as enterprises with fewer than 300 employees and less than 100 million yen in capital; in wholesale trade as firms with not more than 100 employees and 30 million yen in capital; and in retail trade as enterprises with less than 10 million yen in capital and fewer than 50 employees (Fujita 1993: 55).

8. Most likely, the weight of Japanese SMEs in total FDI is larger when measured by number of investments than when measured by the value of the capital outflow. Unfortunately, the Japanese government does not disclose the monetary value of overseas investment by SMEs.

Chapter 3: Japan's Regulatory Regime Governing Capital Outflows

1. Krause and Sekiguchi (1976) provide a good analysis of balance-of-payments policy in Japan during the early postwar period.

2. The full name of the law was the Foreign Exchange and Foreign Trade Control Law.

3. For an excellent study of Japanese policy on inward foreign direct investment see Encarnation and Mason 1990.

4. The rapid advance of Japanese corporations into Southeast Asia in the early 1970s increased tensions with some host countries, which often complained of Japanese "over-presence." These tensions escalated in the spring of 1974 when a tour by the Japanese prime minister in the region generated a wave of protests known as the "Tanaka riots."

5. The reasons for the demise of the proposed Foreign Economic Law remain obscure in MITI's account (1993: 306). MITI asserts that the law failed to pass because of the upheaval created in the Diet by the security treaty crisis. However, the ministry does not explain why the law was never presented to the Diet again if bad timing was the problem. MITI (1993) also does not discuss the next round of negotiations over revising the Foreign Exchange Law that took place in 1963.

6. The IMF's eighth clause called for free foreign exchange transactions, currency convertibility, and the elimination of currency discriminatory measures. And the OECD passed a code on capital liberalization that member countries were to emulate.

7. The following paragraphs draw heavily on Horne 1985: 153–63.

8. In order to secure the stability of the financial system, MOF's regulation of the banking sector resembled a convoy system in that all financial institutions were to move like ships in a convoy at the same pace, and the government would guarantee that they stay afloat.

9. On the loss of competitiveness of the Japanese financial system, Dekle (1998: 237) notes that while Tokyo and New York reported similar stock market turnover

in the early 1990s, by the end of the decade Tokyo's turnover was only one-fifth of New York's.

10. Under the previous regime, private firms could bypass the FOREX bank only if MOF granted specific permission to carry out a foreign exchange transaction. This process was very cumbersome (approval could take as long as a month) and was rarely used. Modest exemptions to the monopoly of the FOREX banks were granted to the *sōgō shōsha* in 1956 (they could hold a certain amount of foreign currencies to carry out their international trading activities), and to designated securities firms in 1978 (they could process FOREX transactions when investing in foreign securities or when assisting their customers with foreign currency bond issues) (Masunaga 1997: 2). Nevertheless, both the general traders and the securities houses were dissatisfied with their very restricted access to FOREX transactions.

11. General trading houses (Mitsui Bussan, Itochu), securities firms, and manufacturing firms with extensive international dealings (Nissan, NEC) were well represented in the committee on FOREX reform ("Gaitamehō no Kaisei Sagyō ga iyoiyo gutaika," 1996: 6).

12. In fact, owing to foreign pressure, inward FDI had already been operating under an ex post facto reporting system since 1992. There were, nevertheless, notable exceptions where the prior notification system would still apply (for restricted sectors, or if the Japanese government deemed that the project could damage the national economy) (Geist 1994: 9). This means that in the area of FDI, formal liberalization—ex post facto notification—moved ahead more quickly for inward flows (where Japan's reputation for strict control is most developed) than for outward flows.

13. Response to a written questionnaire submitted by the author to MITI officials, December 2001.

14. My conclusion on the importance of domestic politics to capital outflow liberalization in Japan parallels Encarnation and Mason's (1990) contention that foreign pressure to ease restrictions on inward investment succeeded only when it was seconded by a domestic support group.

Chapter 4: Public FDI Credit and the Expansion of Japanese Multinational Corporations

1. Three laws in particular spelled out the ample powers of bureaucratic intervention: the FECL and FIL (discussed at length in the previous chapter), and the 1953 Anti-Monopoly Law.

2. Several social institutions helped reconcile conflicting preferences of regulators and firms: close contact between public and private elites who share family and educational backgrounds (Johnson 1982), the inclusion of the private sector in the policymaking process through deliberation councils or *shingikai* (Schwartz 1998), and the practice of *amakudari*—descent from heaven—whereby top bureaucrats retire to high-level positions in private enterprises (Calder 1989; Schaede 1995).

3. See, for example, the works of Horiuchi and Sui (1993); Ogura and Yoshino (1988; 1985); Cho and Hellmann (1993); Kato et al. (1994); Calder (1993); Vittas and Kawaura (1995); and Calomiris and Himmelberg (1995).

4. For example, Horiuchi and Sui (1993) concluded that JDB loans stimulated firms' investment expenditure and private sector borrowing because they facilitate

the generation of information and the monitoring of borrowing firms. Calomiris and Himmelberg (1995) assert from their study of the machine tool industry that direct credit "was effective in promoting investment, supporting growing firms, crowding in private funds, and avoiding capture of policy funds by particular firms." On the other hand, Calder (1993: 120–22) offered a much more temperate view of the impact of the JDB in spurring industrial transformation. He described a conservative and rigid pattern in JDB credit allocation, with the bank rarely stepping out of the "circle of compensation" established with its traditional credit recipients.

5. Only in 1994 with the establishment of the World Trade Organization (WTO) were some performance requirements eliminated: local content and foreign trade balancing. In other words, for most of the postwar period, host governments have been free to impose performance conditions on incoming foreign multinationals. (Of course mobile transnational enterprises could disinvest if they found the performance requirements too onerous, but for multinationals with large fixed assets the price of exit was too high.) Moreover, no international arbitration mechanism to mediate investment disputes between multinational corporations and foreign governments has been yet established at the multilateral level. One of the most heated ongoing debates in the WTO is over a possible investment agreement.

6. The other FILP funds are the Postal Life Insurance Fund, the Industrial Investment Special Account, and Government Guaranteed Bonds and Borrowings. The Industrial Investment Special Account is funded through transfers from the general account, dividend income from NTT and Japan Tobacco Corp., and operating income generated by payments from investment by institutions such as JDB and the Japan Eximbank (Kato et al. 1994, 14; Nakagawa et al. 1994, 1–2; and Ishi 1986: 83).

7. In that year, the Diet approved the Law concerning Special Measures for Long-Term Investment of the Trust Fund Bureau Funds and Funds accumulated from Postal Annuities and Postal Life Insurance Annuity Funds to include all four FILP funds in the Diet's budgetary review process (Y. Suzuki 1987: 274). Diet oversight has not extended to all crucial stages of FILP, however. There is no legislative review of the lending portfolio of public financial institutions, and the second budget's "flexibility clause," by which increases of up to 50 percent of the original budget do not require Diet review, gives Treasury bureaucrats freedom to rapidly expand outlays (Hanano et al. 1991: 7).

8. Author's estimates using MOF data.

9. Later on, the bank was permitted to supplement its financial resources through bond issues (see Japan Eximbank 1992, 1; Nakagawa et al. 1994: 349–50).

10. Despite these similarities, there has always been an important difference in the export credit offered by the US and Japanese Eximbanks. The US Eximbank mostly provides credit to buyers, while the Japan Eximbank limited its export credit to Japanese suppliers.

11. Project finance refers to a lending scheme in which repayment is made solely from the cash flow generated by the project and the collateral is circumscribed to the assets of the project. This kind of financing is known as "nonrecourse" because the company is not liable for the repayment obligations of the project.

12. McKinney and McVay (1997) report that Japan Eximbank project finance totaled $4,031 million between 1986 and 1996. In contrast, the US Eximbank (which

created its Project Finance Division only in 1994) provided $5,622 million for twenty-two projects in only four years (from 1993 to April 1997).

13. Arase (1995: 78–79) provides numerous examples of industrial restructuring concerns that guided ODA policy. For instance, in 1979 a push was given to the depressed Japanese shipbuilding industry through the granting of ODA loans to Thailand, the Philippines, and Bangladesh to buy electrically powered barges. And to help the chemical fertilizer industry, the government created a new category of grant aid in 1977 to subsidize the pesticide and fertilizer industries.

14. These four ministries were MITI, MOF, the Ministry of Foreign Affairs (MOFA), and the Economic Planning Agency (EPA).

15. The Japan International Cooperation Agency was the other institution in the ODA machinery with a program targeting the investment activities of Japanese corporations. This agency provided long-term low-interest loans to projects for which it is difficult to obtain funds from the Japan Eximbank or the OECF, that do not pay on a commercial basis, and that are related to the construction or improvement of public facilities such as transportation, communications, and sanitation. The scale of this program was very modest, though. Between 1974 and 1993 a total of 11,881 million yen was spent in this category, representing only 0.8 percent of its total commitments (Japan International Cooperation Agency 1994: 413).

16. Interview with OECF officials, Tokyo, October 1995.

17. The OECF was authorized to hold up to 50 percent of the equity in a Japanese investment corporation carrying out an economic cooperation project in the developing world (Matsuzawa 1993: 101). As noted earlier, in 1989 the Japan Eximbank was allowed to acquire equity ownership in investment projects in the developed world, but rarely did so given the higher risks involved. Other government corporations, such as the Japan National Oil Corporation and the Metal Mining Agency of Japan, could extend equity financing to overseas projects, but their range of operation was limited to their specific target industries.

18. A project is designated as "national" by the cabinet after a consortium of Japanese manufacturers forms an investment company under MITI's guidance for the sole purpose of participating in the venture overseas.

19. This was perhaps the last major initiative of the OECF in manufacturing equity investments. The number and amount of industrial FDI projects supported by the OECF declined during the 1990s, and in the second half of the decade it made no equity investments in manufacturing.

20. These formally private, noncommercial foundations are important for the placement of retired bureaucrats (*amakudari*) and to the flexible implementation of policies since ministries can directly fund them without MOF's authorization (Johnson 1978: 49–50). The supervising ministry exerts strong budgetary, lending, and personnel influence over the *zaidan hōjin*.

21. According to Keidanren and JAIDO officials, the OECF did not heavily influence the decision-making process at JAIDO, despite its position as a major shareholder. The only privileges that the OECF enjoyed were one seat on JAIDO's board of directors and access to detailed information about each project. JAIDO's freedom of action was not unlimited, however. Even though no formal approval was necessary from the four ministries in charge of economic cooperation, informal consulta-

tions took place, and the implementation of a project would be delayed until an understanding was obtained from the bureaucracy (interview with Keidanren and JAIDO officials, Tokyo, August and October 1995).

22. Interview with Keidanren and OECF officials, Tokyo, August and October 1995.

23. Interview with JAIDO officials, Tokyo, October 1995.

24. Shōko Chūkin is the oldest SME financial institution in Japan. It was established in 1936 to help small enterprises cope with the financial instability of the early Shōwa years. Shōko Chūkin is the only public SME financial institution that accepts deposits from member cooperatives in addition to capital contributions and FILP loans from the government. The government created the People's Finance Corporation in 1949 to provide operating funds for very small firms. A conspicuous feature of the lending record of this institution is its frequent authorization of noncollateralized loans to companies endorsed by local chambers of commerce (Takabashi 1991: 198). In the past, LDP members and local chambers used their influence to secure noncollateralized loans to serve their political interests (see Calder 1993: 122).

25. Estimated by the author with data provided by JODC.

26. Interview with JODC officials, August 1995.

27. Since 1987, JFS, Shōkō Chūkin, and the People's Finance Corporation have offered "loans for overseas expansion."

28. Its full name was the Law for Smoothing the Advance of Small and Medium-Sized Firms into New Fields.

29. MITI (1994: 3–7) documented well the severe environment in which SMEs struggle to survive: an economic slump, yen appreciation, rising competition from ASEAN and China, and foreign sourcing by large firms operating overseas. As Japanese assemblers purchased more abroad, SMEs were saddled with faltering export sales and more intense competition in the domestic market in the form of reverse imports (MITI 1994a: 151–52). MITI conceived of the following adjustment strategies for SMEs: the move into higher-value-added production in the same industry/product, the minimization of risk through the development of supplier relations with several customers, foreign direct investment to avoid losing markets to local suppliers, and entry into new industrial fields (ibid.: 171–72).

30. The Association for Small and Medium-Sized Businesses was established in 1980 under MITI's supervision. It received capital contributions from the national budget and borrowed money from the FILP. Its finance operations, however, were not very large. For example, in the early 1990s the lending volume of JFS was ten times larger than that of the association (see Nakagawa et al. 1994: 274, 460).

31. The official name of this new loan program was: "loans to cope with economic changes overseas," but I will simply refer to these credits as "Asia crisis loans."

32. Interview with JFS officials, Tokyo, January 2001.

33. Interview with JFS officials, 1995.

34. The revised Restructuring Law cited the shift from the production of plain white T-shirts to golf T-shirts as an example of sufficient product innovation for credit approval (MITI 1995: 4).

35. Interview with officials of the Planning Division at MITI's Small Enterprise Agency, Tokyo, June 1995.

36. Kijima (1995: 5) makes the same point. For instance, in the decade between 1985 and 1994, the OECF reported losses in seven years, which ranged between $2 million and a $100 million (OECF, *Annual Report*, 1995: 169).

37. The interest burden reduction was estimated as follows: (Japan Eximbank loan) x (LTPR–TFBR) and (OECF equity investment) x (LTPR−0). The long-term prime rate (LTPR) is charged by trust banks and long-term banks to corporations with the highest credit rating and is considered the "de facto lower limit for longer-term lending" (Y. Suzuki 1987: 147). The Trust Fund Bureau rate is the capital procurement rate for public institutions when they contract loans from the Treasury and is the lowest rate they themselves can charge to their private sector clients in the absence of interest rate subsidies from the general account.

Several qualifications are in order. My estimation of the interest burden reduction is based on the lowest interest rate the Japan Eximbank could charge its clients. Obviously, the Japan Eximbank did not always apply that preferential interest rate. In fact, the standard interest rate charged by public financial institutions was usually equivalent to the LTPR, which with my estimation procedure would eliminate the subsidy element in public financing. However, it is equally true that not all firms contracted debt from private banks at the best interest rate available in the market (LTPR), especially when they were investing overseas in higher-risk projects.

Finally, in my estimation I relied on the nominal interest rate offered by private banks, but it is widely recognized that in Japan effective interest rates have been much higher because of compensating balances: banks require firms to maintain certain levels of deposits earning a lower interest rate, effectively increasing the real interest rate at which companies borrow money (Y. Suzuki 1980: 46–47).

The figures in Table 4.6 should therefore be understood as an assessment of the "open subsidy" delivered through government FDI financing, since my calculation is based on the differential in posted interest rates. A more precise estimation was not feasible because no reliable data exist on the actual interest rates charged by commercial and public financial institutions for overseas projects.

38. Author interviews with Japan Eximbank and OECF officials, Tokyo, September–October 1995.

39. The system of bureaucratic supervision has remained largely intact. MOF continues to be the sole supervisor of the international financial activities account. MOFA is now formally in charge of overseeing the overseas economic cooperation operations account, but must consult with MOF and MITI, which in January 2001 became the Ministry of Economy, Trade, and Industry—METI (interview with JBIC officials, January 2001). At that time too, EPA disappeared as a separate ministry and was attached to the prime minister's office as a result of the administrative reform campaign.

40. MOF bureaucrats had always occupied the position of chairman of the board of directors of both the Japan Eximbank and the OECF. With the merger, MOF lost one of these top slots, but MITI also surrendered one *amakudari* position at the level of executive director on the board.

41. MOPT is well backed by the LDP in this realm. Whereas reform of the FECL created little controversy in political quarters, postal savings have been heavily politicized. Well aware of the electoral consequences of displeasing the vast num-

ber of postal savers, the LDP's postal savings support group has been large and active. As Horne (1985) points out, throughout the 1970s the LDP supported MOPT in resisting interest rate cuts and in opposing the transfer of interest rate policy to MOF's Banking Bureau.

42. Since the early 1980s, MOPT through a subsidiary organization had retained and invested 12 percent of the postal insurance funds and 3 percent of the postal savings resources. Yet the investment record of this institution has been so dismal (requiring the familiar first budget injections to keep it afloat), that there are good reasons to worry about MOPT's ability to effectively manage the mammoth second budget (Lincoln 2001). During the transition period, MOPT will mostly use the postal savings resources to buy FILP agency bonds and FILP bonds, but after that the direction and quality of MOPT's investment decisions remains an open question.

43. It is too soon to fully assess the extent of FILP reform, though. The election of Junichiro Koizumi as prime minister in 2001 fueled speculation of more dramatic change, since Koizumi had long proposed privatizing postal savings. At the time of this writing in late 2003, intra-LDP politics had managed to derail this initiative. The majority of the party opposed Koizumi's ideas because the Association of Postal Masters is a bastion of support for conservative politicians, whom the party did not want to alienate.

Chapter 5: Textiles

1. The standard demarcation of the textile industry is as follows: upstream: production of man-made fibers or natural yarn (spinning); midstream: weaving, dyeing and knitting of fabrics; downstream: apparel and distribution.

2. For example, Dore (1986: 158) reported that sales of the Big Ten firms in cotton spinning accounted for 75 percent of the market, whereas the share of the Big Nine synthetic firms was as high as 90 percent. The major-league spinners are Tōyōbō, Kanebō, Nisshin Bōseki, Kurabō, Fuji Bōseki, Daiwa Bōseki, Shikibō, Omikenshi, Unitika, and Nittō Bōseki. The leaders in synthetic fiber manufacturing are Tōray, Teijin, Asahi Kasei, Unitika, Kuraray, Tōhō Rayon, Mitsubishi Rayon, Tōyōbō, and Kanebō.

3. The synthetic textile industry was exempted from the compulsory registration system for three years (M. Fujii 1971: 198).

4. Diversification into other industries has been a major domestic adjustment strategy for some textile companies. For instance, by the mid-1990s, Asahi Kasei derived only 14 percent of its total sales from textiles, and Nittō Bōseki a somewhat larger 29 percent. In general, fiber companies have pursued the diversification strategy more vigorously because they enjoy sufficient financial resources and have technological expertise that is applicable to other fields. Only a few of the large spinners have divested from textiles (such as Nittō), and for the vast majority of small spinners, weavers, knitters, and apparel makers the textile industry has remained the battleground for survival (Solís 1998: 391).

5. The position of Japanese labor on the domestic and international prescriptions for textile adjustment is discussed more fully later in this chapter.

6. The share of total manufacturing FDI has remained small (3 percent) because of the massive overseas investments carried out by other Japanese sectors adversely influenced by the yen appreciation (electronics and automobiles).

7. In the interwar period, Japanese cotton spinners invested actively abroad, especially in China, where between 1914 and 1925 seventeen Japanese cotton spinning firms opened thirty-three factories. By 1923 one-third of all spindles in China were located in Japanese factories (Nakatase, Maruyama, and Ikeda 1979: 217–18). The Japanese spinning and weaving base in China developed further between 1923 and 1937. During those years, Japanese-owned spindles increased from 961,000 to 2.3 million, and weaving looms from 3,777 to 33,304 (ibid.: 227). Although a more exhaustive analysis of prewar FDI in Japanese textiles is beyond the scope of this chapter, it is important to note that government support played a key role. Japanese textile firms operated in occupied territories and were very protected by the new colonial governments (ibid.: 220).

8. Cotton spinning FDI in Brazil is noteworthy as well because it did not exhibit two characteristics that have been frequently attributed to Japanese textile FDI: group investment and minority-owned joint ventures (Ozawa 1978). In the late 1950s, Japanese spinners were not accompanied by general trading companies and established wholly or majority-owned ventures in Brazil.

9. Unfortunately, more complete FDI statistics (with a breakdown by textile subsector) are no longer available because the Japan Chemical Fiber Association stopped printing them in their yearbook.

10. Both overseas and domestically, the fiber makers moved out of textiles more rapidly than the spinners. But some fiber makers and spinners do not produce textiles at all in their offshore subsidiaries. This is true for Kuraray and Nittō Bōseki.

11. For a more detailed analysis of the impact of *keiretsu* relations on the overseas expansion of Japanese MNCs, see Solís 1998.

12. The textile industries of two other Asian nations, South Korea and Taiwan, have also undertaken some overseas investment. At the end of 1995, South Korea's textile FDI amounted to $730 million, and Taiwan's to $802 million (Van Hoesel 1999: 100, 108). Textile FDI from these two countries is still much smaller than Japanese FDI in this industry ($9.3 billion as of 1999). Yet these are the three countries identified in Chapter 1 as having large government FDI credit programs. A more systematic comparison of the role of state FDI financing in the multinationalization of the Asian textile industry is a promising area for future research.

13. There has been more FDI in synthetic fibers precisely because those conditions prevail.

14. For a good review of the evolution of textile trade policy in the United States, see Aggarwal with Haggard 1983; and Friman 1990.

15. In 1998 the textile industry filed a second suit against Korea for dumping knitted sweaters. Once more, MITI encouraged an informal settlement that resulted in Korean VERs in February 1989. Only in 1995 did the JSA succeed in persuading MITI to take action in an antidumping case against cotton yarn imports from Pakistan (Yoshimatsu 2000: 137–38).

16. Trade tensions between Japan and China escalated in the spring of 2001 when Japan for the first time imposed safeguards against three agricultural products

imported from China: leeks, shiitake mushrooms, and tatami rushes. No safeguards on textiles were imposed largely because the apparel industry opposed them ("Zantei yunyū seigen o shohatsudō, nihon kigyō no katsuryoku sogu osore" [Provisional import restrictions are invoked, Japanese firms' vitality dampens fears], *Nihon Keizai Shimbun*, April 24, 2001).

17. For example, the Retailing Association lodged protests against the imposition of textile quotas ("Sensan shinteigen 'yunyū kisei' ni yureru gyōkai" [Industry rocked by the proposal from the textile deliberation council to "regulate imports"], *Nihon Keizai Shimbun*, May 18, 1994).

18. The role of the Japanese government in discouraging reverse importing during the first boom in textile FDI was in no way minor. In the early 1970s some "firms were required to submit sworn documents that they would not reimport textile products to Japan" (Yoshimatsu 2000: 152).

19. China and ASEAN were the largest suppliers of downstream textile products to the Japanese market. MITI (1994b: 196) estimated that 22.5 percent and 34.6 percent of the Chinese and ASEAN exports to Japan were from Japanese companies.

20. In 1987, Domei was dissolved with the creation of Rengō (the Japanese Trade Union Council). Zensen transferred its affiliation to the newly created labor federation.

21. Dore notes that at its 1973 conference Zensen brought up the issue of organizing part-timers. But this initiative never prospered, since "regular tenured workers in the union are well aware that their privileges depend in part on the existence of others less privileged" (Dore 1986: 210).

Chapter 6: The Offshore Rebirth of Japanese Aluminum Smelting

1. Bauxite is the key raw material for the production of aluminum. The ore is crushed and ground into a powder called alumina, which is used as the main input in aluminum smelting.

2. In 1970, Alcoa (US), Alcan (Canada), Pechiney (France), Alusuisse (Switzerland), Reynolds (US), and Kaiser (US) produced 63 percent of the bauxite, 66 percent of the alumina, and 54 percent of aluminum ingot in market economies (UNCTC 1981: 1).

3. For this reason, aluminum ingot has been called "canned electricity."

4. Sumitomo Chemicals established Sumitomo Aluminum Smelting, Shōwa Denko created Shōwa Aluminum Smelting, and Mitsubishi Chemicals formed Mitsubishi Light Metals.

5. The original MITI proposal was to reduce tariffs for the specified quota to 0 percent. However, MOF strongly opposed this idea and only a 3.5 percent cut was obtained (Imuta 1993: 108).

6. Under MITI's sponsorship the Light Metals Stockpiling Association was established in July 1976. Immediately after its creation, the association bought 9,570 tons of ingot from the domestic industry. The Metal Mining Agency of Japan (under MITI's supervision) financed the stockpiling system by borrowing from commercial banks and receiving government guarantees and interest subsidies from the general budget (Imuta 1993: 111). In 1982, as the aluminum industry's situation deteriorated,

the government approved the purchase of over 100,000 tons of domestic ingot (Samuels 1983: 504).

7. The government considered anathema the protection of an energy-intensive industry. Therefore, the Electricity Industry Act both forbade preferential treatment for individual customers and, in 1974, applied a rate system to punish the largest consumers of electricity.

8. Interestingly, labor was not a major actor in the definition of aluminum policies, for two reasons: the size of the workforce was very small (14,000 employees), and the smelting firms relied on their *keiretsu* connections to shuffle their workers, without resorting to layoffs. Labor had only one representative on the Aluminum Subcommittee (Uriu 1996: 179, 181), and personnel adjustment never became a political issue in the drafting of aluminum restructuring packages.

9. The same was true for alumina production. Mitsubishi was by far the most important buyer of alumina sold on the open market (Stuckey 1983: 126).

10. This interdependence was recognized by both sides, and in Stuckey's (1983: 124) opinion, it explains Comalco's sympathy for the Japanese smelters' plight in the post–oil shock years, and its willingness to provide ore at low cost to help these firms stay afloat.

11. Tensions between host governments and the six international majors reached high levels with the 1971 nationalization of bauxite mines in Guyana, as well as Jamaica's decision to impose a special levy on its ore in 1973. The limited development of a bauxite market had prevented host nations from receiving an adequate return on their resources since they had to rely on the value estimations submitted by multinationals for tax purposes. Jamaica eliminated this problem by linking tax obligations to the price of aluminum ingot. It also demanded a role in the management of the mines (Holloway 1988: 39, 55).

12. The MMAJ was founded in 1963 and placed under MITI's jurisdiction. Its funding originated from general budget appropriations and subsidies, capital injections from the Trust Fund Bureau and the Industrial Investment Special Account, and loans from commercial banks (Jūkagaku 1976: 61). MMAJ's assistance program for overseas mining comprised subsidies for general survey work and initial drilling, low-interest loans for detailed follow-up exploration, loan guarantees for the debt incurred by Japanese firms to develop foreign mines, and later, equity contributions (MMAJ 1983, 19; Crowson 1983: 162). By 1982, MMAJ had disbursed 7.2 billion yen to assist overseas mining projects (H. Tanaka 1993: 395).

13. Although bauxite is abundant, ore deposits are concentrated in four countries: Australia (68.1 percent), Guinea (26.7 percent), Brazil (10.7 percent), and Jamaica (9.5 percent) (Bunker and Cicantell 1994: 41). But Australia (holder of the largest deposits) did not support the policies of the International Bauxite Association, compromising the prospects of this cartel to significantly influence the market.

14. However, Alcoa decided to idle the operations of Intalco in May 2001 because of high electricity prices in the wake of the energy crisis in the western United States.

15. Some overseas projects for natural resource exploitation received this official designation because they fostered relations with resource-abundant nations, contributed to industrial upgrading in Japan, and secured the stable supply of minerals

and metals. Private enterprises were willing to jointly undertake the investment project in order to disperse financial risk, internalize business links, and make politically feasible the disbursal of subsidies (Ozawa 1993: 119–20). An implicit understanding lies at the core of government-business cooperation in national projects: the private sector obtains access to preferential government financing in exchange for remaining vested in the project (interview with OECF officials, Tokyo, August 1996).

16. There was one domestic project in Okinawa, and two others overseas in Bintang (Malaysia) and Ghana.

17. Author's estimates are based on documents provided by Nippon Asahan Aluminum.

18. The *sōgō shōsha* members of NAA were Sumitomo Trading (2.5 percent), Mitsubishi Shōji (2.5 percent), Mitsui Bussan (2.5 percent), Marubeni (for Shōwa Denko, 2.5 percent) and C. Itoh, Nissho Iwai, and Nichimen (for Nippon Light Metals, each 0.835 percent).

19. Interview with Nippon Asahan Aluminum officials, Tokyo, August, 1996.

20. Interview with Nippon Asahan Aluminum officials, Tokyo, August 1996.

21. Internal document provided by Nippon Asahan Aluminum.

22. According to Arase (1995: 90), there were also disagreements over pricing the aluminum. Trying to make the ingot less expensive, the Japanese suggested that the price be determined by the futures market instead of the spot market on the LME (London Metals Exchange). However, the existence of a conflict over this issue could not be confirmed in my discussions with NAA's officials. The supply of alumina to the Asahan smelter was another point of contention among partners. Currently, each partner sells to Inalum an amount of alumina equivalent to its equity share (40 percent for Indonesia and 60 percent to Japan). The Indonesian government and the Japanese trading companies in turn buy the alumina from other companies (Alcoa, Clarendon, Billiton). The original idea of feeding the smelter with bauxite mined in Indonesia did not materialize. Moreover, procurement costs for Inalum were high because all alumina is supplied by the partners as a resale. Both partners insisted on retaining their role as alumina suppliers; otherwise they would have had to forfeit their handling commissions (interview with NAA officials, Tokyo, August 1996).

23. Interview with NAA officials, Tokyo, January 2001.

24. At the end of 1999, NAAC was capitalized at 57.35 billion yen, a figure below that of the original Asahan project (68.3 billion, which has since augmented to 97.5 billion yen)(based on documents provided by NAAC and NAA).

25. Equity shares were modified over time. In 1996 the OECF held 45 percent, the smelters 25.4 percent, trading companies 15.62 percent, and fabricators 10.29 percent. In contrast to NAA, the five smelting companies did not contribute equally to NAAC: Mitsui Aluminum contributed 8.30 percent; NLM 7.94 percent; Sumitomo Chemicals 4.59 percent; Shōwa Denko 2.75 percent; and Mitsubishi Materials 1.84 percent. Import quotas for Amazonian ingot are based on equity shares, so the largest importers are the Mitsui and NLM groups with more than one-fifth of total imports each. These two companies are the most involved in the daily operations of the Amazon aluminum project, since they staff the Tokyo offices of NAAC (interview with NAAC officials, Tokyo, August 1996).

26. Interview with NAAC officials, Tokyo, August 1996 and January 2001.
27. Interview with NAAC officials, Tokyo, August 1996.
28. All figures come from documents provided by NAAC.
29. Interview with NAAC and Japan Eximbank officials, Tokyo, August 1996.
30. In January 2000 a Norwegian firm, Norsk Hydro, invested $160 million to expand Alunorte's capacity. Once more, the Japanese side declined to invest additional money in the alumina plant (NAAC, internal document).
31. Tilton (1996: 60) found evidence suggesting that the Japanese government also encouraged FDI through the tariff/quota system. According to his informant in the Japan Aluminum Federation, one criterion employed by MITI in tariff rebate allocations was how actively the company intended to invest overseas.
32. Interview with NAAC and Japan Eximbank officials, Tokyo, August 1996.
33. The Iran-Japan Petrochemical Complex (IJPC) is another well-known example of the inherent tensions of state/business overseas undertakings. Originally a Mitsui group venture, the $730 billion project was transformed into a national project after the Iranian revolution of 1979. Mitsui demanded a stronger public commitment to maintain the petrochemical complex, and the OECF poured in 20 billion yen (*Japan Economic Newswire*, November 29, 1980). But the misfortunes of the project continued with the outbreak of the Iran-Iraq War in 1980.

In 1982 the Japan Eximbank announced it would not allow repayment delays on the 125 billion yen it had lent with a syndicate of Japanese private banks to Mitsui's investment company (the Iran Chemical Development Corporation). Mitsui continued to shoulder the burden of the project by maintaining the scheduled payments, but Iraqi bombings brought construction to a halt in 1984 with the complete withdrawal of Japanese engineers. Tensions escalated in 1986 when the Iranian oil company (the local partner to IJPC) suspended payment on the loans received both from the Japanese investment consortium and the Japanese government. Mitsui kept pressing for its withdrawal from a project that it considered unfeasible given the substantial war damage, and for the prompt recovery of the insurance claim it had acquired from MITI to cover 90 percent of its exposure. The Japanese government, however, was unwilling to let Mitsui abandon the national project, and was also afraid of harming relations with Iran and losing the chance to ever collect its bilateral official loans.

The Japanese government was equally preoccupied with Mitsui's FDI insurance claim on MITI. The Export Insurance Division of MITI had a deficit of $683 million in 1986. In order to meet Mitsui's claim it would have had to resort to public subsidies ("The Japanese Ministry of Trade and Industry's Export Insurance Division [MITI/EID] is gearing up for a test case insurance claim from Mitsui & Co.," *Euromoney*, September 28, 1987). In 1988, MITI injected 115 billion yen and transformed the agency into the Trade Insurance Agency.

In 1989 both governments finally terminated IJPC. Negotiations in Japan intensified for the settlement of the Mitsui insurance claim, which business circles deemed a showcase for the government's credibility as an insurer of overseas investment projects. In 1991 the final resolution of the insurance dispute was announced: MITI granted only 77.7 billion yen, even though the private consortium had asked for as much as 93 billion yen ("Hoken gaku ukeire [IJPC] de Mitsui Bussan nado" [Mitsui & Co. receives insurance amount for IJPC], *Nihon Keizai Shimbun*, August 17, 1991).

The protracted IJPC controversy illustrates well the discrepancies between a corporate logic of profitability and a state strategy for key resource procurement.

Chapter 7: Consumer Electronics and the Limits of State FDI Financing

1. Even after 1977, when quotas were imposed on Japanese exports in the form of an Orderly Market Agreement (OMA), Japanese products continued to enjoy a larger share of the US market (17.1 percent in 1979) (Hiramoto 1994: 197).

2. The Japanese government supported HDTV technologies mostly because of the positive externalities it expected—specifically, increased consumption of semiconductors. But it provided only a modest level of subsidization (Busch 1999). And worldwide demand for HDTVs has not picked up enough to make this product a new engine of growth for Japanese consumer electronics.

3. Interview by the author with National Thai managers, Bangkok, February 1996.

4. Local production in advanced country markets was not limited to the United States. During these years, Japanese TV manufacturers actively invested in the UK to create a supply base for European markets. Sony and Matsushita were the first companies to move to the UK in 1974. They were followed by Tōshiba in 1978, Hitachi in 1979, and Sanyō in 1982 (Hiramoto 1994: 162).

5. Ten out of eighteen consumer electronics plants operating in Singapore in the 1990s were established during the 1970s (EIAJ 1995: iv).

6. Interview by the author with Hitachi officials in Singapore, February 1995.

7. From a sample of forty-eight Japanese electronics part makers operating in North America, I was able to trace the existence or not of *keiretsu* affiliations for thirty-seven firms. Of these, thirty-one were independent component makers. In other words, 84 percent of those overseas investors operated outside the *keiretsu* umbrella.

8. Capannelli (1996: 65) obtained similar results from his fieldwork in Malaysia. Japanese consumer electronic firms mostly provided technical assistance to their suppliers, such as product design specifications or technical expertise.

9. The sample size was of ninety-seven subcontractors for Hitachi and fifty-one for Matsushita. The list of subcontractors was obtained from the publication *Assembly-Maker List* (1990), which prints a list of each company's subcontractors as provided by the companies themselves. Therefore, it is possible to avoid the problem of determining the operationalization of the *keiretsu* membership (for example, the stock-ownership ratio). This problem is particularly acute in electronics, where capital relations between assemblers and affiliated suppliers are weak.

10. This law was in effect from 1957 to 1971.

11. In 1985 the Japanese government's R&D expenditures as a share of total R&D was 24 percent; in West Germany it was 42 percent, in the United States 46 percent, in the UK 50 percent, and in France 58 percent (Todd 1990: 216).

12. MITI controlled the introduction of foreign technology through the licensing system. MITI's intervention aimed to reduce the price of know-how purchased abroad and to disseminate the new technology to several companies in the industry. Nevertheless, "before 1968 MITI gave priority to intermediate goods, such as chem-

icals and machine tools, and suppressed the domestic demand for foreign technology in such areas as consumer goods" (Baranson 1981: 67).

13. Domestic shortages, however, forced MITI to permit the import of key components for TV manufacturing. In 1954 it allowed imports of 82,000 picture tubes for fourteen- and twenty-one-inch sets (Hiramoto 1994: 27).

14. Capital and foreign exchange controls are not the only NTBs, of course. Other barriers include quotas, government procurement of domestic goods, and closed distribution channels.

15. Interview by the author with Denki Rengō officials, May 1996.

16. A study by Denki Rengō (1986: 1) concluded that Japanese FDI until 1984 was responsible for 95,000 jobs lost (or 5.3 percent of domestic employment in the electronics industry). J. Goto (1990: 181) calculated FDI led to the loss of 31,0000 jobs in 1987–88. In a more recent Denki Rengō study (1995: 37), the employment loss attributed to FDI was 95,000 by 1993, and by the year 2000 it was expected to increase to between 106,000 and 313,000. These analyses take into account both FDI's negative consequences (export substitution and reverse imports) and positive effects (sales of parts and equipment to overseas subsidiaries). The wide range of results reported by the studies reflects the arbitrary selection of the replacement ratio of exports by FDI (30 percent or 100 percent). Goto (1990) avoided this problem by estimating the elasticity of exports to FDI.

17. Although at the time, Zenith and Sylvania operated some overseas plants, they were the only American companies that still assembled all their color television sets in the United States (Millstein 1983: 128).

Conclusion: Crafting Comparative Advantage Through FDI

1. The same rules apply to the international financial operations account of the JBIC, which took over FDI financing in 1999.

2. Calder (1993) makes a persuasive argument that MITI bureaucrats had limited powers over preferential financing to bring about their vision of economic transformation. Calder points out that MITI's industrial strategy was severely curtailed by the loss of its power over foreign exchange quotas, by the contraction of the funding provided through the Industrial Investment Special Account that it supervised (together with MOF), and by its lack of regulatory jurisdiction over banks and securities. My findings corroborate Calder's thesis by showing that those institutions influenced by MITI have operated much smaller lending programs.

3. As Busch (1999) reminds us, export credit competition has focused on high-technology sectors with significant spillover effects in the economy. States fight for these high-value-added industries when they can both consume and internalize the positive externalities.

4. Another remarkable similarity with Japan is the visible role that small enterprises played in the relocation of labor-intensive manufacturing to neighboring Asian nations. In 1999 the share of SMEs in accumulated FDI stock was 17 percent (Park 2000: 591).

5. For a good account of the tight policies governing FDI inflows, see Mardon 1990.

6. According to Woo-Cummings (1991: 151), foreign lending played such a pivotal role in Korean industrialization during 1962–82 that in its absence annual growth would have been only a little more than half its actual rate: 4.9 percent rather than 8.2 percent.

7. Estimates based on data released by the Korea Eximbank to the author.

8. Estimates based on data released by the Korea Eximbank to the author.

Bibliography

Abraham, Katharine, and Susan Houseman. 1989. "Job Security and Work Force Adjustment: How Different Are US and Japanese Practices." *Journal of the Japanese and International Economies* 3: 500–21.

Aggarwal, Vinod K., with Stephan Haggard. 1983. "The Politics of Protection in the US Textile and Apparel Industries." In John Zysman and Laura Tyson, eds., *American Industry in International Competition*. Ithaca, N.Y.: Cornell University Press.

Akamatsu, Kaname. 1962. "A Historical Pattern of Economic Growth in Developing Countries." *Developing Economies* 1 (March–August): 1–23.

Amsden, Alice H. 1989. *Asia's Next Giant: South Korea and Late Industrialization*. New York: Oxford University Press.

Anzai, Masao. 1971. *Aruminiumu Kōgyō Ron* [The aluminum industry]. Tokyo: Daiyamondosha.

Aoki, Takeshi. 1994. *Ajia Taiheiyō Keizaihen no Seisei* [The creation of an economic sphere in the Asia-Pacific region]. Tokyo: Chuo Keizai Sha.

Arase, David. 1995. *Buying Power: The Political Economy of Japan's Foreign Aid*. Boulder, Colo.: Lynne Rienner.

Arpan, Jeffrey S., Mary Barry, and Tran Van Tho. 1984. "The Textile Complex in the Asia-Pacific Region." In Peter H. Gray, ed., *Research in International Business and Finance*. Vol. 4. Greenwich: JAI Press.

Assembly-Maker List. 1990. Tokyo: Denshi Keizai Kenkyujō.

Bailey, David, George Harte, and Roger Sugden. 1994. *Transnationals and Governments: Recent Policies in Japan, France, Germany, the United States, and Britain*. London: Routledge.

Baldwin, Robert. 1985. *The Political Economy of US Import Policy*. Cambridge, Mass.: MIT Press.

Banerji, Kunal, and Rakesh B. Sambharya. 1996. "Vertical Keiretsu and International Market Entry: The Case of the Japanese Automobile Ancillary Industry." *Journal of International Business* 27, no. 1: 89–113.

Bank of Japan. Various years. *Economic Statistics Annual*. Tokyo: Bank of Japan.

Baranson, Jack. 1981. *The Japanese Challenge to US Industry*. Lexington, Mass.: Lexington Books.

Beason, Richard, and David Weinstein. 1993. "Growth, Economies of Scale, and Targeting in Japan (1955–1990)." Discussion paper 1644. Harvard Institute of Economic Research.

Behrman, Jack N., and Robert E. Grosse. 1990. *International Business and Governments: Issues and Institutions*. Columbia: University of South Carolina Press.

Belderbos, Rene, and Leo Sleuwaegen. 1993. "Japanese Firms and the Decision to Invest Abroad: Business Groups and Regional Core Networks." Mimeograph.

Bergsten, Fred C., Thomas Horst, and Theodore H. Moran. 1978. *American Multinationals and American Interests*. Washington, D.C.: Brookings Institution.

Bernard, Mitchell, and John Ravenhill. 1995. "Beyond Product Cycles and Flying Geese." *World Politics* 47, no. 2: 171–209.

Bhagwati, Jagdish N. 1988. *Protectionism*. Cambridge, Mass.: MIT Press.

———. 1987. "Structural Adjustment and Factor Mobility." In Karl Jungenfelt and Douglas Hague, eds., *Structural Adjustment in Developed Open Economies*. London: Macmillan.

———. 1982. "Shifting Comparative Advantage, Protectionist Demands, and Policy Response." In Jagdish N. Bhagwati, ed., *Import Competition and Response*. Chicago: University of Chicago Press.

Bluestone, Barry, and Bennett Harrison. 1982. *The Deindustrialization of America: Plant Closings, Community Abandonment, and the Dismantling of Basic Industry*. New York: Basic Books.

Borrus, Michael. 2000. "Asian Production Networks and the Rise of Wintelism." In Michael Borrus, Dieter Ernst, and Stephan Haggard, eds., *International Production Networks in Asia. Rivalry or riches?* New York: Routledge.

Brennglass, Alan C. 1983. *The Overseas Private Investment Corporation: A Study in Political Risk*. New York: Praeger.

Brewer, Thomas L., and Stephen Young. 1998. *The Multilateral Investment System and Multinational Enterprises*. Oxford: Oxford University Press.

Buckley, Peter J. 1989. *The Multinational Enterprise: Theory and Applications*. London: Macmillan.

———. 1983. "Macroeconomic Versus International Business Approach to Direct Foreign Investment: A Comment on Professor Kojima's Interpretation." *Hitotsubashi Journal of Economics* 24 (June): 95–100.

Buckley, Peter J., and Casson, M.C., eds. 1976. *The Future of the Multinational Enterprise*. London: Macmillan.

Bunker, Stephen G. 1994. "Flimsy Joint Ventures in Fragile Environments." In Bradford Barham, Stephen G. Bunker, and Denis O'Hearn, eds., *States, Firms and Raw Materials: The World Economy and Ecology of Aluminum*. Madison: University of Wisconsin Press.

Bunker, Stephen G., and Paul S. Cicantell. 1994. "The Evolution of the World Aluminum Industry." In Bradford Barham, Stephen G. Bunker, and Denis O'Hearn, eds., *States, Firms and Raw Materials: The World Economy and Ecology of Aluminum*. Madison: University of Wisconsin Press.

Bunker, Stephen G., and Denis O'Hearn. 1993. "Strategies of Economic Ascendants for Access to Raw Materials: A Comparison of the United States and Japan." In Ravi Arvind Palat, ed., *Pacific Asia and the Future of the World System*. Westport, Conn.: Greenwood.

Busch, Marc L. 1999. *Trade Warriors: States, Firms, and Strategic-Trade Policy in High-Technology Competition*. Cambridge: Cambridge University Press.

Calder, Kent E. 1993. *Strategic Capitalism: Private Business and Public Purpose in Japanese Industrial Finance*. Princeton, N.J.: Princeton University Press.

———. 1990. "Linking Welfare and the Developmental State: Postal Savings in Japan." *Journal of Japanese Studies* 16, no. 1: 31–59.

———. 1989. "Elites in an Equalizing Role: Ex-Bureaucrats as Coordinators and Intermediaries in the Japanese Government-Business Relationship." *Comparative Politics* 21, no. 4 (July): 379–403.

———. 1988. *Crisis and Compensation: Public Policy and Political Stability in Japan, 1949–1986*. Princeton, N.J.: Princeton University Press.

Callon, Scott. 1995. *Divided Sun: MITI and the Breakdown of Japanese High-Tech Industrial Policy, 1975–1993*. Stanford, Calif.: Stanford University Press.

Calomiris, Charles W., and Charles P. Himmelberg. 1995. "Directed Credit and Industrial Performance: Evidence from the Japan Machine Tool Industry, 1963–1991." World Bank Working Paper Series, Washington, D.C.

Capannelli, Giovanni. 1996. "Industry Relocation and Technology Transfer: Japanese Consumer Electronic Firms in Malaysia." Working paper 5, APEC Study Center, Hitotsubashi University and Institute of Developing Economies, Tokyo.

Carlile, Lonny E. 1998. "The Politics of Administrative Reform." In Lonny E. Carlile and Mark C. Tilton, eds., *Is Japan Really Changing Its Ways? Regulatory Reform and the Japanese Economy*. Washington, D.C.: Brookings Institution Press.

Caves, Richard E. 1982. *Multinational Enterprise and Economic Analysis*. New York: Cambridge University Press.

———. 1971. "International Corporation: The Industrial Economics of Foreign Investment." *Economica* 38, no. 149: 1–27.

Cho, Yoon Je, and Thomas Hellman. 1993. *The Government's Role in Japanese and Korean Credit Markets*. World Bank Policy Research Working Paper 1190, Washington, D.C..

Cho, Yoon Je, and Joon-Kyung Kim. 1995. "Credit Policies and the Industrialization of Korea." World Bank Discussion Paper 286, Washington, D.C.

Choy, Jon. 1997. "Financial Market Reform in Japan: Big Bang or Just Fizz? *JEI Report*, no. 3 (January 24) http://www.jei.org/Archive/JEIR97/9703.html.

Chung, Un-Chan. 1990. "Korean Economic Growth and Financial Development." In Chung H. Lee and Ippei Yamazawa, eds., *The Economic Development of Japan and Korea*. New York: Praeger.

Clark, D. P., W. C. Sawyer, and R. L. Sprinkle. 1989. "Determinants of Industry Participation Under Offshore Assembly Provisions in the United States Tariff Code." *Journal of World Trade* 23, nos. 4–6: 123–30.

Clegg, Jeremy. 1987. *Multinational Enterprises and World Competition*. London: Macmillan.

Cline, William R. 1987. *The Future of World Trade in Textiles and Apparel*. Washington: Institute for International Economics.

Cohen, Stephen D. 1998. *An Ocean Apart: Explaining Three Decades of US-Japanese Trade Frictions*. Westport, Conn.: Praeger.

Committee on Foreign Exchange and Other Transactions. 1997. "Concerning the

Amendment of the Foreign Exchange and Foreign Trade Control Law." http://www.mog.go.jp/english/e1702f1.htm.

Council on Foreign Economic Cooperation. 1987. *Waga Kuni Keizai Kyōryoku no Suishin* [On the promotion of our country's economic cooperation]. Tokyo: Office of the Prime Minister.

Crowson, Phillip. 1983. "Non-Fuel Mineral Procurement Policies." In Nobutoshi Akao, *Japan's Economic Security: Resources as a Factor in Foreign Policy*. Aldershot, UK: Gower.

Dekle, Robert. 1998. "The Japanese 'Big Bang' Financial Reforms and Market Implications." *Journal of Asian Economics* 9, no. 2: 237–49.

Denki Rengō. 1995. *Sōzō to Kakushi e no Chōsen* [The challenge of creation and innovation]. Tokyo: Denki Rengō.

———. 1994. *Denki Rengō no Seisaku Shishin* [Manual on the policies of Denki Rengō]. Tokyo: Denki Rengō.

———. 1993. "Chokumen suru Endaka to Denki Sangyō Kōzō Tenkan ni kansuru Denki Rengō no kangaekata to taiō ni tsuite" [The opinion and response of Denki Rengō to the yen appreciation and the structural transformation of the electric industry]. Photocopy.

———. 1986. "Denki Sangyō no Kaigai Shinshutsu to Koyō e no Eikyō Suikei" [Estimation of the effect on employment of the overseas expansion of the electric industry]. *Seisaku Shiryō Geppo* no. 131 (October): 1–5.

Denshi Kōgyō Nenkan [Yearbook of the electronics industry]. Several years. Tokyo: Denpa Shinbunsha.

Dicken, P. 1992. *Global Shiji—The Internationalization of Economic Activity*. London: Paul Chapman.

Doi, Takero, and Takeo Hoshi. 2002. "Paying for the FILP." NBER Working Paper Series 9385, Cambridge, Mass.

Doner, Richard F. 1993. "Japanese Foreign Investment and the Creation of a Pacific Asian Region." In Jeffrey A. Frankel and Miles Kahler, eds., *Regionalism and Rivalry: Japan and the United States in Pacific Asia*. Chicago: University of Chicago Press.

———. 1991. *Driving a Bargain: Automobile Industrialization and Japanese Firms in Southeast Asia*. Berkeley: University of California Press.

Dore, Ronald. 1986. *Flexible Rigidities: Industrial Policy and Structural Adjustment in the Japanese Economy, 1970–80*. Stanford, Calif.: Stanford University Press.

Doremus, Paul N., William W. Keller, Louis W. Pauly, and Simon Reich. 1998. *The Myth of the Global Corporation*. Princeton., N.J.: Princeton University Press.

Dunning, John H. 1993. "Governments and Multinational Enterprises: From Confrontation to Cooperation?" In Lorraine Eden and Evan H. Potter, eds., *Multinationals in the Global Political Economy*. New York: St. Martin's.

———. 1992. *Multinational Enterprises and the Global Economy*. Suffolk, UK: Addison-Wesley.

Dunning, John H., and Howard Archer. 1987. "The Eclectic Paradigm and the Growth of UK Multinational Enterprise, 1870–1983." *Business and Economic History* 16: 19–49.

Dunning John H., and John Cantwell. 1987. *IRM Directory of Statistics of International Investment and Production.* New York: New York University Press.

Eaton, Jonathan. 1986. "Credit Policy and International Competition." In Paul R. Krugman, ed., *Strategic Trade Policy and the New International Economics.* Cambridge, Mass.: MIT Press.

Elder, Mark. 2003. "METI and Industrial Policy in Japan: Change and Continuity." In Ulrike Schaede and William Grimes, eds., *Japan's Managed Globalization: Adapting to the Twenty-First Century.* Armonk, N.Y.: M.E. Sharpe.

Electronics Industry Association of Japan (EIAJ). 2000. *Kaigai Hōjin Ristō* [List of corporations overseas]. Tokyo: EIAJ.

———. 1998. *EIAJ Half-Centennial: A Look at 50 Years of the Japanese Electronics Industry.* Tokyo: EIAJ.

———. 1995. *Denshi Kōgyō Nenkan* [Electronics industry yearbook]. Tokyo: EIAJ.

Encarnation, Dennis J., and Mark Mason, eds. 1994. *Does Ownership Matter? Japanese Multinationals in Europe.* New York: Clarendon.

———. 1990. "Neither MITI nor America: The Political Economy of Capital Liberalization in Japan." *International Organization* 44 (Winter): 25–54.

Ernst, Dieter. 2000. "The Asian Production Networks of Japanese Electronic Firms." In Michael Borrus, Dieter Ernst, and Stephan Haggard, eds., *International Production Networks in Asia: Rivalry or Riches?* New York: Routledge.

Evans, Peter C., and Kenneth A. Oye. 2001. "International Competition: Conflict and Cooperation in Government Export Financing." In Gary Clyde Hufbauer and Rita M. Rodriguez, eds., *The Ex-Im Bank in the 21st Century: A New Approach?* Washington, D.C.: Institute for International Economics.

Evans, Peter C., Dietrich Rueschemeyer, and Theda Skocpol, eds. 1985. *Bringing the State Back In.* New York: Cambridge University Press.

Farrel, Roger. 2000. "Japanese Foreign Direct Investment in the World Economy 1951–1997." Pacific Economic Paper 299. Australia-Japan Research Centre, Canberra.

Frieden, Jeffry A. 1994. "International Investment and Colonial Control: A New Interpretation." *International Organization* 48 (Autumn): 559–93.

Friedman, David. 1988. *The Misunderstood Miracle: Industrial Development and Political Change in Japan.* Ithaca, N.Y.: Cornell University Press.

Friman, Richard H. 1990. *Patchwork Protectionism: Textile Trade Policy in the United States, Japan, and West Germany.* Ithaca, N.Y.: Cornell University Press.

Fujii, Kiyotaka. 1971. "Kokusaika jidai ni chōsensuru aruminiumu shigen no kaihatsu" [Development of aluminum resources in the international era]. In Shigeru Nishio, ed., *Kinzoku Shigen. Kaihatsu to Riyō no Senryaku* [Metal resources: strategy for development and use]. Tokyo: Kinzoku Kakō Shuppankai.

Fujii, Mitsuo. 1979. "Sen'i Sangyō ni Okeru Kaigai Tōshi Katsudō no Tenkai [Development of the textile industry's overseas investment activities]. In Mitsuo Fujii, Taichi Nakase, Yoshinari Maruyama, and Masataka Ikeda, eds., *Nihon Takokuseki Kigyō no Shiteki Tenkai* [Historical development of the Japanese multinational corporation]. Tokyo: Otsuki Shōten.

———. 1971. *Nihon Sen'i Sangyō Keieishi: sengō—menbō kara gōsen made* [Managerial history of the Japanese textile industry: postwar—from cotton to synthetics]. Tokyo: Nihon Hyōronsha.

Fujita, Masahisa, and Ryoichi Ishii. 1995. "Global Location Behavior and Organization Dynamics of Japanese Electronics and Their Impact on Regional Economies." Discussion Paper 423. Kyoto Institute of Economic Research.

Fujita, Masataka. 1993. *Small and Medium-Sized Transnational Corporations: Role, Impact and Policy Implications*. New York: United Nations Centre on Transnational Corporations.

Fukuhara, Genichi. 1969. "Aruminiumu Kōgyō no Genjō to Kadai" [Current situation and topics in the aluminum industry]. In Shigeru Nishio, ed., *Kaigai Arumi Shigen no Kaihatsu* [Overseas development of aluminum resources]. Tokyo: Institute of Developing Economies.

"Gaitamehō Kaiseigō no Hōkoku Gyōmu wa nihyaku man en chō ni." 1997. [After the liberalization of the Foreign Exchange Law, reporting requirement for over 2 million yen]. *Kinyū Zaisei Jijō* (September 29): 35.

"Gaitamehō no Kaisei Sagyō ga iyoiyo gutaika." 1996. [Preparations for the revision of the Foreign Exchange Law are becoming more and more concrete]. *Kinyū Zaisei Jijō* (September 23): 6.

Gann, Lewis H. 1984. "Western and Japanese Colonialism: Some Preliminary Comparisons." In Ramon H. Myers and Mark R. Peattie, eds., *The Japanese Colonial Empire, 1895–1945*, Princeton, N.J.: Princeton University Press.

Geist, Michael. A. 1994. "Foreign Direct Investment in Japan: A Guide to the Legal Framework." *Banking and Finance Law Review* 9: 305–57.

General Accounting Office (GAO). 2000. *The Overseas Private Investment Corporation's Investment Funds Program*. Washington, D.C.: General Accounting Office.

———. 1997. *Issues Related to the Overseas Private Investment Corporation's Reauthorization*. Washington, D.C.: General Accounting Office.

Gilpin, Robert A. 1975. *US Power and the Multinational Corporation: The Political Economy of Foreign Direct Investment*. New York: Basic Books.

Goodman, John B., and Louis W. Pauly. 1993. "The Obsolescence of Capital Controls? Economic Management in an Age of Global Markets." *World Politics* 46, no. 1: 50–82.

Goto, Akira. 1988. "Japan: A Sunset Industry." In Merton J. Peck, ed., *The World Aluminum Industry in a Changing Energy Era*. Baltimore: Johns Hopkins University Press for Resources for the Future.

Goto, Junichi. 1990. *Labor in International Trade Theory: A New Perspective on Japanese-American Issues*. Baltimore: John Hopkins University Press.

Gourevitch, Peter. 1986. *Politics in Hard Times: Comparative Responses to International Economic Crises*. Ithaca, N.Y.: Cornell University Press.

Graham, Edward M. 2000. *Fighting the Wrong Enemy: Antiglobal Activists and Multinational Enterprises*. Washington, D.C.: Institute for International Economics.

Grieder, William. 1997. *One World, Ready or Not: The Manic Logic of Global Capitalism*. New York: Simon and Schuster.

Haley, John O. 1987. "Governance by Negotiation: A Reappraisal of Bureaucratic Power in Japan." In Kenneth Pyle, ed., *The Trade Crisis: How Will Japan Respond?* Seattle: Society for Japanese Studies.

Hall, Anthony. 1989. *Developing Amazonia: Deforestation and Social Conflict in Brazil's Carajas Programme*. Manchester: Manchester University Press.

Hall, Maximilian J.B. 1998. *Financial Reform in Japan: Causes and Consequences*. Cheltenham: Edward Elgar.

Hall, Peter A. 1995. "The Japanese Civil Service and Economic Development in Comparative Perspective." In Hyung-Ki Kim, Michio Muramatsu, T. J. Pempel, and Kozo Yamamura, eds., *The Japanese Civil Service and Economic Development*. Oxford: Oxford University Press.

Hall, Peter A., and David Soskice. 2001. "An Introduction to Varieties of Capitalism." In Peter A. Hall and David Soskice, eds., *Varieties of Capitalism: The Institutional Foundations of Comparative Advantage*. New York: Oxford University Press.

Hanano, Akio, et al. 1991. *Zusetsu: Zaisei Toyushi* [Diagrams: the fiscal investment and loans program]. Tokyo: Toyo Keizai.

Hara, Masayuki. 1992. *Kaigai Chokusetsu Tōshi to Nihon Keizai* [Foreign direct investment and the Japanese economy]. Tokyo: Egusa Tadataka.

———. 1989. "Kigyōnai Sangyō Chōsei—Takokuka to Chokusetsu Tōshi" [Intrafirm industrial adjustment—diversification and direct investment]. *Sekai Keizai Hyōron* 33, no. 8: 25–31.

Hashimoto, Juro. 1990. "Sen'i Kōgyō no Anteika Seisaku" [Stabilization policy for the textile industry]. In MITI, ed., *Tsushōsangyō Seisakushi* [History of trade and industrial policies]. Tokyo: MITI.

Hashimoto, Toshiro. 1990. "Denki-Denshi Kōgyō no Ikusei" [Nurturing the electric-electronics industry]. In MITI, ed., *Tsushōsangyō Seisakushi* [History of trade and industrial policies]. Tokyo: MITI.

Hatch, Walter, and Kozo Yamamura. 1996. *Asia in Japan's Embrace: Building a Regional Production Alliance*. Cambridge: Cambridge University Press.

Higuchi, Hirotaro. 1998. "Gaitamehō Kaisei no Eikyō to En no Kokusaika" [The influence of the reform to the Foreign Exchange Law and the internationalization of the yen]. *Keidanren Gekkan* 46 (August): 9–15.

Hillman, Arye L. 1989. *The Political Economy of Protection*. New York: Harwood Academic Publishers.

———. 1982. "Declining Industries and Political-Support Protectionist Moves." *The American Economic Review* 72 (December): 1180–87.

Hirai, Toko, and Hiroyushi Iwasaki. 1985. *Sen'i Gyōkai* [The textile industry]. Sangyō Series 46. Tokyo: Kyōiku Shashinsho.

Hiramoto, Atsushi. 1994. *Nihon no Terebi Sangyō* [The Japanese television industry]. Tokyo: Minerva.

Hiwatari, Nobuhiro. 2000. "The Reorganization of Japan's Financial Bureaucracy: The Politics of Bureaucratic Structure and Blame Avoidance." In Takeo Hoshi and Hugh Patrick, eds., *Crisis and Change in the Japanese Financial System*. Boston: Kluwer.

Hoekman, Bernard M., and Michel M. Kostecki. 1995. *The Political Economy of the World Trading System: From GATT to WTO*. Oxford: Oxford University Press.

Holloway, Steven. 1988. *The Aluminum Multinationals and the Bauxite Cartel*. London: Macmillan.

Horaguchi, Haruo. 1992. *Nihon Kigyō no Kaigai Chokusetsu Tōshi: Ajia e no Shinshutsu to Tettai* [Overseas investment by Japanese firms: expansion and withdrawal from Asia]. Tokyo: Tokyo Daigaku Shuppankai.

Horiuchi, Akiyoshi. 2001. "The Big Bang: Idea and Reality." In Takeo Hoshi and Hugh Patrick, eds., *Crisis and Change in the Japanese Financial System*. Boston: Kluwer.

Horiuchi, Akiyoshi, and Qing-Yuan Sui. 1993. "Influence of the Japan Development Bank Loans on Corporate Investment Behavior." *Journal of the Japanese and International Economies* 7: 441–65.

Horne, James. 1985. *Japan's Financial Markets: Conflict and Consensus in Policymaking*. Sydney: George Allen and Unwin.

Hoshi, Takeo, and Anil K. Kashyap. 2001. *Corporate Financing and Governance in Japan: The Road to the Future*. Cambridge, Mass.: MIT Press.

Hufbauer, Gary C. 1991. "United States: Adjustment Through Import Restriction." In Hugh Patrick, ed., with Larry Meissner. *Pacific Basin Industries in Distress*. New York: Columbia University Press.

Ietto-Gillies, Grazia. 1992. *International Production: Trends, Theories, Effects*. Cambridge: Polity Press.

Ike, Brian. 1980. "The Japanese Textile Industry: Structural Adjustment and Government Policy." *Asian Survey* 20 (May): 532–51.

Ikeda, Masataka. 1982. "Kara Terebi no Seisan Kōzō to Shitauke Kigyō" [The production structure of color television and subcontracting firms]. *Chūō Daigaku Keizai Kenkyujō Nenpō* 13: 25–49.

———. 1979. "Minseiyō Denshi Kikai Kigyō no Kaigai Shinshutsu to Takokuseki Kigyōka [Overseas expansion of consumer electronics companies and multinationalization]. In Fujii Mitsuo, ed., *Nihon Takokuseki Kigyō no Shiteki Hatten* [Historical evolution of Japanese multinationals]. Tokyo: Daigetsu Shoten.

Imuta, Toshimitsu. 1993. "Kinzoku" [Metals]. In MITI, ed., *Tsūshōsangyō Seisakushi* [History of trade and industrial policies]. Vol. 14. Tokyo: MITI.

Industrial Structure Council. 1972. *Nihon no Taigai Keizai Seisaku* [Japan's economic cooperation policy]. Tokyo: Daiyamondosha.

Ishi, Hiromitsu. 1986. "The Government Credit Program and Public Enterprises." In Tokue Shibata, ed., *Public Finance in Japan*. Tokyo: University of Tokyo Press.

Ishii, Masashi. 1996. "Nihon no Buhin Mêkâ no Ajia Jigyō Senryaku—Jidōsha Buhin, Denshi-Denki Buhin o chushin ni shite" [The Asian business strategy of Japanese part makers—focusing on automobile parts and electric-electronic parts]. In Sueo Sekiguchi and Hiroshi Tanaka, eds., *Kaigai Chokusetsu Tōshi to Nihon Keizai* [Overseas direct investment and the Japanese economy]. Tokyo: Toyo Keizai Shinjōsha.

Ishiyama, Yoshihide. 1999. "Is Japan Hollowing Out?" In Dennis J. Encarnation, ed., *Japanese Multinationals in Asia: Regional Operations in Comparative Perspective*. Oxford: Oxford University Press.

Ito, Masaaki. 1993. "Sen'i" [Textiles]. In MITI, ed., *Tsūshōsangyō Seisakushi* [History of trade and industrial policies]. Tokyo: MITI.

Itoh, Motoshige, Kazuharu Kiyono, Masahiro Okuno-Fujiwara, and Kotaro Suzumura. 1991. *Economic Analysis of Industrial Policy*. San Diego: Academic Press.

Iwami, Makoto. 1977. "Sen'i Sangyō ni miru Nihon no Kaigai Tōshi" [Japan's overseas investment in textiles]. In *Nihon no Kaigai Tōshi no Sangyō betsu Kentō* [A sectoral examination of Japan's overseas investment]. Tokyo: Institute of Developing Economies.

Japan Aluminum Federation. 2000. *Aruminiumu Dêtabukku* [Aluminum databook]. Tokyo: Japan Aluminum Federation.

Japan Bank for International Cooperation (JBIC). 2002. *Annual Report*. Tokyo: JBIC.

Japan Eximbank. *Gyōmu Binran* [Operations manual]. Several issues. Tokyo: Export-Import Bank of Japan.

———. 1996. "Project Finance: Part I." *Highlights of JOI Review* 28 (July): 8–17.

———. 1995. "Nihon Yushutsunyū Ginkōhō Kaisei no Suido" [Evolution of reforms to the law of the Export-Import Bank of Japan]. Internal document.

———. 1994. *Guide to the Export-Import Bank of Japan*. Tokyo: Export-Import Bank of Japan.

———. 1993. *The Export-Import Bank of Japan: Articles of Incorporation*. Tokyo: Export-Import Bank of Japan.

———. 1992. *The Course: Forty Years of the Export-Import Bank of Japan*. Tokyo: Export-Import Bank of Japan.

———. 1983. *Sanjūnen no Ayumi* [Thirty-year course]. Tokyo: Export-Import Bank of Japan.

Japan Institute of Labor. 1984. *Kaigai Tōshi to Koyō Mondai* [Overseas investment and the employment problem]. Tokyo: Nihon Rōdo Kyōkai.

Japan International Cooperation Agency. 1994. *Annual Report*. Tokyo: Japan International Cooperation Agency.

Japan International Development Organization (JAIDO). 1995. *Annual Report*. Tokyo: JAIDO.

Japan Statistical Yearbook. Several years. Tokyo: Sorifu, Tokeikyoku.

Japan Textile News. May 1990: 55–63.

Johnson, Chalmers. 1982. *MITI and the Japanese Miracle: The Growth of Industrial Policy, 1925–1975*. Stanford, Calif.: Stanford University Press.

———. 1978. *Japan's Public Policy*. Washington, D.C.: American Enterprise Institute.

Jones, Geoffrey. 1996. *The Evolution of International Business*. New York: Routledge.

Jūkagaku Kōgyō Tsūshinsha. 1976. *Nihon no Kaigai Shigen Kaihatsu* [Japan's development of overseas resources]. Tokyo: Jūgaku Kōgyō Tsūshinsha.

Kaigai Tōshi Kenkyūkai. 1978. *Gosen Sen'i Kōgyō* [The synthetic textile industry]. Tokyo: Kaigai Tōshi Kenkyūkai Hōkokusho.

Kaisha Shikihō [Quarterly report of companies]. 1996. Tokyo: Toyo Keizai Shinposha.

Kang, David C. 2002. "Bad Loans to Good Friends: Money Politics and the Developmental State in South Korea." *International Organization* 56 (Winter): 177–207.

Kasen Handōbukku [Handbook of chemical textiles]. 1997. Tokyo: Nihon Kagaku Sen'i Kyōkai.

Kato, Kozo, et al. 1994. *Policy-Based Finance: The Experience of Postwar Japan*. World Bank Discussion Paper 221, Washington, D.C.

Katz, Richard. 1998. *Japan, the System That Soured: The Rise and Fall of the Japanese Economic Miracle*. Armonk: M.E. Sharpe.

Katzenstein, Peter J. 1985. *Small States in World Markets: Industrial Policy in Europe*. Ithaca, N.Y.: Cornell University Press.

Kawahara, Isao, and Shoji Ishii. 1980. "Waga Kuni Minseiyō Denshi Kōgyō no Kokusaika" [The internationalization of our consumer electronics industry]. *Kaigai Tōshi Kenkyūjōhō* (April): 1–29.

"Kawase Kanrihō ni Kawaru Shinpō Settei e" [Toward the establishment of a new law to replace the Foreign Exchange Law]. 1963. *Kinyū Zaisei Jijō* (March): 8.

Kernell, Samuel. 1991. "The Primacy of Politics in Economic Policy." In *Parallel Politics: Economic Policy-Making in the United States and Japan*. Washington, D.C.: Brookings Institution.

Kijima, Kanetaka. 1995. "The Export-Import Bank of Japan and Japan-Europe Relations." Photocopy.

Kikai Shinkō Kyōkai Keizai Kenkyūjō. 1987. *Kikai Sangyō ni Okeru Kokusaika no Shinten to Shitauke Bungyō Kōzō no Henka ni tsuite no Chōsa Kenkyū* [Survey research on the internationalization of the machinery industry and changes in the structure of subcontractors' division of labor]. Tokyo: Machinery Promotion Association.

Kim, Seungjin. 1998. "Effects of Outward Foreign Direct Investment on Home Country Performance: Evidence from Korea." Working Paper, Korea Development Institute, Seoul.

Kimura, H. 1983. "Arumi Seirengyō no Tesshū to Kongo no Kadai" [Withdrawal from the aluminum smelting industry and future problems]. *Chōgin Chōsa Geppō* no. 202: 1–33.

Kimura, Yiu, and Thomas A. Pugel. 1995. "Keiretsu and Japanese Direct Investment in US Manufacturing." *Japan and the World Economy* 7 (November): 481–503.

Kindleberger, Charles P. 1969. *American Business Abroad*. New Haven, Conn.: Yale University Press.

Kinoshita, Takeo. 1984. "Denki Sangyō ni Okeru Koyō Chōsei no Tenkai to Koyō Kōzō no Hendō" [The unfolding of employment adjustment in the electric industry and changes in the structure of employment]. In Seichiro Hasegawa, Yonosuke Koshi, and Toshio Aida, eds., *Denki Sangyō ni Okeru Rōdō Kumiai* [Labor unions in the electric industry]. Tokyo: Heichi Toru.

Kinoshita, Toshihiko. 1992. "Chikuseki Saimu Mondai to Shikin Kanryū" [The accumulated debt problem and the recycling of funds]. In Ito Takahashi, ed., *Kokusai Kinyū no Genjō* [The current situation of international finance]. Tokyo: Egusa.

Kōgyō Tōkeihyō [Census of manufacturing]. Several years. Tokyo: MITI.

Koike, Kazuo. 1987. "Human Resource Development and Labor-Management." In Kozo Yamamura and Yasukichi Yasuba, eds., *The Political Economy of Japan: The Domestic Transformation*. Stanford, Calif.: Stanford University Press.

Kojima, Kiyoshi. 1978. *Direct Foreign Investment: A Japanese Model of Multinational Business Operations*. New York: Praeger.

Kojima, Kiyoshi, and Terutomo Ozawa. 1984. *Japan's General Trading Companies: Merchants of Economic Development*. Paris: OECD.

Kolenda, T. E. 1985. "Japan's Develop-for-Import Policy." *Resource Policy* 11 (October): 257–66.

Komiya, Ryutaro. 1988. "Japan's Foreign Direct Investment: Facts and Theoretical Considerations." In Silvio Borner, ed., *International Finance and Trade in a Polycentric World*. New York: St. Martin's.

Kong, Tat Yan. 1995. "From Relative Autonomy to Consensual Development: The Case of South Korea." *Political Studies* 43: 630–44.

Koo, Bohn-Young, and Eon-Oh Lee. 1985. "Korean Business Ventures Abroad: Patterns and Characteristics." Working Paper 8502, Korea Development Institute, Seoul.

Koo, Hagen. 2000. "The Dilemmas of Empowered Labor in Korea: Korean Workers in the Face of Global Capitalism." *Asian Survey* 40, no. 2: 227–50.

Korea Eximbank. 1996. *Korea's Outward Direct Investment.* Seoul: Export-Import Bank of Korea.

———. *Annual Report*, several years. Seoul: Export-Import Bank of Korea.

Krasner, Stephen D. 1978. *Defending the National Interest: Raw Materials Investments and US Foreign Policy.* Princeton, N.J.: Princeton University Press.

Krause, Lawrence B., and Sueo Sekiguchi. 1976. "Japan and the World Economy." In Hugh Patrick and Henry Rosovsky, eds., *Asia's New Giant: How the Japanese Economy Works.* Washington D.C.: Brookings Institution.

Kumar, Krishna, and Kee Young Kim. 1984. "The Korean Manufacturing Multinationals." *Journal of International Business Studies* (Spring/Summer): 45–61.

Kume, Ikuo. 1998. *Disparaged Success: Labor Politics in Postwar Japan.* Ithaca, N.Y.: Cornell University Press.

Laurence, Henry. 2001. *Money Rules: The New Politics of Finance in Britain and Japan.* Ithaca, N.Y.: Cornell University Press.

Lee, Changwon, Dong-One Kim, and Johnseok Bae. 2000. "Globalization and Labour Rights: The Case of Korea." *Asia Pacific Business Review* 6, nos. 3–4: 133–53.

Lee, Chung H. 1994. "Korea's Direct Foreign Investment in Southeast Asia." *ASEAN Economic Bulletin* 10 (March): 280–96.

———. 1990. "Direct Foreign Investment, Structural Adjustment, and International Division of Labor: A Dynamic Macroeconomic Theory of Direct Foreign Investment." *Hitotsubashi Journal of Economics* 31: 61–72.

Lee, Keun. 1995. "Structural Changes in the Korean Economy and Korean Investment in China and ASEAN." In Sumner J. La Croix, Michael Plummer, and Keun Lee, eds., *Emerging Patterns of East Asian Investment in China.* London: M.E. Sharpe.

———. 1994. "Structural Adjustment and Outward Direct Foreign Investment in Korea." *Seoul Journal of Economics* 7, no. 2: 179–211.

Lee, Seong-Bong. 2000. "Korea's Overseas Direct Investment: Evaluation of Performances and Future Challenges." KIEP Working Paper 00-12, Korea Institute for International Economic Policy, Seoul.

Lincoln, Edward J. 2001. "Time to End Postal Savings." http://www.brook.edu/views/articles/lincoln/20010602.

Lincoln, Edward J., and Robert E. Litan. 1998. "The 'Big Bang'? An Ambivalent Japan Deregulates Its Financial Markets." *Brookings Review* 16, no. 1: 37–40.

Lipsey, Robert E. 1991. "Direct Foreign Investment and Structural Change in Developing Asia, Japan and the United States." In Eric D. Ramstetter, ed., *Direct Foreign Investment in Asia's Developing Economies and Structural Change in the Asia-Pacific Region.* Boulder, Colo.: Westview.

Lipson, Charles. 1985. *Standing Guard: Protecting Foreign Capital in the Nineteenth and Twentieth Centuries.* Berkeley: University of California Press.

Machado, R. C. 1994. "The Present and Future of CVRD in the Brazilian Aluminum Industry." In Bradford Barham, Stephen G. Bunker, and Denis O'Hearn, eds., *States, Firms and Raw Materials: The World Economy and Ecology of Aluminum*. Madison: University of Wisconsin Press.

Maeda. 1998. "Kaisei Gaitamehō Jikkō nirami tōgin ga tesuryō kaitei, shinshohin, sâvisu o kaihatsu" [Following the implementation of the revised Foreign Exchange law, city banks revise their fees and develop new products and services]. *Kinyū Zaisei Jijō* (January 5): 83.

Magee, Stephen P., William A. Brock, and Leslie Young. 1989. *Black Hole Tariffs and Endogenous Policy Theory: Political Economy in General Equilibrium*. Cambridge: Cambridge University Press.

Mardon, Russell. 1990. "The State and the Effective Control of Foreign Capital: The Case of South Korea." *World Politics* 43 (October): 111–38.

Marques, Isabel. 1994. "Industrial Organization and Supply Policy in the Japanese Aluminum Industry." In Bradford Barham, Stephen G. Bunker, and Denis O'Hearn, eds., *States, Firms and Raw Materials: The World Economy and Ecology of Aluminum*. Madison: University of Wisconsin Press.

———. 1990. "Albras/Alunorte." In Olivier Bomsel, ed., *Mining and Metallurgy Investment in the Third World: The End of Large Projects?* Paris: OECD.

Mason, Mark. 1999. "The Origins and Evolution of Japanese Direct Investment in East Asia." In Dennis J. Encarnation, ed., *Japanese Multinationals in Asia. Regional Operations in Comparative Perspective*. Oxford: Oxford University Press.

Masunaga, Rei. 1997. "The Deregulation Process of Foreign Exchange Control in Capital Transactions in Post-war Japan." http://www.jcif.or.jp/deregdec2001.pdf.

Matsuzawa, Takeo. 1993. "Ippan Anken (Minkan Sekuta Kaihatsu Kinyū) no Genjō Oyobi Kongo no Kadai" [Present condition and future issues for general finance (development finance for the private sector)]. In *Kokusai Kaihatsu Janaru* 6, no. 78: 97–106.

McKeown, Timothy J. 1984. "Firms and Tariff Regime Change: Explaining the Demand for Protection." *World Politics* 36, no. 2: 215–33.

McKern, R. B. 1976. *Multinational Enterprises and National Resources*. Sydney: McGraw Hill.

McKinney, Jeff, and Megan McVay. 1997. "Project Finance: A Comparative Study of Ex-Im and JEXIM in Chile." Photocopy.

McNamara, Dennis L. 1995. *Textiles and Industrial Transition in Japan*. Ithaca, N.Y.: Cornell University Press.

Metal Mining Agency of Japan (MMAJ). 1983. *Nijūnen no Ayumi* [Twenty-year course]. Tokyo: Metal Mining Agency of Japan.

Michalet, Charles Albert. 1997. "France." In John H. Dunning, ed., *Governments, Globalization, and International Business*. Oxford: Oxford University Press.

Millstein, James E. 1983. "Decline in an Expanding Industry: Japanese Competition in Color Television." In John Zysman and Laura Tyson, eds., *American Industry in International* Competition. Ithaca, N.Y.: Cornell University Press.

Milner, Helen V. 1988. *Resisting Protectionism: Global Industries and the Politics of International Trade*. Princeton, N.J.: Princeton University Press.

Ministry of Finance (MOF). 2002. *FILP Report 2002. Extension Volume: Policy Cost Analysis of FILP Projects.* http://www.mof.go.jp/english/zaito.

———. 2001. *Zaisei Toyūshi Report* [FILP report]. Tokyo: MOF.

———. 1992. *Shōwa Zaisei Shi, 1952–73* [History of Shōwa's public finance, 1952–73]. Tokyo: Toyo Keizai.

———. Several issues. *Zaisei Kinyū Tokkei Geppo* [Monthly financial statistics]. Tokyo: MOF.

Ministry of Foreign Affairs (MOFA). 1991. *Nihon no ODA to Kokusai Chijō* [Japanese ODA and the international order]. Tokyo: Nihon Kokusai Mondai Kenkyūjō.

Ministry of International Trade and Industry (MITI). 1998. *Waga Kuni Kigyō no Keiei Bunseki* [Managerial analysis of Japanese enterprises]. Tokyo: MITI.

———. 1995. *Kaisei Chūshō Kigyō Shinbunya Shinshutsu nado Enkatsuka hō no Tebiki* [Guide to the reformed Law for Smoothing the Advance of Small and Medium-Sized Firms into New Fields]. Tokyo: MITI.

———. 1994. *Chūshō Kigyō Shinbunya Shinshutsu nado Enkatsukahō no Gaiyō* [Outline of the Law for Smoothing the Advance of Small and Medium-Sized Firms into New Fields or Other]. Tokyo: MITI.

———. 1994a. *Chūshō Kigyō no Dōkō ni Kansuru Nenji Hōkoku* [Annual report on the direction of small and medium-sized enterprises]. Tokyo: MITI.

———. 1994b. *Sekai Sen'i Sangyō Jijō. Nihon no Sen'i Sangyō no Ikinokori Senryaku* [Condition of the world textile industry: survival strategy for Japan's textile industry]. Tokyo: MITI.

———. 1994c. *Kaigai Tōshi Tokei Sōran* [Comprehensive statistics on overseas investment]. Tokyo: MITI.

———. 1993. "Kaigai Tōshi no Josei" [Fostering overseas investment]. In *Tsushōsangyō Seisakushi* [History of international trade and industrial policies], ed. MITI. Tokyo: MITI.

———. 1993a. *Chūshō Kigyō Shinbunya Shinshutsu nado Enkatsukahō no Tebiki* [Guide to the Law for Smoothing the Advance of Small and Medium-Sized Firms into New Fields or Other]. Tokyo: MITI.

———. 1993b. *Kaigai Tōshi Tokei Sōran* [Comprehensive statistics on outward investment]. Vol. 5. Tokyo: MITI.

MITI, Small Business Agency. 1994. *Chūshō Kigyō no Dōkō ni Kansuru Nenji Hōkoku* [Annual report on the evolution of small and medium-sized firms]. Tokyo: MITI.

———. *Chūshō Kigyō Hakushō* [White paper on small and medium-sized enterprises]. Several issues. Tokyo: MITI.

"Minkatsu Jūshi Rosen to OECF Kaigai Toyūshi" [The importance of private activity and OECF's private sector investment finance]. *Kokusai Kaihatsu Janaru* 4: 24–30.

Minns, John. 2001. "Of Miracles and Models: The Rise and Decline of the Developmental State in South Korea." *Third World Quarterly* 22, no. 6: 1025–43.

Minotani, Chiohiko, ed. 1996. *Sangyō Kūdōka: Nihon no Makuro Keizai.* [Industrial hollowing-out: Japanese macroeconomics]. Tokyo: Taga Shuppan.

Miyawaki, Jun. 1995. *Zaisei Toyūshi no Kaikaku* [Reform of the fiscal investment and loans program]. Tokyo: Toyo Keizai.

Moran, Theodore H. 1985. "Multinational Corporations and the Developing Countries: An Analytical Overview." In Theodore H. Moran, ed., *Multinational Corporations. The Political Economy of Foreign Direct Investment.* Lexington, Mass.: Lexington Books.

Moran, Theodore H., ed. 1993: *Governments and Transnational Corporations.* Vol. 7. The United Nations Library on Transnational Corporations. London: Routledge.

Moravcsik, Andrew M. 1989. "Disciplining Trade Finance: The OECD Export Credit Arrangement." *International Organization* 43: 173–205.

Murakami, Jintarō. 1977. "Sen'I Sangyō no Kaigai Shinshutsu. Mikuroteki Sokumen" [Overseas expansion of the Japanese electronics industry]. In *Nihon no Kaigai Tōshi no Sangyō betsu Kentō* [Sectoral examination of Japan's overseas investment]. Tokyo: Institute of Developing Economies.

Muramatsu, Michio, and Ellis S. Krauss. 1987. "The Conservative Policy Line and the Development of Patterned Pluralism." In Kozo Yamamura and Yasukichi Yasuba, eds., *The Political Economy of Japan.* Vol. 1, *The Domestic Transformation.* Stanford, Calif.: Stanford University Press.

Nagaoka, Sadao. 1995. "Endaka to Nihon no Seizōgyō" [Yen appreciation and Japanese manufacturing]. Paper presented at the Conference on the Yen Appreciation and the Japanese Economy (95-5-1) Tokyo: MITI.

Nakagawa, Masaharu, et al. 1994. *Zaisei Toyūshi* [Fiscal investment and loans program]. Tokyo: Okurasho Zaimu Kyokai.

Nakahira, Yukinori, and Zembei Mizoguchi. 1992. *Kawasehō no Jitsumu* [Business practice in the Foreign Exchange Law]. Tokyo: MOF.

Nakajima, Takayuki, and Sumio Muratsu. 1976. *Arumi Gyōkai* [Aluminum business world]. Tokyo: Kyōikusha.

Nakamura, Yoshiaki, and Minoru Shibuya. 1995. *The Hollowing Out Phenomenon in the Japanese Industry.* Tokyo: Research Institute of International Trade and Industry.

Nakaoka, Nozumu. 1998. "Gaitamehō Kaisei ni yotte nani ga dō kawatta no ka?" [What changed with the revision of the Foreign Exchange Law?]. *Keidanren Gekkan* 46 (August): 28–29

Nakatase, Taichi, Yoshinari Maruyama, and Masataka Ikeda. 1979. "Sen'i Sangyō no Kaigai Shinshutsu to Zaikabō no Tenkai" [The overseas expansion of the textile industry and the development of Chinese spinning]. In *Nihon Takokuseki Kigyō no Shiteki Tenkai* [Historical development of Japanese transnational corporations]. Vol. 1. Tokyo: Otsuki Shoten.

Nelson, Douglas. 1988. "Endogenous Tariff Theory: A Critical Survey." *American Journal of Political Science* 32, no. 3: 796–837.

Nicolas, Françoise. 2001. "A Case of Government-Led Integration into the World Economy." In Frédérique Sachwald, ed., *Going Multinational: The Korean Experience of Direct Investment.* London: Routledge.

Nihon Kagaku Sen'i Kyōkai. *Sen'i Handobukku* [Textile handbook], several issues. Tokyo: Nihon Kagaku Sen'i Kyōkai.

Nippon Light Metals. 1991. *Nihon Keikinzoku Gojūnenshi* [Fifty-year history of Nippon Light Metals]. Tokyo: Nihon Keikinzoku.

Nishiguchi, Toshihiro. 1994. *Strategic Industrial Sourcing: The Japanese Advantage.* New York: Oxford University Press.

Nishimura, Atsushi. 1977. "Hong Kong Sen'i Sangyō to Nihon no Tōshi [Hong

Kong's textile industry and Japanese investment]. In *Nihon no Kaigai Tōshi no Sangyō betsu Kentō* [A sectoral examination of Japan's overseas investment]. Tokyo: Institute of Developing Economies.

Noguchi, Yukio, 1995. "The Role of the Fiscal Investment and Loan Program in Postwar Japanese Economic Growth." In Hyung-ki Kim, Michio Muramatsu, T. J. Pempel, and Kozo Yamamura, eds., *The Japanese Civil Service and Economic Development.* New York: Oxford University Press.

Ogura, Seiritsu, and Naoyuki Yoshino. 1988. "The Tax System and the Fiscal Investment and Loan Program." In Ryutaro Komiya, Masahiro Okuno, and Kotaro Suzumura, eds., *Industrial Policy of Japan.* Tokyo: Academic Press.

———. 1985. "Tokubetsu Shōkyaku-Zaisei Toyūshi to Nihon Sangyō Kōzō" [Impact of accelerated depreciation and government loan programs on Japanese industrial structure]. In *Keizai Kenkyū* 36 (April): 110–20.

Ohmae, Kennichi. 1996. *The End of the Nation State.* New York: Free Press.

Oishi, Takayoshi. 1994. "Kaigaibō 25 nen no Kaiko to Tenbō" [Recollections and views of JODC's Twenty-five years]. In Kaigai bōeki kaihatsu kyōkai (Japan Overseas Development Corporation), ed., *25–shūnen tokushu-gō* (Twenty-five-year special review). Tokyo: JODC.

Okamoto, Yasuo. 1989, 1990. "Takokuseki Kigyō to Nihon Kigyō no Takokuseika" [Multinational firms and the multinationalization of Japanese firms]. *Keizai Gaku Ronshū* 55, no. 7: 43–76; 56, no. 4: 53–100.

———. 1988a. "Takokuseki Kigyō to Nihon Kigyō no Takokusekika" [Transnational corporations and the transnationalization of Japanese corporations]. *Keizaigakuron* 54, no. 3 (October): 67–92.

———. 1988b. "Waga Kuni no Denshi Sangyō no Keisei-Hatten to sono Tokushitsu" [The creation-development of the Japanese electronics industry and its characteristics]. *Denshi* 5: 42–57; 7: 27–37; 8: 34–44.

Okimoto, Daniel I. 1989. *Between MITI and the Market: Japanese Industrial Policy for High Technology.* Stanford, Calif.: Stanford University Press.

———. 1988. "Political Inclusivity: The Domestic Structure of Trade." In Takashi Inoguchi and Daniel I. Okimoto, eds., *The Political Economy of Japan: The Changing International Context.* Stanford, Calif.: Stanford University Press.

Olson, M. 1971. *The Logic of Collective Action.* Cambridge, Mass.: Harvard University Press.

Onoda, Kinya, Hiroshisa Kohama, and Shujiro Urata. 1991. "Nihon Kigyō ni yoru Sangyō Chōsei to Seifu no Seisaku" [Industrial adjustment by Japanese companies and government policy]. In Ippei Yamazawa and Akira Hirota, eds., *Senshinshokoku no Sangyō Chōsei to Hatten Tojōkoku* [Industrialized countries' industrial adjustment and developing countries]. Tokyo: Ajia Keizai Kenkyūjō.

Organization for Economic Cooperation and Development (OECD). Several years. *International Direct Investment Statistics Yearbook.* Paris: OECD.

Osaka Chemical Research. 1973. *Waga Kuni Sen'i Sangyō no Kaigai Shinshutsu no Jittai Chōsa* [Fact-finding survey of the overseas expansion of our country's textile industry]. Osaka: Osaka Chemical.

Overseas Economic Cooperation Fund (OECF). Several years. *Annual Report.* Tokyo: OECF.

———. 1982. *Kaigai Keizai Kyōryoku Kikin. Nijūnenshi* [Overseas Economic Cooperation Fund: twenty-year history]. Tokyo: OECF.

Overseas Private Investment Corporation (OPIC). 1997. "Program Handbook." http://www.opic.gov/subdocs/what/ph-intro.htm.

Ozawa, Terutomo. 1993. "Foreign Direct Investment and Structural Transformation: Japan as a Recycler of Market and Industry." *Business and the Contemporary World* (Spring): 129–49.

———. 1986. "Japan's Largest Financier of Multinationalism," *Journal of World Trade Law* 70, no. 6: 599–614.

———. 1978. *Multinationalism, Japanese Style: The Political Economy of Outward Dependency*. Princeton, N.J.: Princeton University Press.

Park, Yong Soo. 2000. "The Korean Chaebol's Dash for Globalization: Has It Really Been Driven by Government Policy?" *Korea Observer* 31 (Winter): 579–605.

Patrick, Hugh. 1991. "Concepts, Issues and Selected Findings." In Hugh Patrick, ed., with Larry Meissner. *Pacific Basin Industries in Distress*. New York: Columbia University Press.

Patterson, Dennis. 1994. "Electoral Influence and Economic Policy: Political Origins of Financial Aid to Small Business in Japan." *Comparative Political Studies* 27, no. 3 (October): 425–47.

Pauly, Louis W., and Simon Reich. 1997. "National Structures and Multinational Corporate Behavior: Enduring Differences in the Age of Globalization." *International Organization* 51, no. 1 (Winter): 1–30.

Peck, Merton J. 1988. "Introduction." In Merton J. Peck, ed., *The World Aluminum Industry in a Changing Energy Era*. Baltimore: Johns Hopkins University Press for Resources for the Future.

Peck, Merton J., Richard C. Levin, and Akira Goto. 1987. "Picking Losers: Public Policy Toward Declining Industries in Japan." *Journal of Japanese Studies* 13, no. 1 (Winter): 79–123.

Pempel, T. J. 1999. "Structural Gaiatsu. International Finance and Political Change in Japan." *Comparative Political Studies* 32 (December): 907–32.

———. 1998. *Regime Shift: Comparative Dynamics of the Japanese Political Economy*. Ithaca, N.Y.: Cornell University Press.

Pempel, T. J., and Keiichi Tsunekawa. 1979. "Corporatism Without Labor? The Japanese Anomaly." In Philippe C. Schmitter and Gerhard Lembruch, eds., *Trends Toward Corporatist Intermediation*. Beverly Hills, Calif.: Sage.

Piazza, James A. 2002. *Going Global: Unions and Globalization in the United States, Sweden and Germany*. Boston: Lexington Books.

Radin, Robin. 1998. "The Evolution of Japan's Economic and Regulatory System: A Brief History," Harvard Law School, Program on International Financial Systems. http://www.us-japan.org/boston/radin.htm.

Ramseyer, Mark J. 1981. "Letting Obsolete Firms Die: Trade Adjustment Assistance in the United States and Japan." *Harvard International Law Journal* 22, no. 3: 595–619.

Ramseyer, Mark J., and Frances McCall Rosenbluth. 1993. *Japan's Political Marketplace*. Cambridge, Mass.: Harvard University Press.

Ramstetter, Eric D. 1991. "US Direct Investment in Developing Asia and Structural Adjustment in the US Manufacturing Industry." In Eric D. Ramstetter, ed., *Direct*

Foreign Investment in Asia's Developing Economies and Structural Change in the Asia-Pacific Region. Boulder, Colo.: Westview.

Ray, John E. 1995. *Managing Official Export Credits: The Quest for a Global Regime*. Washington, D.C.: Institute for International Economics.

Reed, Steven R. 1993. *Making Common Sense of Japan*. Pittsburgh: University of Pittsburgh Press.

Reinert, Kenneth A. 2000. "Give Us Virtue, but Not Yet: Safeguard Actions under the Agreement on Textiles and Clothing." *The World Economy* 23, no. 1: 25–55.

Research Association on Subcontracting Firms. 1986. *Kokusaika no Naka no Shitauke Kigyō* [Internationalization and subcontracting firms]. Tokyo: Tsūshōsangyō Chōsakai.

Robinson, Richard D. 1976. *National Control of Foreign Business Entry*. New York: Praeger.

Rodman, K.A. 1993. "Sanctity versus sovereignty." In Theodore H. Moran, ed., *Governments and Transnational Corporations*. New York: Routledge.

Rodriguez, Rita M. 2001. "Ex-Im Bank: Overview, Challenges, and Policy Options." In Gary Clyde Hufbauer and Rita M. Rodriguez, eds., *The Ex-Im Bank in the 21st Century: A New Approach?* Washington, D.C.: Institute for International Economics.

Roundtable on the Long-Term Prospects for the Home Appliances Industry. 1991. "Report." Photocopy.

Ruggie, John Gerard. 1983. "International Regimes, Transactions, and Change: Embedded Liberalism in the Postwar Economic Order." In Stephen D. Krasner, ed., *International Regimes*. Ithaca, N.Y.: Cornell University Press.

Rugman, A.M. 1982. *New Theories of the Multinational Enterprise*. London: Croom Helm.

Sachwald, Frédérique. 2001. "Emerging Multinationals: The Main Issues." In Frédérique Sachwald, ed., *Going Multinational: The Korean Experience of Direct Investment*. London: Routledge.

Safarian, A.E. 1993. *Multinational Enterprise and Public Policy: A Study of the Industrial Countries*. Hants, U.K.: Edward Elgar.

———. 1993a. "Firm and Government Strategies." In Theodore H. Moran, ed., *Governments and Transnational Corporations*. New York: Routledge.

Sakurai, Masao. 1972. *Waga Kuni no Keizai Kyōryoku* [Our country's economic cooperation]. Tokyo: Ajia Keizai Kenkyūjō.

Samuels, Richard J. 1987. *The Business of the Japanese State: Energy Markets in Comparative and Historical Perspective*. Ithaca, N.Y.: Cornell University Press.

———. 1983. "The Industrial Destructuring of the Japanese Aluminum Industry." *Pacific Affairs* (Fall): 495–509.

Samuels, Richard J., and Eric Heginbotham. 1998. "Mercantile Realism and Japanese Foreign Policy." *International Security* 22 (Spring): 171–203.

Sasaki, Takeo, and Edokoro Hidenori. 1987. Nihon Denki Sangyō Kaigai Shinshutsu [Oversease expansion of the Japanese electronics industry]. Tokyo: Hosei Daigaku Shuppansha.

Sazanami, Yoko, Shujiro Urata, and Hiroki Kawai. 1995. *Measuring the Costs of Protection in Japan*. Washington, D.C.: Institute for International Economics.

Schaede, Ulrike. 2000. *Cooperative Capitalism: Self-Regulation, Trade Associations, and the Anti-Monopoly Law in Japan*. New York: Oxford University Press.

———. 1995. "The 'Old Boy' Network and Government-Business Relations in Japan." *Journal of Japanese Studies* 21, no. 2: 293–317.

Schoppa, Leonard J. 1997. *Bargaining with Japan: What American Pressure Can and Cannot Do*. New York: Columbia University Press.

Schwartz, Frank J. 1998. *Advice and Consent: The Politics of Consultation in Japan*. Cambridge: Cambridge University Press.

Sekiguchi, Sueo. 1994. "An Overview of Adjustment Assistance Policies in Japan." In Hong W. Tan and Haruo Shimada, eds., *Troubled Industries in the United States and Japan*. Scranton, Penn.: Hadden Craftsmen.

———. 1991. "Japan: A Plethora of Programs." In Hugh Patrick, ed., with Larry Meissner. *Pacific Basin Industries in Distress*. New York: Columbia University Press.

"Sengō Gojūnen to Nihon Yushutsunyū Ginkō" [Fifty years after the war and the Export-Import Bank of Japan]. 1995. In *Kokusai Kaihatsu Janaru* 458: 98–125.

Shafer, Michael. 1985. "Capturing Mineral Multinationals: Advantage or Disadvantage?" In Theodore H. Moran, ed., *Multinational Corporations. The Political Economy of Foreign Direct Investment*. Lexington, Mass.: Lexington Books.

Sheard, Paul. 1991. "The Role of Firm Organization in the Adjustment of a Declining Industry in Japan: The Case of Aluminum." *Journal of the Japanese and International Economies* 5: 14–40.

Shelp, Ronald K. 1980. "Private Sector Investment and Political Risk: A Comparative Study of OPIC and Other Schemes." In Geoffrey Goodwin and James Mayall, eds., *A New International Commodity Regime*. London: Croom Helm.

Shields, Janice C. 1999. "In Focus: Overseas Private Investment Corporation." http://www.foreignpolicy-infocus.org/briefs/vol4/v4n19opic.html.

Shimada, Haruo. 1980. "The Japanese Employment System." Japan Industrial Relations Series, no. 6. Japan Institute of Labor, Tokyo.

"Shinkawase Kanrihō no Osuji Matomaru" [Outline of the new Foreign Exchange Control Law]. 1963. *Kinyū Zaisei Jijō* (April): 9.

Solís, Mireya. 1998. "Exporting Losers: The Political Economy of Japanese Foreign Direct Investment." Ph.D. diss., Harvard University.

———. 1997. "Vertical *Keiretsu* and Foreign Direct Investment: The Creation of a Japanese Supply Network in North America." Working Paper. Center for US-Mexican Studies, University of California at San Diego.

Spinanger, Dean. 1999. "Textiles Beyond the MFA Phase-Out." *The World Economy* 22, 4: 455–76.

Stopford, John M., and Louis Turner. 1985. *Britain and the Multinationals*. Chichester: John Wiley.

Stuckey, John A. 1983. *Vertical Integration and Joint Ventures in the Aluminum Industry*. Cambridge, Mass.: Harvard University Press.

Sumitomo Chemicals. 1981. *Sumitomo Kagaku Kabushiki Gaishashi* [History of Sumitomo Chemicals Industries Limited]. Tokyo: Sumitomo Chemical.

Suzuki, Tsuneo. 1991. "Sen'i Kōgyō no Kōzo Kaizen" [Structural improvement of the textile industry]. In MITI, ed., *Tsūshōsangyō Seisakushi* [History of trade and industrial policies]. Tokyo: MITI.

Suzuki, Yoshio. 1987. *The Japanese Financial System*. Oxford: Oxford University Press.

———. 1980. *Money and Banking in Contemporary Japan*. New Haven, Conn.: Yale University Press.

"Taigai Keizaihō no Kōbōsen" [Offensive/defensive battle over the Foreign Economic Law]. 1963. *Kinyū Zaisei Jijō* (November): 14–15.

Takabashi. 1991. *Senshinkoku no Chūshō Kigyō to Kinyū* [Small firms and finance in industrialized countries]. Tokyo: Chūshō Kigyō Research Center.

Take, Kazuteru. 1982. "Waga Kuni Sen'i Sangyō to Kaigai Tōshi" [Our country's textile industry and overseas investment]. *Kaigai Tōshi Kenkyū Jōhō* 8 (March): 4–28.

Takeuchi, Kenji. 1990. "Japan's Experience in Linking Foreign Direct Investment and Imports of Minerals." *Resources Policy* (December): 307–12.

Takisawa, Kikutaro. 1982. *Chūshō Kigyō no Kaigai Shinshutsu* [Overseas expansion of small and medium-sized firms]. Tokyo: Egusa Tadamitsu.

Tamaki, Masami. 1969. "Aruminiumu Kokusai Dokusen Shihon no Shigen Kakutoku Kyōso" [Aluminum's international monopolistic capital and the competition for resources acquisition]. In Shigeru Nishio, ed., *Kaigai Arumi Shigen no Kaihatsu* [Overseas development of aluminum resources]. Tokyo: Institute of Developing Economies.

Tan, Hong W., and Haruo Shimada, eds. 1994. *Troubled Industries in the United States and Japan*. Scranton, Penn.: Hadden Craftsmen.

Tanaka, Hiroshi. 1993. "Overseas Direct Investment and Trade: Investment by Japanese Consumer Electrical Appliance Industry in ASEAN and the Import of Such Products into Japan." *Exim Review* 13, no. 1: 2–41.

Tanaka, Naoki. 1991. "Shigen Seisaku" [Resource policy]. In MITI, ed., *Tsūshōsangyō Seisakushi* [History of trade and industrial policies]. Tokyo: MITI.

Tanikawa. 1996. "Kokusai CMS no ga kokunai kokyaku o kakoi komu" [The winner of international CMS will fence in domestic clients]. *Zaisei Kinyū Jijō*, April 1: 22–23.

Tashita, Masaaki. 1976. "Aruminiumu Seirengyō no Kokusai Kyōsoryoku to Setsubi Tōshi no Dōkō" [The international competitiveness of the aluminum smelting industry and trends in capital investment]. *Chōgin Chōsa Geppō* 146: 1–31.

Tilton, Mark. 1996. *Restrained Trade: Cartels in Japan's Basic Materials Industries*. Ithaca, N.Y.: Cornell University Press.

Todd, Daniel. 1990. *The World Electronics Industry*. London: Routledge.

Tomita, Toshiki. 2000. "Reform of Japan's Fiscal Investment and Loan Program." *Capital Research Journal* 3: 2–27.

Toyo Keizai. 1995. *Kaigai Shinshutsu Kigyō Sōran* [Comprehensive survey of firms expanding abroad]. Tokyo: Toyo Keizai.

Trebilcock, Michael. 1986. *The Political Economy of Economic Adjustment*. Toronto: University of Toronto Press.

Uemura. 1969. "Aruminiumu Seizōgyō Genryō Shigen" [Raw materials for aluminum manufacturing]. In Shigeru Nishio, ed., *Kaigai Arumi Shigen no Kaihatsu* [Overseas development of aluminum resources], Tokyo: Institute of Developing Economies.

Ueno, Akira. 1977. "Sen'i Sangyō no Burajiru e no Tōshi" [The textile industry's investment in Brazil]. In *Nihon no Kaigai Tōshi no Sangyō betsu Kentō* [A Sectoral examination of Japan's overseas investment]. Tokyo: Institute of Developing Economies.

United Nations (UN). Several years. *International Trade Statistics Yearbook.* New York: UN.

United Nations Centre for Transnational Corporations (UNCTC). Several years. *World Investment Report.* New York: UN.

———. 1987. *Transnational Corporations in the Man-Made Fibre, Textile and Clothing Industries.* New York: UNCTC.

———. 1981. *Transnational Corporations in the Bauxite/Aluminum Industry.* New York: UNCTC.

United States Department of Commerce. Several issues. Bureau of Economic Analysis. *Survey of Current Business.* Washington, D.C.: BEA.

Upham, Frank K. 1987. *Law and Social Change in Postwar Japan.* Cambridge, Mass.: Harvard University Press.

Uranishi, Tomogi. 1996. "Kinyū Shihon Shijō no Isso no Kasseika wa Shobi no kyū de aru" [On the urgency of revitalizing the financial capital markets]. *Kinyū Zaisei Jijō,* July 1: 24–27.

Urata, Shujiro. 1991. "The Rapid Increase of Direct Investment Abroad and Structural Change in Japan." In Eric D. Ramstetter, ed., *Direct Foreign Investment in Asia's Developing Economies and Structural Change in the Asia-Pacific Region.* Boulder, Colo.: Westview.

Urata, Shujiro, and Hiroshisa Kohama. 1991. "Denshi Sangyō" [The electronics industry]. In Ippei Yamazawa and Akira Hirota, ed., *Senshinshokoku no Sangyō Chōsei to Hatten Tojokoku* [Industrialized countries' industrial adjustment and developing countries]. Tokyo: Ajia Keizai Kenkyujō.

Uriu, Robert M. 1996. *Troubled Industries: Confronting Economic Change in Japan.* Ithaca, N.Y.: Cornell University Press.

Uryu, Fujio. 1990. "Industrial Adjustment in Japan and the US: The Case of the Textile Industry." USJP Occasional Paper 90–16, Program on US-Japan Relations, Harvard University.

Van Hoesel, Roger. 1999. *New Multinational Enterprises from Korea and Taiwan.* London: Routledge.

Van Tho, Tran. 1992. *Sangyō Hatten to Takokuseki Kigyō* [Industrial development and multinational enterprises]. Tokyo: Toyo Keizai.

Vernon, Raymond. 1983. *Two Hungry Giants: The United States and Japan in the Quest for Oil and Ores.* Cambridge, Mass.: Harvard University Press.

———. 1971. *Sovereignty at Bay: The Multinational Spread of US Enterprises.* New York: Basic Books.

———. 1970. "Future of the Multinational Enterprise." In Charles P. Kindleberger, ed., *The International Corporation: A Symposium.* Cambridge, Mass.: MIT Press.

———. 1966. "International Investment and International Trade in the Product Cycle." *Quarterly Journal of Economics* 80: 190–207.

Viner, Jacob. 1948. "Power vs. Plenty as Objectives of Foreign Policy in the Seventeenth and Eighteenth Centuries." *World Politics* 1: 1–29.

Vittas, Dimitri, and Akihiko Kawaura. 1995. *Policy-Based Finance, Financial Regulation, and Financial Sector Development in Japan*. Policy Research Working Paper 1443, World Bank.

Vogel, Ezra F., and David L. Lindauer. 1997. "Toward a Social Compact for South Korean Labor." In David L. Lindauer et al., eds., *The Strains of Economic Growth: Labor Unrest and Social Dissatisfaction in Korea*. Cambridge, Mass.: Harvard University Press.

Vogel, Steven K. 1996. *Freer Markets, More Rules: Regulatory Reform in Advanced Industrial Countries*. Ithaca, N.Y.: Cornell University Press.

Wakasugi, Ryuhei. 1989. *Bōeki-Chokusetsu Tōshi to Nihon no Sangyō Sōshiki* [International trade, foreign direct investment, and Japanese industrial organization]. Tokyo: Toyo Keizai Shinposha.

Watanabe, Makoto. 1963. *Kawase Kanri Kaisō* [A retrospective on Foreign Exchange Control]. Tokyo: Gaikoku Kawase Bōeki Kenkyūkai.

Wilkins, Mira. 1988. "European and North American Multinationals, 1870–1914: Comparisons and Contrasts." *Business History* 30 (January): 8–45.

———. 1974. *The Maturing of Multinational Enterprise: American Business Abroad from 1914 to 1970*. Cambridge, Mass.: Harvard University Press.

Williamson, Oliver E. 1985. *The Economic Institutions of Capitalism. Firms, Markets, Relational Contracting*. New York: Free Press.

Woo-Cummings, Meredith. 1991. *Race to the Swift: State and Finance in Korean Industrialization*. New York: Columbia University Press.

World Bank. 1993. *The East Asian Miracle: Economic Growth and Public Policy*. New York: Oxford University Press.

Yamashita, Shoichi. 1986. "Ōgata Enjō Purojecto no Keizai Hakyū Kōka. Asahan Purojecto o Hitotsu no Jirei Toshite" [The economic impact of large-scale aid projects: the case of the Asahan project]. *Nenpō Keizaigaku* (Hiroshima University) (March): 1–31.

Yamawaki, Hideki. 1992. "International Competition and Japan's Domestic Adjustments." In Kym Anderson, ed., *New Silk Roads: East Asia and World Textile Markets*. Cambridge: Cambridge University Press.

Yamazawa, Ippei. 1988. "The Textile Industry." In Masahiro Okuno and Kotaro Suzumura, eds., *Industrial Policy of Japan*. Tokyo: Academic Press.

———. 1984. *Nihon no Keizai Hatten to Kokusai Bungyō* [Japanese economic development and the international division of labor]. Tokyo: Toyo Keizai.

———. 1980. "Increasing Imports and Structural Adjustment of the Japanese Textile Industry." *The Developing Economies* 18 (September): 441–62.

Yamin, Mohammad. 1991. "A Reassessment of Hymer's Contribution to the Theory of the Transnational Corporation." In Christos N. Pitelis and Roger Sugden, eds., *The Nature of the Transnational Firm*. London: Routledge.

Yanaga, Chitoshi. 1968. *Big Business in Japanese Politics*. New Haven, Conn.: Yale University Press.

Yoon, Young-Kwan. 1990. "The Political Economy of Transition: Japanese Foreign Direct Investment in the 1980s." *World Politics* 43 (October): 1–27.

Yoshihara, Kunio. 1978. *Japanese Investment in Southeast Asia*. Honolulu: University of Hawaii Press.

Yoshimatsu, Hidetaka. 2000. *Internationalization, Corporate Preferences, and Commercial Policy in Japan*. London: Macmillan Press.

Yoshino, M. Y. 1976. *Japan's Multinational Enterprises*. Cambridge, Mass.: Harvard University Press.

Yoshioka, Masayuki. 1979. "Sen'i Sangyō ni Okeru Kaigai Tōshi" [Overseas investment in the textile industry]. In Hiroshi Kitamura and Takeshi Mori, eds., *Waga Kuni no Kaigai Tōshi to Kokusai Bungyō o meguro Shomondai* [Problems surrounding our country's overseas investment and the international division of labor], Tokyo: Institute of Developing Economies.

———. 1978. "Overseas Investment by the Japanese Textile Industry." *The Developing Economies* 18 (December): 3–44.

"Yugin to OECF Tōgō ni Nokoru Mujun to Sōten" [Remaining issues and contradictions in the JEXIM-OECF merger]. 1995. *Kokusai Kaihatsu Janaru* 5: 12–13.

Zhang, Xiaoke. 2003. *The Changing Politics of Finance in Korea and Thailand: From Deregulation to Debacle*. London: Routledge.

Zysman, John. 1983. *Governments, Markets, and Growth: Financial Systems and the Politics of Industrial Change*. Ithaca, N.Y.: Cornell University Press.

Index

Milton Keynes UK
Ingram Content Group UK Ltd.
UKHW011515020624
443455UK00003B/24/J